WILDERNESS *The Edge of Knowledge*

## CONTRIBUTORS

Richard W. Behan
David R. Brower
Jeffery Cohelan
Richard A. Cooley
Harry B. Crandell
Robert R. Curry
Paul R. Ehrlich
Brock Evans
R. Buckminster Fuller
John L. Hall
Garrett Hardin
H. Albert Hochbaum
Celia M. Hunter
Henry M. Jackson
W. Howard Johnson
Norman B. Livermore, Jr.
William B. Lord
Daniel B. Luten
George Macinko
Ferren MacIntyre
J. Michael McCloskey
John P. Milton
Margaret E. Murie
Roderick Nash
Urban C. Nelson
Richard L. Ottinger
Douglas R. Powell
George W. Rogers
Raymond J. Sherwin
Burton W. Silcock
Elvis J. Stahr
Lee M. Talbot
Marty Talbot
Willard A. Troyer
Edgar Wayburn
Robert B. Weeden

# WILDERNESS
## the Edge of Knowledge

Edited by *Maxine E. McCloskey*

Sierra Club • San Francisco • New York

Designed by Robert Reitz
Copy Editor: Constance L. Stallings
Production by Heliographic, Inc., New York
Copyright © 1970 by the Sierra Club
Library of Congress Catalog Card No. 71-127135
International Standard Book No. ISBN 87156-044-5
Manufactured in the United States by Vail-Ballou Press, Inc.

We are grateful for permission to use quotations from the
following sources:
Benét, Rosemary and Stephen Vincent. The poem "Daniel Boone"
by Stephen Vincent Benét, from A Book of Americans, copyright © 1933
by Stephen Vincent Benét copyright renewed 1961 by
Rosemary Carr Benét. Published by Holt, Rinehart & Winston, Inc.
Eiseley, Loren. The Immense Journey, © copyright 1957 by
Random House Inc.
Galbraith, John Kenneth. The New Industrial State,
copyright © 1967 by John Kenneth Galbraith. Reprinted by permission
of the publisher, Houghton Mifflin Company.
Gilliam, Harold. The Natural World of San Francisco,
copyright © 1967 by Doubleday and Company, Inc.
Leopold, Aldo. A Sand County Almanac, with Other Essays on
Conservation from Round River, copyright © 1949, 1953, 1966
by Oxford University Press, Inc.
MacKaye, Benton. The New Exploration: A Philosophy of Regional
Planning, copyright © 1962 by University of Illinois Press.
Marshall, Robert. Alaska Wilderness: Exploring the Central Brooks Range,
copyright © 1970 by University of California Press.
Service, Robert. The poem "The Land of Beyond" from The Collected
Poems of Robert Service, copyright © 1959 by Dodd, Mead and
Company, Inc.

# EDITOR'S PREFACE

The Eleventh Biennial Wilderness Conference, on which this book is based, was held in San Francisco, California, March 14 and 15, 1969. Sponsored by the Sierra Club and the Sierra Club Foundation, the conference attracted a capacity audience—the largest in the 20-year history of the biennial conferences. At the time, a new ecology movement was just beginning to gather strength across America.

The challenging program, under the chairmanship of Dr. Daniel B. Luten, presented participants with a wide-ranging portrayal of the wilderness values of Alaska even as oil discoveries at Prudhoe Bay on the Arctic coast and the proposed pipeline to transport that oil across the state to an all-weather port at Valdez were announced. The oil blowout at Platform A in the Santa Barbara Channel off southern California's coast shortly before the conference simply demonstrated the dangers that might soon confront Alaska, its wilderness and wildlife.

This was the first conference in the series to explore the role of wildlife in wilderness. In the words of historian Roderick Nash, "Wildlife is built into the very meaning of wilderness." To extend this discussion, I have included in the Appendices a list of species that are considered endangered; the text of the Endangered Species Conservation Act of 1969, which is designed to protect endangered species throughout the world by eliminating the market in the United States for products made from their hides, pelts, or feathers, and a special essay by Margaret W. Owings on the return of the sea otter.

The text of the Bureau of Land Management's regulations for public recreational use of its lands is included in Appendix D. Wilderness advocates need to know how this agency provides for such use on its vast land holdings. One of the maps in this volume reveals that much of the State of Alaska is administered by the BLM; thus, its regulations for primitive area protection are particularly relevant. In addition, this appendix completes the reprinting in conference books of regulations by federal agencies that have significant amounts of designated or potential wilderness land under their jurisdiction. (The book based on the Tenth Biennial Wilderness Conference, *Wilderness and the Quality of Life*, included wilderness regulations of the Forest Service, the National Park Service, and the Bureau of Sport Fisheries and Wildlife.) A conference book, in short, is designed not only to serve as a source of inspiration and knowledge, but also to provide a manual of helpful tools for those working actively in the wilderness cause.

There is a growing movement for a constitutional amendment providing for a Bill of Environmental Rights. While several proposals have been put forth, one of the most widely circulated proposed amendments was submitted by a conference speaker, Congressman Richard L. Ottinger. It is reprinted as Appendix E.

The reader will note that some of the problems discussed have been updated through footnotes. Also, wherever possible, the biographical sketches reflect the status of those described as of the spring of 1970.

Three persons deserve special recognition for their contributions to this book. They are: Sonya Thompson for preparing the list of endangered species from a number of sources, and for assistance with the biographical sketches; Adrienne E. Morgan for the maps of Alaska, based on information provided by the Bureau of Land Management, the Bureau of Sport Fisheries and Wildlife, the Forest Service, and Brock Evans; and Margaret W. Owings for the essay on revival of the sea otter, Appendix A.

Before there can be a conference book there must first be a conference. And a conference can only take place through the generosity of many individuals and organizations. Major financial contributions from the following are gratefully acknowledged:

Sierra Club Foundation
Ansel Adams
Horace M. Albright
Belvedere Scientific Fund
Robert K. Cutter
Helen M. Land
Norman B. Livermore, Jr.
Daniel B. Luten

Nathaniel and Margaret W. Owings
Pacific Gas and Electric Company
Mrs. William P. Roth
Standard Oil Company of California
Harold L. Zellerbach

Indispensable to the success of any wilderness conference are the devotion, knowledge, and volunteer time contributed by the members of the conference planning and arrangements committees. Their names are listed in Appendix F.

Maxine E. McCloskey

# *FOREWORD*

Ecology has become a familiar word at last. Yet paradoxically its popular use obscures its relationship with wilderness. While the term describes the scientific bonds between organisms and their environments, popular usage implies an *ideal* relationship, a norm, if you will. And in seeking this norm in an urban society, the concept seems far removed from wilderness.

Thinking of ecology in terms of a norm makes practical sense because it leads toward defining programs of public action. But the search for this norm is futile without wilderness. As the tiny part of the world that man has not yet spoiled, wilderness is a reference point for finding our way back to a saner relationship with nature. Without wilderness, we cannot know what a rich and stable ecosystem really is; and without enough wilderness everywhere, we will not have enough models to guide us in restoring the numberless habitats we have abused so badly.

Because we need to look now in universal terms at the problem of preserving wilderness, the Eleventh Biennial Wilderness Conference shifted its focus beyond the boundaries of the contiguous United States. In its opening and closing sessions, the conference explored the way people in other lands look at wilderness, particularly as it is symbolized by wild animals. Too few people understand the value of preserving the earth's residue of wild places, as country after country has become caught in the crush between population and resources. Yet how can Americans tell other peoples what should be done when we fail to do it ourselves? On that note, the conference turned to the fate of America's greatest remaining wilderness in Alaska. In examining our plans for that last frontier, an exceptional group of analysts revealed how little we have learned from our mishandling of older frontiers despite the pledges and rhetoric of those who are charting that great state's demise.

With wilderness, we are truly at "the edge of knowledge"; we are at the threshold of discovering what we need to know to maintain the fullness of life. Without it, we are engaged in guesswork of the most hazardous sort. This conference report will help keep us from such hazards, and hopefully too, encourage us to begin the process of discovery on a new scale.

Michael McCloskey
*Executive Director*
*Sierra Club*

*San Francisco, California*
*May 14, 1970*

# TABLE OF CONTENTS

*Maxine E. McCloskey:* Editor's Preface                              v
*J. Michael McCloskey:* Foreword                                   vii
*Edgar Wayburn:* Introduction                                     xiii
*Daniel B. Luten:* Welcoming Address                                 1
*Paul R. Ehrlich:* Keynote Address—Population and
   Conservation: Two Sides of a Coin                   3


## Part One.
## THE ROLE OF WILDLIFE IN WILDERNESS

*David Brower:* Introduction                                        13
*Lee M. Talbot:* An International View of Wildlife
   in Wilderness                                       16
*H. Albert Hochbaum:* Wilderness Wildlife in Canada                 23
*Roderick Nash:* "Wild-deor-ness," The Place of Wild
   Beasts                                              34
*H. Albert Hochbaum, Roderick Nash, Marty Talbot,*
   *Lee M. Talbot, and David Brower, Session*
   *Chairman:* Discussion                               38

## Part Two. ALASKA'S WILDERNESS

*Richard A. Cooley:* Introduction                                   53
*Maps*                                                              55

ix

*Douglas R. Powell:* Alaska's Wilderness:
A Geographic Appraisal                                      62
*Burton W. Silcock:* Alaska, the Last Great
Opportunity                                                73
*W. Howard Johnson:* National Forest Wilderness
Planning in Alaska                                         81
*Brock Evans:* A Conservationist Views Alaskan
Wilderness                                                 88
*R. W. Behan, Brock Evans, John L. Hall, W. Howard
Johnson, William B. Lord, Burton W. Silcock, and
Richard A. Cooley, Session Chairman:* Discussion          101

## Part Three. BANQUET

*Elvis J. Stahr:* The Most Glaring Gap in Education        119
*Richard L. Ottinger:* The Empty Horn of Plenty           128
*Norman B. Livermore, Jr.:* Closing Remarks by
Master of Ceremonies                                       139

## Part Four. ALASKA'S WILDERNESS WILDLIFE

*George W. Rogers:* Keynote Address—Alaska in
Transition: Wilderness and Development                     143
*Margaret E. Murie:* Introduction                         154
*Robert B. Weeden:* Arctic Oil: Its Impact on
Wilderness and Wildlife                                    157
*Urban C. Nelson:* Alaskan Wilderness Wildlife
Today                                                      168
*Willard A. Troyer:* Wilderness Studies on Alaska
Wildlife Refuges                                           175
*Harry B. Crandell, Celia M. Hunter, and
Urban C. Nelson:* Discussion                              183

## Part Five. LUNCHEON

*Jeffery Cohelan:* Remarks                                    193
*Henry M. Jackson:* The Legislative Path to
    Wilderness                                           195
*Edgar Wayburn:* Presentation of the John Muir
    Award                                                204

## Part Six. WILDERNESS PLANNING AND PEOPLE

*Raymond J. Sherwin:* Introduction                            209
*John P. Milton:* Earth: The End of Infinity                  211
*R. Buckminster Fuller:* Conserving the Assets of
    Spaceship Earth                                      224
*George Macinko:* Constructing the Man-Made
    Wilderness                                           237
*Robert R. Curry, Ferren MacIntyre, George Macinko,*
    *John P. Milton, and Raymond J. Sherwin:*
    Discussion                                           246
*Garrett Hardin:* We Must Earn Again for Ourselves
    What We Have Inherited                               260

## APPENDICES

A—The Return of the Sea Otter                                 269
B—Endangered Species                                          271
C—Endangered Species Conservation Act of 1969                 274
D—Regulations on Public Outdoor Recreation Use of
     Bureau of Land Management Lands                 282
E—National Conservation Bill of Rights                        293
F—The Eleventh Biennial Wilderness Conference—
     Planning Committee and Arrangements
     Chairmen                                        294
G—Biographical Sketches                                       295

# INTRODUCTION

*Edgar Wayburn*
President, Sierra Club*

This marks the twentieth anniversary of the founding of the wilderness conferences. From a beginning as a sort of local get-together of administrators, packers, and travelers of the Sierra Nevada, the wilderness conference has grown beyond its founders' biggest dreams. The issues which it explored and defined in its earliest conclaves proved to be broad and basic, applicable to wilderness everywhere—and, more significantly, applicable beyond wilderness to all of man's environment. Today, the wilderness conference has grown to be a principal national forum for the enunciation of major environmental concerns.

In 1969 the overriding issue that faces all of us is that we have come another year closer to the ecological crisis which may threaten man's ultimate survival on this planet.

For years we have closed our eyes to what we have been doing to our physical environment, and what this could mean to us. The natural resources we have been so busy toying with—and too often destroying—comprise a good part of man's supporting habitat. And man is as perilously dependent upon particular physical requirements as is any other kind of animal, as the bald eagle, the condor, or the grizzly bear. By our continuing disregard of this fact, demonstrated by our massive pollution of water, air, soils, and watersheds, and by attenuation of space and beauty and quietness, we are endangering what is to us the most important species of all—ourselves.

Half of this conference will be concerned with this profoundly disturbing issue; and we are fortunate to have a number of outstandingly knowledgeable and thoughtful people here to discuss various aspects of it with us.

* In May, 1969, Dr. Wayburn was elected to the office of vice-president of the Sierra Club.

The other half of this conference will deal with Alaska—the great land that has such vast assets of wildlife, timber, minerals, and, pre-eminent of all, superlative scenery. Alaska is the last mighty frontier of our wilderness and one of the last frontiers of conservation opportunity left on earth. The challenges and the problems are enormous: our speakers will take up some of these and explore them in depth.

Hopefully, certain solutions will come out of this conference. Unquestionably, new ideas, new approaches, and new challenges will result from the coming together of so many stimulating participants—both in the audience and on the platform. We anticipate that this, the Eleventh Biennial Wilderness Conference, will serve not only as a forum but as a take-off point for immediate and future action. For action, swift, informed, and intelligent, we must have if mankind is to survive.

To be possible, a conference like this must have both dedicated people and funds. The Sierra Club is grateful to all those who contributed the latter (the major ones are listed in the Editor's Preface) and most particularly to the Sierra Club Foundation.

I join my personal appreciation to that of the club for the immense efforts of the many people who have put this conference together—especially its hard-working chairman, Daniel Luten. The credit for the conference's success is rightfully theirs—and his. We are all in their debt.

WILDERNESS *The Edge of Knowledge*

"There are a thousand hacking at the branches
of evil to one who is striking at the root."

Henry David Thoreau

# WELCOMING ADDRESS

*Daniel B. Luten*
Chairman, Eleventh Biennial Wilderness Conference

Wilderness conferences have been, and continue to be, heterogeneous. They are neither a completely scholarly inquiry nor a gathering and exhortation of clans of wilderness advocates, nor indoctrination for the laymen. This might be deplorable in a well-established discipline. However, in any inquiry into wilderness we must first recognize the complexity of the matter and also that inquiry is exploratory in a way rather different from established disciplines.

In the latter, probing fingers of exploration have long since clarified the major outlines and the basic patterns of the field. Subsequent inquiry serves largely to fill in the gaps, to flesh out the bones, to complete a structure whose outlines are already visible.

In contrast, in any inquiry into wilderness we are still in exploratory phases on many counts. We see simultaneously the need for statutory protection for wilderness as we understand it at this moment. We see also the need for education of those who are puzzled by our concern. And we remain puzzled intellectually about the idea itself. And so a wilderness conference may turn in any direction, and perhaps at any moment. Because no other recognized medium for reporting the results of inquiry into wilderness exists, new ideas are likely to turn up here.

People ask me the meaning of the theme of the conference, "Wilderness, The Edge of Knowledge." Usually I just shrug my shoulders and say that a conference has to have a theme. After you have heard one theme, how many more? Others know immediately what it means. In these divergent reactions there is a clue to our feelings about wilderness. To some, wilderness is acreage to be set aside, protected

1

by statute, and perhaps managed. To others, it is an edge of knowledge and what lies beyond that edge. To resolve these differences is itself an edge of knowledge.

Through most of the millennia of human existence, of human consciousness of surroundings, explicit terra incognita always lay just beyond. Only in recent millennia, have men in fact inhabited all the habitable earth. While gradually we have come to suspect that our wilderness is another man's back yard, still for us it is wilderness, because it is beyond the edge of our knowledge. Even though Utah cattlemen ran cattle in and rounded them up out of Glen Canyon's Cathedral in the Desert, it was still Eliot Porter's *Place No One Knew*. But now with an explosion of information, explicit terra incognita is almost gone. Even ultima Thule becomes an air base. It is no longer necessary to go around the world to count the cats in Zanzibar, for they are numbered in some statistical abstract. Where then lies the edge of knowledge?

To sum up, the question of wilderness does not end with the signing of the Wilderness Act of 1964 and completion of the details of wilderness classification. It is also in the blood and in the mind. We are faced with an enigma. Do we destroy wilderness by learning more of it, or as we lengthen the edge of knowledge do we add to it? This is why we have quoted from Thoreau in the conference program: "We need the tonic of wildness . . . At the same time that we are earnest to explore and learn all things, we require that all things be mysterious and unexplorable, that land and sea be infinitely wild, unsurveyed and unfathomed by us because unfathomable. We can never have enough of nature."

# POPULATION AND CONSERVATION: TWO SIDES OF A COIN

*Paul R. Ehrlich*
Professor of Biology, Stanford University

Perhaps the most serious aspect of the current population—environment crisis is the continuing delusion, particularly among economists, demographers, and politicians, that environmental problems can in some way be separated from the population explosion, isolated, and cured in isolation. Actually, of course, population growth and environmental deterioration are extremely closely connected. The relationship between population size and man's impact on his environment can be seen most clearly through a simple consideration. As an organism, every individual man is a part of his environment and has an impact on it. Therefore, the aggregate impact of all men on the world's environment *will always be proportional to the population size.* Whatever life style is adopted, fewer people employing it will mean less impact on the environment. No permanent solution to any of our environmental problems will be possible until we bring population growth under control, and probably not until we reduce the size of the human population on earth.

The most obvious interrelationship between population growth and environmental deterioration is that, unless they are allowed to starve to death, more people need more food. In this country, unfortunately, producing more food means two things—heavy use of inorganic nitrogen fertilizers and intensive application of synthetic organic pesticides. When one puts a pollutant into the medium in which organisms live, often it does not remain evenly dispersed throughout the medium; it is concentrated by the biological systems. Generally, there can only be about one-tenth as much weight of animals eating plants as there is of plants, and only one-tenth as much weight of animals eating animals as there is of animals who eat plants and so on. Consequently, substances which are consumed with food but are not readily broken down in or excreted from the consumers, tend to build up in increasing concentrations at each step in a food chain—algae to crustacean to fish to bird or man, for example. DDT and polychlorinated bi-

3

phenyls are such substances. When they build up in high concentrations in organisms, the organisms tend to turn their toes to the sky, and that is the end of the game.

Around the world we are in danger of losing our carnivorous birds, with potentially devastating consequences for ecosystem stability. So we have a serious problem of general environmental deterioration, traceable directly to the use of pesticides that are used primarily in attempts to grow more food for more people. Of course, the more subtle effects of these pesticides on ecological systems are extremely serious. It is not just a matter of losing the bald eagle, we may eventually lose ourselves.

As another example, the overuse of inorganic nitrogen fertilizers very drastically alters the nitrogen cycle in the soil. There are two general results. One is that water percolating through the soil tends to wash more nitrates out of the soil. When the soil is high in humus content, the nitrates tend to remain in the soil, close to the plant roots where they are needed. But when inorganic nitrogen is used as a substitute for humus, the nitrates wash out and become a heavy pollution burden in our rivers and streams. Places like Lake Erie have already undergone a process that ecologists call eutrophication. Essentially, this means chronic overfertilization—too many nutrients in the water lead to population explosions among algae, whose subsequent die-offs lead to oxygen depletion and fish kills.

Another result of the use of inorganic fertilizers gives some support to what were once called health food nuts. When inorganic fertilization first came into use, there were a lot of people who said the food was not as good as when it was grown using natural manuring techniques, and the biologists laughed at them. At the time they had a right to laugh because, of course, it does not matter whether the nitrogen for building proteins in crops comes from inorganic fertilizer or organic fertilizer. However, the general effect on the soil cycle is to make it necessary to put much too much nitrogen into the soil. Some of this is taken up by the plants in the form of nitrate. There is so much that not all of it is converted into amino acids and then into proteins. Some of it remains in the leaves of the plants where it is eaten by animals and by us. Human adults are in no danger, but babies and cattle often have in their digestive tracts bacteria that convert relatively harmless nitrate into nitrite. Nitrite binds with hemoglobin, reducing the oxygen-carrying capacity of the blood in the same manner as does carbon monoxide. This, unfortunately, can happen to babies from eating too much of certain kinds of baby foods (as it has in Europe) or from drinking too much water in areas where the nitrate load in water is very high, as in much of the Central Valley of California. In these ways, an increasing demand for greater food production results in the deterioration of our environment, and, not infrequently, a deterioration in the quality of the food itself. I hardly need mention the thin film of poison on our apples which has replaced the worm that was good protein to begin with.

What are some other consequences of population growth? Not only do we need more food, but the people have to live somewhere. They can be concentrated in cities, but cities are frequently found in the middle of the best farmland. Thus, as the cities grow, first-class farmland disappears under concrete. In fact, at the moment, an area equivalent to the state of Rhode Island is developed in the United States every six months. Consequently, as the population grows, more and more effort must be made to get higher and higher yields of food from progressively worse land. This, of course, leads the giants of the petrochemical industry to continue to promote their various materials for increasing yields, regardless of other consequences.

In addition, people have the curious habit (again with the co-operation of those same giants of the petrochemical industry) of driving cars with 300 horsepower under the hood. People use electricity generated by plants that burn fossil fuels. People burn trash. In short, people produce smog. It is quite true that smog may cause and certainly aggravates lung cancer, emphysema, and cardiovascular difficulties. If you live in Los Angeles or San Jose, your life may be shortened by smog. If you raise your children in these areas, you are increasing the risk that they will develop cancer or something else equally unpleasant because you live there. And, not surprisingly, smog also affects plants. In various agricultural areas of California, smog damage is beginning to reduce the amount of food that can be produced. This is likely to appear on a global scale more and more in the immediate future. So as there are more and more people, the agricultural situation becomes increasingly more desperate because we have to produce more food than the planet can provide on a sustained basis and the side effects of the activities of people themselves make the task all the more difficult.

What about some new solutions that offer great possibilities for feeding the hungry millions? What about food from the sea? While we are trying to increase our food production on the land, soil water percolates into streams and rivers and flows out to sea. Rather than being simple $H_2O$, this water carries a very heavy load of pesticides, fertilizers, and an array of other chemicals. When they reach the sea, these chemicals differentially affect photosynthesis in marine phyto-plankton, the little plants that generate all the food in the sea. The basic process that produces food for all the life in the ocean is being disrupted by pollution from farmlands. There has been a series of experiments showing exactly how chlorinated hydrocarbons affect the photosynthetic activities of marine phytoplankton. It was to be expected; chlorinated hydrocarbons are oil soluble. In single cell organisms one of the places they are sure to turn up is in the lipid layer of the cell membranes—precisely where photosynthesis goes on. Thus, agricultural development on the land is very much reducing our potential for getting food from the sea.

What about food from the sea? We will be extraordinarily lucky to raise our present yield of something on the order of 59 million metric tons of fish a year to about 70 million metric tons by 1980. Now, if population growth continues at its present rate, by 1980, 70 million metric tons will be a slight per capita *decrease* in the amount of food that comes from the sea. Although food from the sea accounts for approximately three percent of the world's total calorie consumption, it accounts for nearly one-fifth of the total animal protein, with the other four-fifths consumed in the form of meat, eggs, and dairy products. Therefore, food from the sea is an extraordinarily important component of the human diet in many parts of the world. The significance of this in a world where protein malnutrition is already a serious problem should be obvious.

What is likely to happen to our supply of food from the sea, even if we do not destroy life in the sea by pollution? A tremendous race to harvest the sea has developed, particularly among the Soviet Union, Japan, and some European nations. An example is provided by the whaling industry. Biologists who advise the International Whaling Commission were able to make remarkably accurate predictions about how many whales could be taken each year. In the face of predictions that the whales would be driven to extinction, the whalers have continued on a course that will run them out of business. In fact, Norway had dropped out of the whaling industry, leaving only Japan and Russia in the game. They have been given about four to five years before all whaling is finished because they have overexploited the stocks. Needless to say, biologists are extremely distraught because whales are fascinating animals, although they no longer supply anything of major significance to the human economy of the world as a whole. The whale oil they produce is something like one-quarter of the yield from that other well-known oil source, rapeseed. But a few people make fortunes from slaughtering whales.

Precisely the same thing is going on with the rest of the fishing industry. A single Rumanian factory ship with extremely sophisticated sonar fish-finding equipment was able in New Zealand waters to outfish all 1,500 ships of the New Zealand fishing fleet.

To illustrate some of the attitudes prevalent in the fishing industry, here are some quotations. First, from a 1966 edition of a sonar fishing equipment manufacturer's house organ, Simrad Echo. The manufacturers were bragging about their industrialized herring fishing off the Shetland Islands, with 300 sonar-equipped Norwegian and Icelandic purse seiners landing undreamed-of quantities of herrings. Their publication asked, "Will the British fishing industry turn . . . to purse-seining as a means of reversing the decline in the herring catch?" Another statement from the same magazine further elucidates the attitudes of the captains of industry who are peddling these electronic marvels: "What then are the Shetlands going to do in the immediate future? Are they going to join and gather the bonanza while the going is good—or are they going to continue drifting and if seining is found to have an adverse effect on the herring stocks find their catch dwindling?" We now know the answer. In January, 1969, the newspapers announced that Britain's east coast herring industry had been wiped out. The purse seiners took very fine mesh nets and caught all the little herrings as well as the mature ones, destroying the breeding stock.

For a beautiful example of the fishing industry's reasoning, see the April, 1967, issue of the Simrad Echo. Here is an article discussing a newspaper item announcing that a Norwegian shipyard is building a purse seiner for Peru, which has the largest fishery in the world now, based on anchovies in the rich Humboldt current. Simrad Echo says, "Fish-rich Peru nurses an ever-growing apprehension. Increasingly it is asked: surely the anchovy stocks off the coast—seemingly limitless at present—cannot sustain catch losses running into millions of tons year after year?

"Behind the news item lies what many people consider to be the answer to the Peruvian question—bigger and better equipped boats to augment the hundreds of small 'day-trip' purse seiners engaged in the stupendous coastal fishery.

"They theorize that if the present abundant stocks do start to get scarce, there will be boats on the scene able to go much further afield and be suitably equipped to track fish down.

"They theorize further that now is the time for action, while things are still relatively good, not at the last moment of truth. In the meantime, valuable experience can be gained operating the latest fish-finding devices, such as echo sounders and sonars."

Those people who are talking very irresponsibly about feeding seven billion people in the year 2000, through dream revolutions or the so-called unlimited resources of the sea, really ought to go back to high school and college and learn a little elementary biology, meteorology, maybe some agricultural economics, and anthropology. We cannot come close to feeding three and one-half billion people today. Somewhere between one and two billion people are hungry right now. Between 15 and 20 million people are dying of starvation or malnutrition every year. And yet these optimists run around prattling to laymen that science is going to save them. The trouble with all this noise, of course, is that it delays any kind of action toward population control.

What about the Green Revolution? There is a substantial number of people who think that tropical agriculture can be revolutionized by sending bags of high-yield seeds to farmers. One could only hold this point of view if one knew virtually nothing about economic development of underdeveloped countries, agricultural economics, and agricultural technology.

The high yields that occurred in 1967-68 in India were due not only to planting out large amounts of high-yield grains, but also to extremely good weather in those years. If high-yield grains are planted on a limited basis, a dramatic early rise in production is to be expected. Why? First of all, the seeds go only to the most progressive farmers in the area, the ones who are willing to try them. Second, technicians are on the scene to tell them how to use them. Third, all the problems that develop with the use of pesticides and misuse of fertilizers develop, not in the first year, but in subsequent years.

All of these high-yield grains are fertilizer-sensitive. Average or less-than-average yields result unless fertilizing is done properly and in the right amount. Therefore, fertilizers must be available. To bring fertilizers to the fields, there must be farm roads, fertilizer factories, and transport vehicles. Places like India are very short of these things. All the tremendous ballyhoo about the Green Revolution really means that in a few places, under carefully controlled conditions, in the first year or two, very high yields have been obtained. But what will happen when they attempt to spread this to other farmers who are not particularly interested in using high-yield grains, do not have access to fertilizers, and will not have enough technicians to help them out because the number of agricultural extension people per farmer in a country like India is miniscule?

In addition to all this, there are serious economic problems involved in producing high-yield grains. Here is a single example. There was a very large famine in northern India a few years ago, following two years of very bad monsoons in Bihar and Orissa. There is no longer a very large famine there. There remains, however, considerable localized famine, roughly 20 million people on the brink of starvation. Simultaneously, there is a glut of grain and prices are tumbling. There in microcosm is another of the major problems in generating an agricultural revolution in underdeveloped areas: starving people generate no effective *demand* in most cases. They have no money to pay for the food. What then happens to a progressive farmer who worked hard last year and grew twice as much grain on the same acreage as he had the year before, using the high-yield seeds and giving them all the proper treatment and necessary extra effort? He may find that he made the same amount of money as he made the year before, or even less. So the incentive to put in all that work is often not there.

That is, of course, an oversimplification of agricultural economics. Part of the economic situation is the need for roads, markets, ways of transporting grains to market, and ways of protecting grain from rats and insects once it is harvested. Those who are interested in the problems of tropical agriculture, as tried by very well trained and experienced people from North America, should read the article in the *National Observer* by Darryl G. Cole ("The Myth of Fertility Dooms Development Plans," April 22, 1968) on his attempts over 13 years to farm a highland rain forest area of Costa Rica.

The consensus among people who know something about agricultural economics, the tropics, and the anthropology of food production and consumption is that the very best that can be expected from the high-yield grains is some local relief. In the long run, that is probably just as well. History is very clear; it shows that, whatever the amount of food produced, the population is likely to grow to whatever size will allow bare subsistence for everybody on that amount of food.

If narrowly trained agronomists from developed countries go to the tropics and try to start an agricultural revolution, they are likely to use such great quantities of inorganic fertilizers and pesticides that we could seriously diminish the harvest of food from the sea—not 10 years from now, as we may anyway, but essentially immediately.

Let me say at this point how very happy I am that the Sierra Club has become involved in worldwide conservation. Conservationists have realized for a long time that small parcels of land set aside would not be sufficiently buffered from man's influence to preserve representative flora and fauna. It has now become very clear that the smallest parcel that we can meaningfully preserve in this day and age is the planet Earth itself. Remember that chlorinated hydrocarbon pollution is worldwide. It will not spare the raptorial birds in all of our national parks, and this, in turn, will inevitably lead to dramatic changes in the flora and fauna of those parks.

Smog is now altering the entire climatic pattern of the earth. A recent UNESCO conference gave us 20 years before the entire planet started to become uninhabitable because of smog. The smog curtain goes all the way around the earth. It is reducing the amount of sunlight coming in. There is a variety of drastic things that it can do to the weather. Climates have always changed, but previously they have changed rather slowly. At the moment when we are most over-extended in food production efforts, we are doing the maximum to alter our climatic patterns. Agriculture is completely dependent on climate, and rapidly changing climates in any direction mean greatly reduced agricultural production. And, of course, rapid climatic change would also spell doom for things like redwood groves and the Everglades.

Putting aside a park here and there is laudable, but not enough. Unless we attack the worldwide problem, putting aside parks is a waste of time. There are a great many reasons to be involved in a worldwide conservation and population control program. The main one is that we want to live, and we want to live in a decent world.

Beyond this, there are many reasons besides the aesthetic ones on which we all agree for preserving the diversity of life on the earth. All of the ecological systems that make it possible for us to live depend for their stability on diversity. There are even more obvious and direct reasons for wanting to preserve diversity other than maintaining this stability. What if we had let the rhesus monkey become extinct 50 or 60 years ago when it was not apparent what a marvelous organism it is for medical experimentations? In this connection, I am very glad that the Sierra Club has started to make an effort toward preserving the Galapagos Islands—it may be necessary one of these days to move Darwin's finches to North America to replace the birds that we have killed off here. (Some of Darwin's finches are rather good insectivores, and insectivores are useful.) My colleagues and I, therefore, hope that the Sierra Club will become much more deeply involved in world conservation, because, after all, success in the world conservation and population battle is the only hope we have of conserving ourselves and the world.

## Part One

# THE ROLE OF WILDLIFE IN WILDERNESS

"When Daniel Boone goes by, at night,
The phantom deer arise
And all lost, wild America
Is burning in their eyes."
                    Stephen Vincent Benét

"And when on the still cold nights, he pointed
his nose at a star and howled long and wolflike,
it was his ancestors, dead and dust, pointing
nose at star and howling down through the centuries
and through him. And his cadences were their
cadences, the cadences which voiced their woe and
what to them was the meaning of the stillness, and the
cold, and dark."
                    Jack London

# INTRODUCTION

*David Brower*
Executive Director, Sierra Club*

All too often the value of wilderness has been calculated by counting the number of recreationist footprints in it, which is something
like appraising the Mona Lisa by weighing the paint. Here are other
evaluations, more in harmony with Nancy Newhall's statement that
"wilderness holds answers to questions man has not yet learned how
to ask."

A physicist, J. H. Rush, has said: "When man obliterates wilderness,
he repudiates the evolutionary force that put him on this planet.
In a deeply terrifying sense, man is on his own."

From Henry David Thoreau, there's a quotation that I think is
quite pertinent to this morning's session: "I take infinite pains to
know all the phenomena of spring, for instance, thinking that I have
here the entire poem, and then, to my chagrin, I learn that it is but
an imperfect copy that I possess and have read, that my ancestors
have torn out many of the first leaves and grandest passages, and
mutilated it in many places. I should not like to think that some
demigod had come before me and picked out some of the best of
the stars. I wish to know an entire heaven and an entire earth."

And then, one of the most beautiful passages from Loren Eiseley.
I think it puts in perspective our time here on the planet and what
we are doing about it. It's from *The Immense Journey*. I think it is
the best thing he ever wrote:

"It was a late hour on a cold, wind-bitten autumn day when I
climbed a great hill spined like a dinosaur's back and tried to take my

* In June, 1969, Mr. Brower was appointed director of the John Muir Institute
for Environmental Studies and in July was elected president of Friends of the Earth.

13

bearings. The tumbled waste fell away in waves in all directions. Blue air was darkening into purple along the bases of the hills. I shifted my knapsack, heavy with the petrified bones of long-vanished creatures, and studied my compass. I wanted to be out of there by nightfall, and already the sun was going sullenly down in the west.

"It was then that I saw the flight coming on. It was moving like a little close-knit body of black specks that danced and darted and closed again. It was pouring from the north and heading toward me with the undeviating relentlessness of a compass needle. It streamed through the shadows rising out of monstrous gorges. It rushed over towering pinnacles in the red light of the sun, or momentarily sank from sight within their shade. Across that desert of eroding clay and wind-worn stone they came with a faint wild twittering that filled all the air about me as those tiny living bullets hurtled past into the night.

"It may not strike you as a marvel. It would not, perhaps, unless you stood in the middle of a dead world at sunset, but that was where I stood. Fifty million years lay under my feet, fifty million years of bellowing monsters moving in a green world now gone so utterly that its very light was travelling on the farther edge of space. The chemicals of all that vanished age lay about me on the ground. Around me still lay the shearing molars of dead titanotheres, the delicate sabers of soft-stepping cats, the hollow sockets that held the eyes of many a strange, outmoded beast. Those eyes had looked out upon a world as real as ours; dark, savage brains had roamed and roared their challenges into the steaming night.

"Now they were still here, or, put it as you will, the chemicals that made them were here about me in the ground. The carbon that had driven them ran blackly in the eroding stone. The stain of iron was in the clays. The iron did not remember the blood it had once moved within, the phosphorus had forgot the savage brain. The little individual moment had ebbed from all those strange combinations of chemicals as it would ebb from our living bodies into the sinks and runnels of oncoming time.

"I had lifted up a fistful of that ground. I held it while that wild flight of south-bound warblers hurtled over me into the oncoming dark. There went phosphorus, there went iron, there went carbon, there beat the calcium in those hurrying wings. Alone on a dead planet I watched that incredible miracle speeding past. It ran by some true compass over field and waste land. It cried its individual ecstasies into the air until the gullies rang. It swerved like a single body, it knew itself and, lonely, it bunched close in the racing darkness, its individual entities feeling about them the rising night. And so, crying to each other their identity, they passed away out of my view.

"I dropped my fistful of earth. I heard it roll inanimate back into the gully at the base of the hill: iron, carbon, the chemicals of life. Like men from those wild tribes who had haunted these hills before me seeking visions, I made my sign to the great darkness. It was not a mocking sign, and I was not mocked."

We have now learned how to make those chemicals of life unusable for any living thing.

One of my favorites is from Aldo Leopold, in *Round River* where he said:

"I have congenital hunting fever and three sons. As little tots, they spent their time playing with my decoys and scouring vacant lots with wooden guns. I hope to leave them good health, an education, and possibly even a competence. But what are they going to do with these things if there is no more deer in the hills, and no more quail in the coverts? No more snipe whistling in the meadow, no more piping of widgeons and chattering of teal as darkness covers the marshes; no more whistling of swift wings when the morning star pales in the east? And when the dawnwind stirs through the ancient cottonwoods, and the gray light steals down from the hills over the old river sliding softly past its wide brown sandbars—what if there be no more goose music?"

One more from Thoreau, just a line:

"We need to witness our own limits transgressed and some life pasturing freely where we never wander."

I hope you will find in the lines from these men—physicist, poet, anthropologist, and zoologist—some background music for what the people here concerned with wilderness have to say, and indeed for what wilderness itself has to say.

# AN INTERNATIONAL VIEW OF WILDLIFE IN WILDERNESS

*Lee M. Talbot*

Resident Ecologist and Field Representative for International Affairs in Ecology and Conservation, Smithsonian Institution

An international view provides a particularly useful perspective on the role of wildlife in wilderness in two ways: biological and conceptual.

The biological role is the role of wildlife in creating and maintaining wilderness; the conceptual role is the role of wildlife in shaping man's concept of that wilderness.

On considering the biological role, we must recognize that wildlife is essential to much wilderness as we know it. Clearly, wildlife does not shape the gross topography of wilderness—its mountains, canyons, and plains. But wildlife does play a vital role in the development and maintenance of the skin of soil and vegetation that covers the wilderness topography. Soils, vegetation, and wildlife are intimately interrelated: they do not exist in isolation one from another.

Wildlife directly affects the soil and vegetation mantle in a variety of ways: dispersal, planting, and germination of seeds; fertilization; conversion of dead plants into organic matter more usable by living plants; pollination; and modification of vegetation and soil.

I will consider briefly these varying roles and will illustrate them with examples from different parts of the world.

A large percentage of the seed plants of the world rely on wildlife to disperse and plant their seeds. Some seeds get a free ride because they have hooks or some other physical adaptation to catch on fur or feathers. Other seeds are packaged in edible fruits or nuts which are eaten by wildlife, frequently carried some distance in the digestive tract, and deposited on another site. Other edible seeds are literally planted by wildlife; squirrels bury nuts, and many other small mammals store seeds and fruits underground. Some of these, of course, are picked up later by the animals and eaten. But a surprisingly large percentage are not; they germinate on the spot and grow.

Most larger herbivores also distribute seeds, even if they don't physically plant them. In Tanzania, for example, it has been shown that the very existence and distribution of groves of the umbrella acacia—one of the commonest trees of the savanna wilderness—are due to the habits of the impala and the baboon. These animals eat the acacia pods, which pass through the animals' digestive tracts and are deposited with the droppings. The distribution of new groves of these typical acacias is dependent on the movements and distribution of the impalas and baboons during the occasional seeding periods.

Flying mammals also serve the same function. Fruit bats, for example, are a key to the dispersal of seeds of many tropical trees in Southeast Asia, tropical America and tropical Africa. The flying foxes are a good example. Some of these massive fruit bats have a wingspan over three feet. They roost in treetops during the day in concentrations sometimes numbering thousands. In the evening they leave the roost and spread out over the forest, flying many miles to harvest the ripe fruit from trees wherever found, and then they return to the roost where the fruit seeds are deposited.

Birds perform the same function in the same way. They not only provide horizontal dispersion, but they also provide vertical dispersion and planting. The hornbill and strangler fig trees of Southeast Asia are a striking example. The strangler fig, one of the most prominent and impressive trees found throughout those lowland tropical forests, is a massive plant standing over 100 feet high. The base of a single tree may occupy more than a quarter of an acre, its multiple trunks extending well over 100 feet from side to side. It becomes a sort of keystone for many of these forested areas for it provides habitat for many forms of wildlife. Because its multiple trunks are remarkably resistant to wind and other factors, these figs frequently are the only trees left standing after a tropical typhoon has flattened the forest around them. And yet, this giant is absolutely dependent upon birds, such as the hornbill, in this way:

The bird eats the fig fruit from a standing tree and then flies to a perch in another tree, possibly some distance away and frequently 50 to 100 feet high. The seed passes through the bird and is deposited with its droppings on the branch, frequently in a hollow where the branch joins the main trunk. Later, the seed germinates and sends out roots. These roots twine down the trunk, eventually reaching the ground. As the fig grows, these intertwining roots, which have now become trunks, totally cover the original tree. The fig also sends down aerial roots, which then become trunks on their own, while at the same time its own trunk grows upward from the original seed site to form part of the forest canopy far above. Eventually the host tree is strangled, its place taken by this forest giant.

In these cases, I have spoken of the role of wildlife in dispersing and planting seeds, but there is another equally important, associated function that wildlife provides. Many seeds will not germinate unless their cover has been opened, either through heat, chemical action, or mechanical action. In many cases, passage through the digestive tract of an animal serves this purpose. In the case of the impala- and baboon-umbrella acacia relationship, it is not only the physical moving of the seed from the place where it is produced to the place where, hopefully, a new grove will start that is required. The seed must pass through the digestive tract of the impala or the baboon. The same is true in the case of many birds. The chewing by animals or the action of the gizzard of birds may physically open the seed cover, or more often, the chemical action of the digestive juices does the trick.

In this way wildlife not only spreads and sometimes plants the seeds, but also enables them to germinate.

We should also not forget that wildlife is usually responsible for pollinating the flowers that produce the seeds or fruits. Most pollination is accomplished by insects; however, some is by birds such as hummingbirds, honeysuckers and sunbirds. It is believed that bats in Java and Trinidad do the same thing.

Wildlife, through its droppings, also fertilizes seeds. In areas of particularly infertile soils, manuring by wildlife can be of considerable importance to wilderness plant life, particularly in areas with high concentrations of large mammals like the east African plains, eastern Javanese savannas, and the savannas of northern Cambodia. Even fertilization by rodents has been shown to be important, especially in arid areas.

Fertilization can also be important to aquatic life. In Uganda, biologists have shown that the rich fish life of some of the lakes is due to the hippopotamus. The hippos feed on land mostly at night, then spend much of their days in the water. Their droppings, which are deposited in the water, enrich the lake waters and contribute to the food chain on which the fish rely.

Another aspect of fertilization is conversion of dead plants directly into organic matter that living plants can use. The tropical rain forests are a good example. We think of them as being massive, permanent, stable, solid. Yet, they are not; they are remarkably fragile, existing in areas of generally extremely infertile soil. Their frequently lush vegetation is the result of a delicate balance, a fine adaptation, and an almost closed cycle of nutrients. The long taproots of some trees bring in some nutrients from the substrate, but mostly nutrients from fallen dead leaves, branches, even tree trunks are almost immediately picked up again by the near-surface roots and recycled back into living vegetation. Wildlife, here in the form mostly of termites and other invertebrates, plays a key role in rapidly transforming the vegetable matter into powder form, facilitating its rapid conversion back to living plants.

The same thing occurs on the open plains. In the grasslands of Africa and Asia the termites harvest a large proportion (in some cases at least as much as the big ungulates) of the growing grasses and in effect powder and store them underground.

One of the more obvious impacts made by wildlife on vegetation is through the physical effect of eating. In wilderness grasslands, grazing ungulates play a significant role in determining the plant species and their abundance. Through overgrazing or undergrazing, in combination with fire, these wild animals can determine whether the area remains grass and what kind of grass, or whether the vegetation changes to bush or forests, or vice versa. Browsing species, such as the giraffe, also alter the distribution, abundance, and composition of part of the tree flora where they live. The most gross example of such impact is that of the elephant, which not only eats a vast amount of vegetation but is capable of further modifying the landscape by pushing down trees and brush, as for example in Africa and in Ceylon where they have literally changed areas from forest to grassland in a few years.

Small mammals also play a significant role. When European rabbits were introduced to Australia they created havoc with the native vegetation. Less well known is what happened when myxomatosis nearly wiped out those transplanted rabbits: the sudden increase in vegetation illustrated dramatically how much influence the little mammals had previously exerted.

Depending on its balance, wildlife can either maintain or virtually destroy the vegetation mantle of wilderness.

Any wildlife that affects vegetation automatically affects the soil also. In addition, some forms of wildlife, big and small, physically modify the soil in significant ways. Larger animals may trample the soil, and the trails of large, migrating mammals, such as American bison, east African wildebeest, and elephants are a characteristic part of the topography of some wilderness. A host of small mammals plow or overturn soil, largely through their burrowing. The actions of squirrels, gophers, and prairie dogs are well known in North America. Other continents have their equivalents, and in some cases larger animals contribute, at least locally, to this effect. In East Africa, hyenas, aardvarks, bat-eared foxes, warthogs, and a number of other medium-sized animals all burrow, or they enlarge other animals' burrows, and in so doing they move about a considerable amount of soil. Pigs are found throughout the world, and their rooting disturbs, turns over, or plows up significant areas of the earth's surface.

The action of worms is well known, but in some areas the effect is much more dramatic than it is in the United States. In northern Cambodia, casts that are thrown up by some worms reach over two feet in height. In East Africa and India, termitaria (the anthills caused by the termites) may become over 10 feet high and they constitute a significant part of wilderness topography.

These few examples show that virtually all forms of wildlife, invertebrate and vertebrate, birds and beasts, directly affect the mantle of soil and vegetation of wilderness; yet they do not do so in isolation from one another. Herbivores have a direct effect; yet predators and scavengers affect the herbivores, and therefore they affect the soil and vegetation mantle indirectly but significantly.

Remove wildlife and there would still be wilderness, in the sense that wilderness is an area uncultivated and unoccupied by man—but it would be a far different wilderness.

Now let us take a brief international overview of the role of wildlife.

In the first place, we must recognize that man's view of wilderness is not always benign. The reverse is frequently true. Man's views of wilderness might be categorized broadly into three stages: (1) fear, (2) challenge, (3) appreciation.

These stages also broadly represent the changing ratio between the culture—or a people—and wilderness. The early stage is fear, partly of the unknown and partly of the known dangers in wilderness. As people gain in numbers, knowledge, and technological capability, there is less to fear and wilderness becomes more of a challenge. It is considered an obstacle to be overcome and conquered in order to provide more land and security. The final appreciation stage comes when people are secure, and they realize that wilderness represents a store of resources—physical and aesthetic.

These stages also broadly represent the changing ratio betwen the amount of wilderness and the numbers of people; in the early fear stage, there is apparently unlimited wilderness and it is overwhelming; in the last stage there is very little, and it is recognized and appreciated as a resource. There is a human behavioral characteristic not to appreciate something until it is lost, or very nearly lost.

Because the concept or the symbol of wilderness to people is some form of wildlife, the three stages might also be characterized as the transition from the "tiger stage" through the "deer stage."

Throughout eastern Asia, from Korea south to Indonesia, and from the Pacific coast westward through India, the tiger is the fear symbol of wilderness. To the villager in the Sumatran forest, the tiger is a very real danger to him and his livestock. This concept is communicated to those much farther removed from actual tigers both in time and in space. To the city dweller, say, in Java or Bali (where tigers are now extinct) as well as to the Chinese merchant in Hong Kong, the wilderness is still thought of as a dangerous place full of tigers.

In Kashmir it is the black and brown Himalayan bears that represent the danger of wilderness, while farther north it is wolves, as it is in parts of North America. Lions take their place farther west into Africa, while jaguars fill it in much of the Latin American tropics.

A further danger to the rural villager in wild areas is damage or loss of his crops or livestock from depredations of other wildlife, particularly beasts like elephants, gaurs, or buffalo, which then become identified with wilderness in these peoples' minds.

In the later challenge stage, wildlife again often provides the symbol. To the Boers occupying South Africa 300 years ago, conquering the wilderness involved decimating the vast herds of mixed African plains game. In much the same way the Americans "conquered" their plains by eliminating bison nearly 200 years later, and east Africans and Arabians rid their plains of game still later. Pigs, deer, and monkeys represent the challenge of wilderness, or what little is left of it, in the Philippines, and the same animals serve as symbols in many other parts of Southeast Asia.

In the appreciation stage there is a much broader attitude toward wildlife, and the symbols become those animals that are of aesthetic value, those that are of general interest, and those that are of resource value—all in contrast to the attitude that wildlife is something to be conquered or something to be feared. This final stage is not necessarily a new thing in human history. In about 300 B.C., sanctuaries were established in India—in effect these were the first national parks or game reserves—and they were described as places "where the wild animals and birds could roam without fear of man."

Man's concept of wilderness closely parallels his relationship with wildlife. Early man was preyed upon by the larger carnivores, and they continued to represent a threat to him and his livestock. His relationship with them was one of fear and aggression, and as a result, the larger predators—that is the bears, the dog family, and cats—have suffered the greatest losses from man. The first recorded extermination was the European lion in about A.D. 80; about 60 percent of the continental mammalian extinctions are larger predators. The next group to go was the larger herbivores, which either represented competition for space or crops or were a source of meat products. Nearly 40 percent of the continental mammalian exterminations are from this group.

Given this relationship between man and wildlife, and since wilderness represents the habitat for the wildlife, it is quite logical that man identifies wilderness in the same terms.

In summary, then, from an international view wildlife plays both a biological and a conceptual role in wilderness. Biologically, wildlife is an integral part of most wilderness. Directly or indirectly it plays a key role in creating and maintaining the conditions of soil, vegetation, and surface topography. Conceptually, wildlife represents the symbol of wilderness for most people at most stages in their existence. The biological-conceptual roles of wildlife in wilderness are basic and essential. Wildlife is an integral part of and is essential to wilderness as we know it.

# WILDERNESS WILDLIFE IN CANADA

*H. Albert Hochbaum*
The Nature Conservancy of Canada

On clear winter evenings I sometimes stand behind my home, looking north across the marsh, beyond the wooded ridge and frozen lake to Polaris. A transect from my eyes to the North Pole would cross but two roads, both gravel. Except for nearby lakeshore cottages, there can be no human dwelling between me and the Siberian plains, 3,000 miles away. My good fortune is to live at the edge of primitive country.

My home is in the village of Delta, in southern Manitoba, near the geographical center of North America. One morning last February, while sipping coffee at my south window, I watched a timber wolf, big-footed, tail fluffed in the wind, trot across the ice beyond the reeds. I am lucky to live and work where wolves are tolerated.

The trail of my breakfast wolf was only 15 miles from a prosperous city of 16,000. Sixty-five miles southeast, across the rich wheat prairie, lies Winnipeg, a thriving metropolitan area of half a million. In March, 1882, Ernest Thompson Seton saw a wolf near the eastern edge of Winnipeg, his "Winnipeg Wolf."[1] In January, 1956, a large wolf was shot by a farmer near Headingly, in sight of Winnipeg's western outskirts. In June, 1960, I saw a wolf cross Highway 12, about 25 miles from Seton's sighting. And in January, 1964, a friend flew over four large timber wolves on frozen marsh not more than 25 miles north of Winnipeg. Far away, a timber wolf, following the railroad grade from his wild home range, found himself in downtown Toronto. I suspect, from evidence in hand, that a wolf this very moment is licking his chops, napping, or following a trail within 100 miles of most of Canada's 21 million citizens. From nearly all our large cities one need travel less than a day's drive to cross a timber wolf track.

[1] Ernest Thompson Seton, *Lives of Game Animals* (1925), I, Part 1, p. 313.

23

I dwell on the wolf's[2] presence near the habitat of Canadian man-kind because this animal, perhaps more than any other, is our criterion of wild country. *Canis lupus* once inhabited most of North America. Where he is now gone, where wolf tracks no longer follow game trails and meet at river crossings, where the voice of lobo never more rings across the night wind, then our country is no longer truly wild, regard-less of wilderness solitude. In some places the departure was inevitable, as where maps are now marked heavily with the names of cities and highways. But there remains much back country where the wolf might have continued had we let him. Here the land is not only tamed by his going, but changed in ways that cannot be mended. "I have lived to see state after state extirpate its wolves," wrote Aldo Leopold. "I have watched the face of many a newly wolfless mountain, and seen the south-facing slopes wrinkle with a maze of new deer trails. I have seen every edible bush and seedling browsed, first to anaemic desue-tude, and then to death. I have seen every edible tree defoliated to the height of a saddlehorn. Such a mountain looks as if someone had given God a new pruning shears, and forbidden Him all other exercise."[3]

In Canada most of us work and play within a short drive of the United States border. But from coast to coast our urban environment is braced against the wilderness, a closeness to the primitive which led Blair Fraser to exclaim, "As long as it is there, Canada will not die."[4] It is easy to suggest that a tolerance of wolves prevailing in much of this cherished neighborhood of wilderness results from an accident of physiography. The Precambrian Shield, the thin-soiled aspen park-land, the rugged eastern highlands, and the mountained west cannot support large numbers of people. This land remains wild and wolves have hung on because civilization could not easily intrude. And yet one of a Canadian's first surprises, when crossing into the United States, occurs when he finds that all wild country is by no means at home. A trip from Alberta to southern Arizona carries one through land as unsettled as much of western Canada: rugged, lonely, often breathtakingly beautiful, but a range entirely without wolves. They

[2] Except where noted, reference in this paper is made to *Canis lupus linné*, in its numerous North American subspecies. On the Great Plains, this was the buffalo wolf, now extinct. It is the gray wolf or timber wolf through most of Canada ex-cept on the Barren Grounds where lives the tundra wolf.

[3] Aldo Leopold, *A Sand County Almanac* (New York: Oxford University Press, 1949), p. 130.

[4] Blair Fraser, *The Search for Identity: Postwar to Present* (Toronto: Doubleday & Co., 1967).

were there, residents of 10 states, in 1915. By 1941 they had all been killed, all of them, several distinct subspecies exterminated.[5]

The edge of Winnipeg is wilder than the whole state of Montana, if one may use the wolf as a criterion of wildness. It is worth noting that several wolf ranges in Canada, as Manitoba's Riding Mountain National Park, are surrounded by settled land. At Riding Mountain, indeed, residual grazing rights have placed the wolf side by side with cattle. Such tolerance is important when we consider that it was the pressure of cattlemen grazing on public lands that brought an end to the wolf in the Rocky Mountain states.

No, it can hardly be said that Canadian topography alone has saved the wolf. There must be an ethic of the people, a tolerance that perhaps marks a cultural difference between Canadians and Americans. Except in northern Minnesota, these Canadian wolves dare not stray across the United States border; when they do, even in wild country, they are quickly dispatched. Only one United States national park south of the Canadian border holds wolves, Isle Royale, a short winter trot across the ice from the Canadian shore. Clearly the wolf ethic is not a force within the 48 contiguous states.

It is worth noting that the red wolf, *Canis niger*, a resident of the southern United States, is rapidly declining, perhaps in danger of becoming extinct. And yet in the face of its impending doom, the United States Fish and Wildlife Service, successor of the bureau that extirpated the gray wolf, continues its trap and poison aggressions against this endangered species.[6] Here is a unique animal, with no members enjoying safety in Canada or Mexico, which may vanish before we have learned the details of its life story.

Perhaps each of us in this human race has an innate fear of the wolf and other large predators. Yet even if this fear is a natural heritage, it is strengthened by learning. Man's folklore, regardless of race or creed, has made sure each youngster learns at an early age that the wolf is his eternal enemy, the perpetual villain. The function of these ancient stories was to prepare the young for the world at large, to warn them of its dangers and of their enemies. So it was always; so it is now, even where the wolf is gone. Modern man aims to thrive in a world that is safe from wolves; and yet "too much safety seems to yield only danger in the long run."[7]

[5] Stanley P. Young and Edward A. Goldman, *The Wolves of North America* (New York: Dover Publications, 1944), p. 58.

[6] Douglas H. Pimlott and Paul W. Joslin, *Status and Distribution of the Red Wolf*, A Transcription of the Thirty-Third North American Wildlife Conference, (1968), p. 386.

[7] Leopold, *loc. cit.*, p. 133.

In the United States, the wolf-fear grew from its folklore into an aggressive, highly successful public assault. In Canada there have been and, in some places there continue similar wolf-killing campaigns. But unlike the United States, the small and more widely spread Canadian population could not afford a massive attack. When such did develop, as in British Columbia, Alberta, Manitoba, and Ontario during the 1950's and early 1960's an ecological conscience by this time was held by enough citizens and newspaper editors to reduce the efficiency of the wolf-control programs. Such a conscience seems to be developing in Alaska where, as in Canada, time, short funds, and an awakened citizenry are in the wolf's favor. The December, 1968, issue of *Alaska Conservation Review* carries this encouraging note:

### "Wolves Return to Kenai"

The flight path of a PA-18 and the route of ten wolves crossed on November 21 this year on Kenai Peninsula, and the first authoritative sighting of these big canines in that part of Alaska in half a century was recorded. Fish and Game biologist Dimitri Bader reported that the wolves—five grays and five blacks—were trotting eastward over crusted snow.

If a proposal made by the Board of Fish and Game this December becomes a regulation, these wolves will be protected from bounty hunting. The Board proposes to authorize no wolf bounty payments in game management units 7 and 15, comprising the entire Kenai Peninsula. Conservationists hope that a modest population of wolves will build up in the wilder parts of the Kenai, enhancing the value of the Kenai National Moose Range and the Chugach National Forest to outdoorsmen and naturalists.

The Board also took a big step forward at their December meeting in Anchorage when they proposed that no bounties be paid on wolverines or coyotes anywhere in Alaska....

If we accept the wolf as a criterion of North American wildness, it is important to wilderness survival in Canada and Alaska that we understand our genetic and social inheritance in regard to wolves and other wilderness wildlife. It is easy for those of us who are engaged in preservation of the wild to believe that we are the anointed ones, holding insights, outlooks, and viewpoints superior to the general run of citizenry. We thus easily become evangelists rather than teachers, preachers rather than practitioners, objectors rather than leaders. Let us humbly understand our beginnings upon which our ethics are founded. The beliefs of all of us evolved as did those of Aldo Leopold. Professor Leopold became the wolf's champion and one of the most articulate in support of predators. And yet as a young forest ecologist in the Southwest, he wrote: "The Biological Survey is making splendid progress in eradication work. But let us remember this: as the work progresses, the remaining animals become fewer, more sophisticated and more expensive to catch. It is going to take patience and money to catch the last wolf or lion in New Mexico. But the last one must be caught before the job can be called fully successful."[8] His subsequent change of mind and the biological research he encouraged have helped to give the wolf a more appropriate position in our world. But most of us, like Aldo Leopold, begin life believing that all wolves are bad.

The wolf ethic came too late to New Mexico and 46 other states. We may continue to hold our wolves in Canada and in Alaska only if we understand the ancient source of our wolf fear and comprehend the natural history of our human need for wild surroundings. Man is just now beginning to relate some of his behavioral diseases to the ecological imbalance he has created within his environment. The wolf ethic may be one evidence that we can, indeed, live in harmony with our surroundings. If this ethic continues to be strong, the wilderness and its wildlife may survive as we strengthen our ties with the land, learning to live as civilized people. Here is the way Blair Fraser put it: "However urban we become, however soft and civilized, we still have the cleansing wild within a few hundred miles, more or less. It is good to know that no matter how much stronger we grow, Canada will still be the same kind of country." If, may I add, we continue to hold the wolf and other wilderness wildlife within this rim of wild country.[9]

The wolf ethic must apply to all wilderness wildlife vulnerable to man: arctic char, the harp seal, all the whales, the polar bear and grizzly, caribou and moose, musk-ox, the whooping crane, all the waterfowl, and countless others living in delicate balance with their surroundings—every animal, indeed, that owes survival to human appreciation of its existence. A sea that has lost its whales to man, an arctic river without its char, a prairie pothole without its canvasback are environments as tame as our Precambrian Shield without timber wolves. It is my contention that if we comprehend how and why the wolf was unable to survive over most of its range in the United States, and if we can understand the reasons for its survival near the urban centers of Canada and Alaska, then we might have the means to hold most or all of our wilderness wildlife within its present environment.

[8] Leopold, "The Game Situation in the Southwest," *Bulletin American Game Protective Association*, IX, No. 2 (1920), p. 5.

[9] At this point a wolf howl, recorded on tape by Dr. Douglas H. Pimlott of the University of Toronto, was played, ringing out wild and clear over the public address system of the Hilton Plaza.

The wolf was finally banished from most of the United States by a federal bureau which reacted strongly to a small and biased public, the cattlemen. I know of no direct federal or provincial aggressions in Canada that threaten the extinction of a species, as may now hold for the red wolf in the United States. But certainly a failure to understand and protect threatens survival of the Barren Ground grizzly in the Northwest Territories. The same holds too, I believe, with some kinds of waterfowl which, as in the case of the canvasback, have not been adequately protected during recent drought years of poor production. As with the wolf in the United States and, indeed, as with the passenger pigeon in times past, knowing officials scoff at the idea that any wild bird or animal could suddenly vanish from what appears to be an abundance. The truth remains that even with some species regularly held on the game lists, we do not understand enough of their life histories to fairly judge the severity of the increasing pressures we place upon these kinds. In respect to the Barren Ground grizzly, Macpherson points out, "Reduction programs against large predators lead easily to local extinctions, for, as familiarity with the animal decreases, those that remain are all the more feared and detested."[10]

The governments of Canada and the United States, acting under legal traditions stemming from the Magna Carta are responsible for the protection of wildlife. This responsibility surely must respect the timber wolf and puma, grizzly and polar bear just as much as it protects songbirds and farm game. But just as a few cattlemen in the western United States commanded the extinction of the wolf, so might oil men, timber and mining interests, and light-conscienced politicians write finis for some kinds of Canadian wildlife. Lobo was exiled from the United States before the citizens or even the sponsors of his departure were aware that he was endangered. All wilderness wildlife is equally vulnerable in Canada unless citizens keep abreast of the times and enforce their influence before it becomes too late. "The citizen group is essential to our social organization where wildland values are concerned. The Civil Service and elected representatives, unguided by the organized conscience of the dedicated, are too vulnerable to the economic religion of our time."[11]

Public interest in Canada is becoming strong and effective through the influence of such organizations as the Federation of Ontario

[10]A. H. Macpherson, "The Barren-Ground Grizzly Bear and its Survival in Northern Canada," *Canadian Audubon*, XXVII, No. 1 (1965), p. 8.

[11] Ian McTaggart Cowan, *Wilderness—Concept, Function, and Management* (VIII Horace M. Albright Conservation Lectureship. Berkeley: University of California School of Forestry and Conservation, 1968), p. 12.

Naturalists, the Canadian Audubon Society, the Canadian Society of Wildlife and Fishery Biologists, and The Nature Conservancy of Canada. The Sierra Club, especially through its publications, has also played an important role in arousing awareness in Canada. The force of such groups, advised by experts within their memberships, recently has given wildlife and wilderness values a more prominent place in Canadian public concern. This is illustrated by the following examples: (1) The strife between polar bears and citizens at Churchill, Manitoba, must now be settled on a basis fair to the bears because of the wide public interest this bear-human conflict has drawn. (2) At this writing, the harvest policy for the harp seal in the Gulf of St. Lawrence is headline news on the prairies, half a continent away from the scene. (3) Listening to wolves has become a thrilling experience to hundreds of people who have learned through Douglas H. Pimlott's studies that wolves inside and out of our national parks will respond to a human imitation of their howl.[12]

Scientists are bringing wilderness wildlife closer to the people through clear reporting. "One of the best places to see a Barren-Ground grizzly bear in the eastern part of the Canadian Arctic," writes A. H. Macpherson, "is on the Thelon River, upstream from Beverly Lake. People have often seen a grizzly here striding along the river bank, neck, shoulders and rump swinging with an undulating rhythm, head swaying from side to side in a characteristic carriage at once shy and defensive, yet menacing, as it moves low between the great curving talons of the forepaws. And overall, there is the aura of wildness and strangeness evoked by the coarse grey mantle of guard hair blowing in the wind."[13] Few Canadians will venture to the Thelon; fewer still will ever see a Barren Ground grizzly bear. But because of Macpherson's account, they will want to know that the Thelon grizzlies survive. It is only this wish of the many that will secure such survival on the remote arctic prairies. So with all wildlife; a public awareness of value is essential for survival.

The wilderness area, as a preserve, is an artificial creation of the white man. In less than 100 years he has wrested most of the wild country from its original inhabitants, tilling the dark soils, grazing the light soils and arid country, removing the forests, overpopulating the gathering places, using rivers and lakes as his sewers. Wilderness preserves were set aside by men of great foresight to protect specimens of North America from our own selves. The national parks of both Canada and the United States are outstanding results of such fore-

[12] Russel J. Rutter and Douglas H. Pimlott, *The World of the Wolf* (Philadelphia: J. P. Lippincott Co., 1968), p. 174.

[13] Macpherson, *loc cit.*, p. 2.

sight. In respect to wildlife, however, the misfortune is that parks and reserves may not include the entire range of a local population, hence parks cannot save or adequately protect some species. An outstanding example, of course, is the Rocky Mountain sheep. Much of its high summer range has been protected, but some of the critical wintering pastures have been exploited and are now untenable. In considering the plight of the red wolf, Mr. Rupert Cutler of The Wilderness Society wondered if the establishment of a wolf refuge might not save this species. Dr. Douglas H. Pimlott, an authority on wolves, pointed out that the effective protection of a limited preserve was questionable because of the large home range of a pack of red wolves. "The emphasis must be on developing a tolerance for wolves," he said, in an attempt to develop public opinion in their favor.[14]

Our challenge is to understand this principle as it relates to species still strong in numbers on their pristine ranges: the polar bear and Barren Ground grizzly, the harp seal and other kinds still thriving on broad ranges where they are increasingly exposed to the presence and pressures of the white man. Establishing boundaries of wilderness areas is not enough. The security of wilderness wildlife hinges upon our public wish to share these environments rather than upon selfish and dangerous desires to take these ranges solely for human use and pleasure. I am not critical of the bounded parks and reserves. But these are not sufficient to maintain the wilderness wildlife of Canada.

Leopold considered that wilderness game consists of species harmful to or harmed by economic land uses.[15] He named seven species— wapiti, caribou, buffalo, grizzly bear, moose, mountain sheep, and mountain goat. Each of us might enlarge this list in our own way, adding polar bear, musk-ox, puma, and many others. I, for one, feel that we must include all of our waterfowl, the ducks, geese, and swans as wilderness wildlife. The slough and pothole nesting range of our prairie provinces is in its way as wild and pristine as when first seen in 1738 by La Vérendrye and his colleagues. The buffalo are gone, to be sure; the surroundings are of agriculture; but the flora and fauna within each rim of marsh is quite the same as before the coming of the white man. Some waterfowl, like the black brant, live close to man's doorstep through fall and winter, then fly to the very northern edges of our arctic wilderness to breed and rear their young where man seldom sets foot. Such wildlife, if only as voices heard at night, is a heritage we are taking for granted, and which cannot survive unless there develops greater public interest in its welfare.

[14] Pimlott and Joslin, *loc. cit.*, p. 389.

[15] Leopold, *Game Management* (New York: Charles Scribner's Sons, 1933), p. 134.

Most North American game ducks nest on private farmland in the Canadian and United States prairies, often in sight of farmhouse windows and at the edges of main roads. Wild ducks, like robins and song sparrows, are territorial, each pair isolating itself from others of its kind during the nesting phase of the breeding season. Thus, while great numbers may gather on small ranges in winter and during migration, ducks must spread far and wide over their nesting grounds in spring. Preserves and refuges cannot save these waterfowl. In some way we must provide the landowner with incentives to preserve waterfowl nesting habitat on farmland.

But the problem of preserving waterfowl is even more complex than this breeding habitat quotient. Because they are migratory, no state or province is completely responsible for their welfare. With such regional irresponsibility, which exists despite our international treaty, wildfowling is becoming socialized as a source of public recreation, resulting in harvests beyond the capacity of the environment to produce. Even in the depths of the recent drought there has been more breeding habitat than ducks to use it. The buffalo wolf is gone from the prairies. Who is to say that the canvasback, as things now stand, may not be far behind? Indeed, because of high mortality during dry years of poor production, the canvasback has already disappeared from many fine bulrush marshes where it bred commonly only 15 years ago.

There is considerable evidence that the ethic keeping wilderness and wildlife close to the people of southern Canada may not be holding on the northern frontiers. "Here the vast, almost uninhabited, northern half of the nation has maintained the illusion that wilderness is present in such abundance that no special concern is needed for its survival."[16] The threat is not simply from complacency in the presence of what appears to be plenty, but from changes being wrought by outsiders who do not plan to live within the environments they alter. They have no permanent ties to the land, few obligations to the countryside or its wildlife. They come and they go; in a twinkling the country is changed forever.

These outlanders appear to be of three sorts.

First, there is the growing company of hunters and fishermen who stand face to face with wilderness wildlife less than a day's scheduled flight from Chicago or other centers of population. Such tourists, now leaving their trail of Seven-Up cans across the Barren Grounds, often have no foundation of wilderness ethics. Out of touch with regular associates and tempering influences, usually at some distance from the law, they tend to behave carelessly in regard to wildlife.

[16] Cowan, loc. cit., p. 26.

When meeting migratory species in their fall and winter concentrations, there is a tendency of man to kill beyond reasonable need. This held for the passenger pigeon in its time; it holds for waterfowl now. Of more sedentary kinds, especially the carnivores, the trophy may be taken without "fair chase." Wildlife that has never seen hunters often shows no fear of man in pristine settings. Indeed, arctic wolves, polar bears and grizzly bears often accept the close presence of man without alarm. The hunter must carry his imagination as well as his rifle to justify a kill. It is possible that hunting may be an important source of income to natives, as with geese on Ontario's James Bay coast, but there must be tighter control of outlanders using wild country. Aircraft and tracked vehicles easily carry soft-handed hunters ever deeper within primitive country where a delicate lady in a red jacket may now slay a grizzly in its bed. And the track of the "weasel" or other vehicle that led to the kill may mar the arctic flora for many years to come.

A sad sidelight on careless hunter use of primitive places is the removal of irredeemable artifacts from settings of great historical importance. The Hudson's Bay Company depot at York Factory, once the seat of western culture and source of its materials, has been ransacked by tourists, much of the vandalism having been accomplished by goose hunters on a wilderness spree. The Royal Canadian Mounted Police have done a magnificent job of enforcement among the tourist hunters of the north. But tourism, encouraged on a booster basis, is moving ahead faster than the means to understand and control it.

The second threat comes from big business and big bureaus which, when planning the exploitation of power, fuel, timber, and minerals, do not consider wildlife in their cost accounting. Thus, the indirect loss of game, fur bearers and fish, and the pristine values of unspoiled country may exceed the immediate cash worth of the resource being exploited. Cowan points out, "We in Canada are still destroying hundreds of miles of potentially magnificent recreation land by flooding forest land without clearing. The results would make strong men weep, but immediate economic arguments prevail."[17]

Regarding floodings, there has been a broad awakening in Manitoba, where citizens from many communities and of many backgrounds have delayed, perhaps thwarted, government plans to flood South Indian Lake, a biological and recreational gem in the central northland, threatened for sacrifice to cheap power. The hard cash talk of big bureaus and big government must be weighed carefully by an enlightened community against losses of those wilderness qualities that Blair

[17] *Ibid.*, p. 28.

Fraser and his colleagues believed fundamental to the survival of Canada.

The third major threat comes from the pioneers. Now they quickly attain their isolated destinations by air, come equipped with motor toboggans, tracked vehicles, and other mechanical paraphernalia. The army and the air force, oil companies, and other private agencies send exploring parties to assay the wilderness. Reckless, uncontrolled use of wildlife about their camps has resulted. Here, it must be noted, even the exploring biologist may be careless when 2,000 miles or more away from his laboratory. A sanctuary against biological collecting has been established in the outskirts of Churchill, Manitoba. This is necessary protection of wildlife near the town; but as yet this has not been a force in preventing naturalists' litter of camera papers and lunch tins from violating the edge of wild country.

Presently, it seems, our goals in the north are mainly industrial. Where mining explorations are not underway, the public land, much of it at least, is open to future exploitation under lease. It is worth noting that tourism itself, which sets about to bring people and their money north for pleasure, is widely handled as an industry. Unless we take care, the north will be managed in accordance with the requirements of industry. "The policies of the state will be subject to similar influence; education will be adapted to industrial need; the disciplines required by the industrial system will be the conventional morality of the community. All other goals will be made to seem precious, unimportant or antisocial. . . . If, on the other hand, the industrial system is only a part, and relatively a diminishing part, of life, there is much less occasion for concern. Aesthetic goals will have pride of place; those who serve them will not be subject to the goals of the industrial system; the industrial system itself will be subordinate to the claims of these dimensions of life."[18] It behooves us, whose children and grandchildren may cherish the north, to become familiar with the threats that endanger this great region and its wildlife.

[18] John Kenneth Galbraith, *The New Industrial State* (New York: Signet, 1967), p. 405.

# "WILD-DĒOR-NESS," THE PLACE OF WILD BEASTS

*Roderick Nash*
Associate Professor of History, University of California at Santa Barbara

Two speakers have already explained how wildlife is a symbol or criteria of wilderness. I would like to probe further the intellectual and spiritual relationship of wildlife and wilderness, arguing that the idea of wildlife is built into the very meaning of wilderness.

Etymology, the science of the origin and derivation of words, offers a key to understanding. In the early Teutonic and Norse tongues, from which the word "wilderness" developed, the root was "will," which had a descriptive meaning of willful, self-willed, or uncontrollable. From "will" came "willd" as an adjective and, by the tenth or eleventh century, this had contracted to "wild," a word used to convey the concept of being lost, unruly, disordered, or confused. In Old Swedish, for instance, "wild" was linked to the image of boiling water, that is water not lying placidly but bubbling and fuming in uncontrollable fashion—wildly. Similarly, a child could be described by an unhappy parent as being wild.

In Old English there was a general term "dēor," which meant animal or beast. "Deer" obviously derives from this term, but "dēor" was a general term for any animal or beast. When the adjective "wild" was prefixed to "dēor"—"wild-dēor"—the connotation was of a creature not under man's control. For convenience one of the d's was dropped, so the word became "wildēor." The earliest use of this term that I have encountered is in the eighth-century epic *Beowulf*, where "wildeor" appears in reference to fantastic, monstrous creatures that live in a dark slimy pool in the forest.

From this point the derivation of "wilderness" is clear. "Wildēor" contracted still further to "wilder." "Ness," indicating a quality (for example, "happiness"), was added. So wilderness means the quality of being the place of wild beasts. Wilderness is the province, the habitat of wild creatures just as civilization is man's habitat. The word "bewilder" is similarly derived: to become like a wildeor—disordered, out of control, beyond guidance and governance.

Those who covet wild country sense the link between wildlife and wilderness. The presence of wildlife, especially some particular kinds, is evidence of the absence of man. It suggests that natural harmonies still exist. Simply knowing that wildlife is present is important to the meaning of wilderness. If wildlife is removed, although everything else remains visibly the same, the intensity of the sense of wilderness is diminished. As Dr. Hochbaum suggested, the knowledge that there are wolves within a hundred miles of every Canadian makes the country seem wilder.

Certain animals have been closely related in the American experience of wilderness: one thinks of the beaver and the buffalo. They are more than animals; they are folk heroes of the wilderness. So is the grizzly. It is significant that in 1967 Andy Russell, the Canadian wildlife expert, entitled his book *Grizzly Country*. He could have just as well entitled it *Wilderness*, because as he explains, grizzly country is wilderness. The loon is closely related to the north country wilderness Sigurd Olson knows so well. Without the loon, what would the Quetico-Superior and the great Canadian northland be? Certainly they would be poorer in a spiritual way.

Looking into the American past we see many expressions of this connection between wildlife and wilderness. There is the early nineteenth-century artist John James Audubon, who went beyond a love of wild birds to an appreciation of the country in which they lived. George Catlin, the almost forgotten originator of the national park idea, also believed that wildlife and wilderness were inseparable. On the upper Missouri in 1832, Catlin witnessed Indians slaughtering 1,400 buffalo merely to take the tongues to the trading post for whiskey. Catlin sadly predicted that if this continued, in time both Indians and buffalo would be extinct—the buffalo because of the Indians, the Indians because of the booze. As an alternative, he conceived the idea of setting aside a strip of land running down the eastern face of the Rocky Mountains from Canada to Mexico and calling it a national park. In this park the buffalo could run, Indians wear their native costumes, and artists come to paint them both.

Henry David Thoreau delighted in wild things. In a little-known passage in his writings he refers to lynx and how they triggered a sense of the wild. The presence of lynx around Concord meant the same thing to him then that being able to sip coffee while watching a wolf trotting across his marsh means to Dr. Hochbaum now. When Thoreau saw even the track of a lynx in Massachusetts in the 1840's, he took hope that the New World was still new and wild.

Theodore Roosevelt was both hunter and lover of big game. I think these things can exist side by side; I think they did in Roosevelt's case. As president of the Boone and Crockett Club, Roosevelt did a great deal, even before the Sierra Club was founded, to alert the country to the need of preserving big game ranges. In Roosevelt's mind these were the equivalents of national parks. Again wildlife and wilderness went hand in hand.

For Aldo Leopold, a pioneer ecologist, awareness expanded from wildlife to wilderness, and then on to the total environment. In fact, as Dr. Hochbaum pointed out, Leopold actually began his career believing in the desirability of predator extermination. But as the concepts of an "ecological conscience" and a "land ethic" took shape in his mind, he came to understand how his early convictions were founded on ignorance of both the biological and spiritual relationship of predators to wild country. He dates the moment of awareness quite precisely. As *A Sand County Almanac* describes it, the incident occurred during Leopold's southwest Forest Service days about 1920. Shots rang out from the rimrock, and, Leopold writes, "We reached the old wolf in time to watch a fierce green fire dying in her eyes. I realized then, and have known ever since, that there was something new to me in those eyes—something known only to her and to the mountain. I was young then, and full of trigger-itch; I thought that because fewer wolves meant more deer, that no wolves would mean hunters' paradise. But after seeing the green fire die, I sensed that neither the wolf nor the mountain agreed with such a view."

Leopold had the same feeling about an old grizzly—the last of its kind roaming the Arizona high country. When a government hunter shot the bear for bounty, Leopold wrote a benediction: "Escudilla still hangs on the horizon, but when you see it you no longer think of bear. It's only a mountain now." The cost of eliminating the grizzly was a diminution in the quality of the wilderness. Using one of those sparkling metaphors for which he was famous, Leopold later told his University of Wisconsin students, "When we attempt to say that an animal is 'useful,' 'ugly,' or 'cruel' we are failing to see it as part of the land. We do not make the same error of calling a carburetor 'greedy.' We see it as part of a functioning motor." When wolves and bears were involved, the land in question was wilderness. Aldo Leopold understood the relationship.

A final example from our own time: I left Santa Barbara this morning at 8:30. As the plane circled to gain altitude before striking north across the coast range, we looked down at the oil-fouled channel. I thought of the lives of birds and sea animals that had been disturbed, if not extinguished, by the blowout at Platform A. And I thought how these creatures had been so much a part of the wilderness of this place. Their value, in an aesthetic or spiritual sense, far transcended their size and number. To hear the bark of a sea lion, to see a spouting whale or a leaping porpoise is to experience wilderness. In Santa Barbara we did not fully comprehend the value of these things until . we lost them.

The presence of wildlife, in sum, is a gesture of humility. By permitting and encouraging other forms of life to share the environment, man indicates his willingness to stop short of complete conquest. He affirms a belief in other orders than his own. And this, it seems to me, is the essence of preserving wild country. In a literal as well as a symbolic way wild-deor defines wilderness.

# DISCUSSION

Marty Talbot, Smithsonian research associate, Office of Environmental Sciences, Smithsonian Institution:

Aesthetics and other aspects of the relationship between wildlife and wilderness have already been mentioned this morning, but for the purposes of this discussion I would like to put them into sharper focus—to show that wildlife is basic to much of the value that wilderness holds for man.

There are at least four aspects of the contribution of wildlife to wilderness for the benefit of man: (1) scientific, (2) reservoir of genetic materials, (3) economic, and (4) enjoyment, which includes recreation.

First, wilderness provides science, or scientists, with two basic essentials on which the survival of mankind and our current world may well depend, by serving as an outdoor laboratory for defining and studying the many components of natural ecosystems and their interractions and processes, and providing ecological reference points that can serve as guidelines and aides in land use. Wildlife is an integral component of almost all natural ecosystems.

More and more of the world is being used, misused, frequently destroyed or changed in some way by the activities of man, principally because the burgeoning population demands more from the land in the way of food and other resources. The growing human population is the problem that underlies all other conservation matters. Everyone now knows—or should know—that the human population is expanding at a constantly increasing rate. It took probably two million years for the earth's population to reach one billion in 1830. It only took 100 years to reach the second billion, 30 years for the third, and it will be about 15 years to the fourth. More people place more demands on the earth's finite resources. But the needs of the increasing numbers are further increased by technology. In a modern technological society,

38

each person requires far more of all resources than in a less industrialized, agricultural society. The United States, with just six percent of the world's population, consumes annually from 40 to 80 percent of the whole world's available renewable and nonrenewable resources. The world's resources—including air, water, land, wilderness, and wildlife—are finite and they clearly cannot support this continued unlimited growth of population and resource consumption. The unlimited growth of both must be stopped, and at the same time we must learn to make more efficient use of the resources we have.

Scientists are expected to provide answers for increasing productivity to meet these demands, but more and more of them are realizing that we lack much of the basic knowledge of the biological processes necessary to achieve it. Some of this knowledge can come from the laboratories, but much of it must come from the study of natural processes under natural conditions—in the outdoor laboratories that wilderness provides.

In recognition of this crisis in the need for basic biological knowledge, biologists from over 60 nations throughout the world are attempting to coordinate their research under the International Biological Program (IBP), a nonpolitical, nongovernmental worldwide program of biological research sponsored by the International Council of Scientific Unions. One of the main objectives of the IBP's Conservation Section is the identification and protection of adequate samples of the world's natural habitats as ecological reference points for scientific research. The importance of this activity is also recognized in a series of resolutions passed by the International Conference on the Resources of the Biosphere organized by UNESCO in Paris in September of 1968, attended by delegates from 63 nations and many international organizations.

Some of the "outdoor laboratories" are protected in national parks, some in various reserves, but all are wilderness in the sense that they are places where natural processes can be investigated. Virtually all of these processes involve or are affected by wildlife. Stated in another way, without wildlife—ranging from the invertebrate fauna through the largest mammals and birds—these wilderness areas would have little if any of this truly great value to both scientific knowledge and to human welfare.

The second main point, which is associated with the first, is that wildlife in wilderness provides a source or reservoir of genetic material for whole species of animals as well as genetic strains for crossbreeding to develop more productive forms that are better able to provide for growing human needs.

It is curious that in the course of history man has domesticated only a very tiny percentage of the large number of the world's species of animals and birds. Each of the conventional domestic animals has a relatively limited range of habitat to which it is adapted. The result is that much of the earth's surface is marginal or submarginal for our conventional domesticates; if we are to use the remaining vast areas for maximum production of food and other human needs, we must either try to modify the habitat to suit our domestic animals—which is far too expensive and impractical in most areas—or seek animals better adapted to the conditions. Wildlife consists of such animals.

The wide spectrum of wild ungulates is adapted to virtually all of the earth's habitats; species can be found to fit virtually any condition, including those places badly degraded through overuse by conventional livestock.

Wilderness areas with their wildlife provide the source of such animals, which can be domesticated as they are or which can be cross-bred with existing domesticates to provide other desired characteristics.

The importance of this "gene bank" aspect of wilderness is now receiving international attention; it is part of the IBP, it was the subject of resolutions by the recent Biosphere Conference, and some gene bank work is now being handled by the Food and Agricultural Organization of the United Nations.

The third consideration is the economic value of wilderness wildlife. This can be divided into two parts: tourism and meat production.

Tourism is an important industry in many parts of the world. And while much of this rapidly growing industry is based on the attractions of cities and other cultural objects, a large and increasing proportion is drawn to wilderness areas. The attraction in most such areas is the wildlife.

In East Africa, tourism is now the second largest foreign-currency-earning industry, and an estimated 97 percent of the tourists come primarily to see the wildlife, predators and herbivores combined.

Without wildlife, the scenery, although grand and inspiring, would not draw tourists. The income from visitors gives wilderness with its wildlife tangible value to the Africans who now have an interest in preserving it. Without this value other kinds of development would be tried in East African wilderness.

Game cropping and hunting are other aspects of the economic value of wilderness wildlife. When based on scientific game management, both can and do contribute an additional economic value on a sustained yield basis without adversely affecting wildlife. In most cases they provide a significant contribution to human nutrition.

My fourth and last point is one we all know very well—enjoyment. The entertainment provided by watching any living creature moving and going about its daily business of eating, preening, playing, defending its territory, is well known. I really think you could accuse many scientists of choosing a life of perpetual entertainment derived from studying the antics of their subject.

Wildlife provides an aesthetic experience in watching the glorious or subtle colors, the graceful, flowing, sensuous lines of both the creature itself or any of its parts, and the lines of its movements. The nerve-tingling, sensuous enjoyment of wildlife has been the subject of man's art works since the earliest cave paintings, and it can still arouse emotions.

Less welcome but perhaps equally important are the adrenalin- or fear-producing experiences—the bear or lion prowling around the camp, perhaps sniffing out a meal of bacon or freshly killed game. The adrenalin and fear and the control of these are of very great value to men and can actually contribute to enjoyment.

One of the what I would call not-quite-enjoyments of wilderness, but certainly a part of the wilderness experience, is the petty annoyance caused by mosquitoes, black flies, and the ants that take over a camp in Africa. Insects too have their value as part of the ecosystem, as well as being a personal challenge to man's capacity for self-control and endurance. Although I might prefer using insect repellents, these character-building experiences are of value to man and by contrast reveal some of the advantages of our modern civilization.

To sum up, then, wilderness wildlife provides much of the value that wilderness holds for men, in terms of economics, enjoyment, aesthetics, scientific knowledge, and general well-being. Through these values, wildlife provides a sort of insurance policy for wilderness itself.

*Session Chairman David R. Brower:* The first question asks if the panel feels that President Wayburn's opening statement that man is the most important species carries the appropriate attitude toward wilderness preservation.

I would say I don't think so but people do. I think the most important thing that operates in our society is self-interest. We can be the greatest threat to other wildlife; we can be the best ally. I think eco-politics will develop where we will realize that a fusing of self-interests, ours and that of other wildlife, will probably lead to our survival and anything else won't.

*Lee M. Talbot:* One can look at the question of the importance of the human species on an aesthetic or philosophical basis. I think that no one species is more important than any other, be it invertebrate,

vertebrate, or whatever. However, from a standpoint of living, of effecting conservation, we have to recognize that people happen to be in the driver's seat. People are the ecological dominant. From that standpoint they are most important whether we like it or not. We have to deal with humans. Hopefully we can educate those of us who do not realize that other creatures are as important philosophically. For example, if predators are to be reestablished, we have to take people into account because they are a critically important factor to deal with. I interpreted President Wayburn's remarks in that way.

*Chairman Brower:* I wasn't clear. I don't disagree with Dr. Wayburn or you on the matter of the importance of people. I was making a joke. I think we may prove to be a short-lived phenomenon, though.

Now another question for Dr. Talbot. Can wolves, other predators, and other wilderness wildlife be reintroduced into wilderness or park areas, and what is the likelihood of their breeding and surviving?

*Lee Talbot:* The simple answer is yes, so long as the park or wilderness area provides all the requirements for the survival of the wildlife involved. This means there must be adequate amounts of food for the yearlong requirements of the animals. There must be adequate water and the vegetation composition must be satisfactory to provide the type of cover, feeding areas, protection, and so forth needed by the animals. The area must be large enough to provide for the yearlong movements of the animals. And the above factors must be available in large enough supply to support a viable animal population. Some species can survive when their population is quite low, while others require fairly large numbers.

All of these factors are interrelated, and the principles hold true for predators or nonpredators. Predators pose two problems that are not usually present with other forms of wildlife. First is the danger that they may move away from the reserved area and threaten livestock living outside. The answer is to recognize that some predators require large ranges and to make sure the parks or wilderness areas are large enough to accommodate them, and, of course, to assure that there is adequate food available within the reserve.

The second problem involves human attitudes toward predators. As has been pointed out, people get emotional about predators, and some think that they cannot be reintroduced because people and predators do not mix. Earlier this morning, our Canadian colleague, Albert Hochbaum, refuted this belief, much to my delight. Elsewhere internationally there are abundant examples of mutual tolerance between predators and man.

In Africa I have frequently been told that it is not possible to develop the country "properly" if you still have lions and other predators around. But it has not been the Africans saying this. It has been the advisors from Europe and America who all too often are trying to develop Africa according to the ideas, techniques, and standards of Europe or America—not in accordance with the very different ecological and sociological conditions of Africa. Fortunately, advisors are not always blindly obeyed, and because in East Africa wildlife is the basis of the tourist industry (the second largest source of foreign currency), the tourist experts point out that the lions and other predators are the largest drawing cards.

India provides another example involving lions. The last surviving Asian lions remain in a small area, the Forest of Gir in northwest India, where they live in intimate association with a large population of Indian herders with their livestock. When I last visited the Gir, several months ago, I walked within less than 20 feet of some of the lions. The local people there are fantastically tolerant of those animals —far more than I felt like being with my experiences with African lions. As has been pointed out earlier today, humans and most predators are not mutually exclusive. Tolerance becomes a matter of knowledge, acquaintance, and mutual respect in some cases, and of assuring that the ecological requirements of the creatures are provided.

*H. Albert Hochbaum:* I would like to add another word about the continuing existence of the wolf in Canada. Undoubtedly Farley Mowat's book, *Never Cry Wolf*, had something to do with the strengthening of the public concept of the "wolf ethic" in Canada. Sympathy for and interest in the wolf must temper government control programs.

*Chairman Brower:* Dr. Nash, if as the Leopold report* pointed out there are a thousand people who want to see wildlife live to only one who wants to kill it, what is lacking in our efforts to make wildlife preservation a reality?

*Roderick Nash:* Lacking is the impetus to translate concern and desire into effective action. We see this constantly in all fields. Most everyone wants peace, for instance, and yet there is war. To bridge the gap in regard to wild things and the environment generally, we need stronger doses of two stimulants: fear and love. If we really did

* Starker Leopold, *Reports of the Special Advisory Board on Wildlife Management for the Secretary of the Interior, 1963-1968.* (Washington, D.C.: Wildlife Management Institute, 1969).

believe Paul Ehrlich, if we really thought that first wildlife and then man himself were going to perish, our conduct would change abruptly. Environmental disaster would scare us into action. But we also need more intense love. How many of those 999 people the Leopold report mentions do you suppose have more than a casual, passing interest in wildlife? It is this casualness that permits them to shrug and turn the other way when effort is demanded. Consequently we need more stimulation such as that provided in the Sierra Club's Exhibit Format books. They show us the great places, the things we are working for, in such dramatic and moving manner as to impel us to act. We need a heaven, in other words, as well as a hell, to move us along the path of righteousness.

*Chairman Brower:* The next question is for Marty Talbot. What is the effect of the Viet Nam war on that country's wildlife?

*Mrs. Talbot:* Vietnamese wildlife has been affected in three ways at least. Wildlife is killed, its habitat is damaged, and it is driven away by the disturbance. Just the other day I was talking with a herpetologist, Simon Campden-Main, who had returned from Viet Nam in 1968. He had made a collection of reptiles in Viet Nam and was working on them at the Smithsonian Institution. He talked about wildlife and the war with Vietnamese villagers in the areas in which he was collecting. He was told that at a village near the Cambodian border the former herds of wild elephant had been destroyed or driven off, and even one of the last surviving Javanese rhinoceros which had lived near the village had disappeared. Our news reports and official releases often report so many "enemy elephants" destroyed, usually by helicopters or other aircraft. Of course, no one knows how many of these enemy elephants were actually pack animals used by the enemy and how many were wild elephants which happened to be in enemy territory.

Lee [Talbot] has worked in Viet Nam and elsewhere in Southeast Asia off and on since 1955, and has made several trips to that area this year. He has frequently been told that our military have orders to destroy any large wildlife they see "to deny them to the enemy." This doubtless results in the needless slaughter of Asia's wildlife.

The war also changes the wildlife habitat through such things as bombing, defoliation, burning, and resettlement. It also increases the hunting pressure on wildlife, through the presence of large numbers of well-armed soldiers and through the destruction of the villagers' livestock. Wildlife provides a major source of protein for the villagers throughout Southeast Asia. When we were in northern Cambodia in

1964 we saw villagers snaring and hunting all kinds of wildlife, and I remember feeling very sorry for a large monitor lizard being carried off to the soup pot. At that time the Cambodian Forest Department personnel were trying to protect the nearly extinct, primitive wild cow, the kouprey, from cart loads of soldiers sent out from their outfits to shoot any wild animals they could find for food. Understandably enough, most troops will shoot wildlife for food, and of course, some do it for sport. We have talked to a number of American servicemen in Southeast Asia in the last few years who have told of the tigers, elephants, deer, and other wildlife they have shot.

*Chairman Brower:* Here are two questions for Dr. Hochbaum. First, what is the attitude of the people of Canada toward wildlife conservation? Second, would you discuss further the forces threatening the wilderness in northern Canada?

*Dr. Hochbaum:* Canadians are well informed about, and in sympathy with, wildlife conservation. Wildlife and resource conservation is the subject of many radio and television news, documentary, and entertainment programs, mostly of high caliber. We are less knowledgeable, less well advised about assaults on the environment, but interest and information regarding environmental conservation is enlarging rapidly.

The interest in the seal hunt on the Gulf of St. Lawrence underlines the importance of the communication media. People did not become widely concerned until they could see what was happening on film.

Forces working against the northern wilderness may be more serious than in the south for two reasons. First of all, violations against the land, as oil spillage, ruts caused by tracked vehicles, trash thrown helter-skelter, are virtually everlasting. In the deep winters and short summers, for instance, a Seven-Up can is nearly indestructible. Where a weasel half-track has gouged a deep rut, the change is permanent. Oil spillage is a catastrophe that may be harmful forever, or almost that long. Secondly, those who violate the north, often in the course of bringing industry and money there, do so without conscience, without threat of reprimand. The country is so big, it seems to the violators, that no harm can come of carelessness. Moreover, because the land is thinly settled, one's peers do not complain; each person feels only a temporary part of a setting, the destruction for which he is not considered accountable. This carelessness may be changing, but great harm has already been done on a wide scale.

*Chairman Brower:* Dr. Nash, can wilderness terms be properly applied to the Santa Barbara Channel? Will it dilute the present concept of wilderness?

*Dr. Nash:* On the contrary, the ocean is one of the few environments virtually devoid of man and his works. It is really an ultimate in a scale of degrees of wildness. I would even argue that the Santa Barbara Channel, and there are 1,800 square miles of it, is wilder than the High Sierra. At least you will see far less of man and civilization, let us say at the western end of San Miguel Island, than you would on the John Muir Trail any August day. At sea even the garbage sinks out of sight. Seriously, we would do well, I believe, to inventory and to cherish forgotten wildernesses such as the sea. One session of the 1967 Wilderness Conference was devoted to the subject of forgotten wilderness, and included a speech by Kenneth S. Norris on marine wilderness.* But we still find it difficult to discern wilderness unless it is labeled such on a map.

*Chairman Brower:* Dr. Talbot, the current newspapers are carrying stories about three dead whales that were washed ashore in southern California. Do you think the oil blowout of January, 1969, offshore at Santa Barbara is responsible for these deaths?

*Lee Talbot:* I do not have all the information on the present status of this subject. However, when the first oil leak was announced, the possibility of danger to whales was one of the things that concerned us at the Smithsonian. I might add here parenthetically that we have an organization called the Center for Short-Lived Phenomena. This is an information center which has a worldwide network of correspondents. The purpose of this center is to quickly notify the scientists concerned whenever a short-lived phenomenon such as an oil spill, the birth of an island, an earthquake, volcano, something like that occurs so that scientists can move in and study them while they still exist. Oil spills unfortunately have been one of our biggest activities.

One of the big worries about the Santa Barbara spill was that the gray whales and others might be in process of migrating through the channel. The question that concerned us was what would be the long-term effect on the gray whale. It was not felt that the oil would kill them on the spot because they are too big; it might kill the young ones, but not an adult. But suppose the whales inhaled or ingested the oil, or suppose there were various other factors that we don't know anything about. Hence, our concern was that there should be a moni-

* The speech is included in the published proceedings of that conference, *Wilderness and the Quality of Life.*

toring of the whales after they had passed through the area. From what I was just told about the three that have washed ashore, it may be we are unfortunately correct. Or it just could be a coincidence. And, of course, the president of the Union Oil Company is reported to have said, "Well, it's only a few birds; they're not very important."

*Chairman Brower:* Margaret Owings has a question for Dr. Talbot. "Dr. Ehrlich's emphasis on pesticides prompts me to ask," she says, "if we in California should not commence a movement to halt the use of persistent pesticides by legislative action?" She notes that Arizona has a moratorium on DDT because of DDT and milk, and comments that some pesticides aren't that hazardous.

*Lee Talbot:* Legislative action may be the only way to do it, and there are two lines of approach. First is to use existing legislation, and second is to pass whatever additional legislation is necessary to accomplish the job. We do have some legislative regulations in this country on the use of some of the more persistent pesticides. There is a highly effective organization, the Environmental Defense Fund, which is devoted to using the courts to enforce existing legislation. They have recently been involved in a highly publicized case in the Wisconsin courts to sue those responsible for the use of such pesticides in that state. Therefore, the first part of the answer is that the movement has already commenced; some legislation exists and we should press state and federal governments to enforce existing legislative controls which in most cases are not being used.

The other part of the approach is to obtain better legislation where it is needed, both at local and national levels. Congress will respond to public pressure, but in view of the potency of the chemical and agricultural industries, it is unlikely that we can get the proper kind of legislation unless there is massive action on the part of the general public writing to their congressmen. When the congressmen are sufficiently convinced that the general public means business, then they will act. But until that time we do not have a chance.

However, the existing legislation has been effective enough to create —or aggravate—another part of the problem. As the use of persistent pesticides has been more and more restricted here, it has resulted in ever-increasing proportions of the production being sent overseas. Several months ago in Pakistan, a series of Pakistani scientists expressed vehement and well-informed complaints to me about our Agency for International Development (AID) program which was dumping large quantities of these persistent pesticides in their country after we were restricting their use in ours. We have seen the same thing in

Latin America, especially in Peru where our AID pesticides nearly destroyed the agriculture they were intended to help, as well as in Africa and southeast Asia. So far as I know, the only foreign country that has passed effective legislation to protect itself from such pesticides is Sabah, in Malaysia.

*Chairman Brower:* There is a question for Dr. Hochbaum that asks what the effect is on the Eskimo of changes now taking place.

*Dr. Hochbaum:* Who knows? The north is a vast and still a mysterious place. But here and there one sees Eskimo boys, whose fathers lived by the caribou, heading out across the barrens on bright red Hondas, wearing tight pants, cowboy shoes, and each with his girl hanging on behind. The native culture of the land is nearly ended; the settlements are filled with people who were once scattered far and wide. What will the modern young men and women do? Who yet knows? But of this we are already aware: these young Eskimos who have given up the ways of their parents are not adjusting easily to the industrial state that is taking over the north.

*Chairman Brower:* I would like to direct this next question to Dr. Nash. Has anyone attempted to show that it is in man's best economic interest to protect and save wildlife and wilderness? Shouldn't conservationists with backgrounds in economics address themselves to this question?

*Dr. Nash:* Of course. Many times in the brass tacks world of politics and management where the wilderness battle is won and lost, the only arguments that carry weight are economic ones. But methods have to be adjusted. For example, in calculating the dollars-and-cents value of a wilderness area as opposed to a hydropower reservoir, economists should take into account what it is worth to just know that the wild country exists. I mean if every American were approached with the question "How much will you pay to keep dams out of the Grand Canyon?" you would end with a sizable sum. It is hypothetical, to be sure; the money is not actually paid. But this is a way of expressing noneconomic values in economic terms, and it should be used more frequently in countering the arithmetic of the dam builders. As for myself, I value a damless Grand Canyon at $5,000. If my decision were crucial, that is the sum I would actually pay to maintain a free-flowing Colorado River in the canyon. Still, there are times when we simply have to stand on ethics and aesthetics. We have to declare we favor wilderness not because it is economically expedient, but because it is beautiful and wonderful. In proposing a dollars-and-cents yardstick for wilderness, I am merely suggesting a way of fighting fire with fire in a way that hard-nosed politicians can understand.

*Chairman Brower:* The last, very important, question will be directed to Marty Talbot. Since education of the public is so important to the conservation cause, please comment on the potential role the public school system and its curriculum can play in getting some of this educating done.

*Mrs. Talbot:* Conservation education has been a concern to many people working with the public school systems. Clearly, in the United States and elsewhere, the most effective way to develop a wide public appreciation and understanding for conservation is to present it in the public schools—and to present it early enough.

The major problems are, first, the curricula are overfull. It is very difficult to add something new without cutting out something old, and the "something old" is usually somebody's sacred cow. It seems terribly difficult to remove anything in the curriculum once it is established.

Second, good instructional materials are needed and few of the teachers have adequate training themselves to present conservation information.

School systems and their curricula have been traditionally inflexible and for this reason many believe that they have lost much of their relevance through the years. Many of us maintain that this is what much of the current turbulence among students is all about. Changes are being made, but until the past few months they have come very slowly. I believe the school systems must play a major role in conservation education, but for them to do it will require a major change in curricula, perhaps in their whole approach to relevance, and it may require a much greater degree of participation by the students themselves.

To better discuss conservation education in general entails a definition of terms. My definition of conservation is based on Theodore Roosevelt's "wisest use, for the longest period of time, for the greatest number of people." This usage refers to all renewable and nonrenewable resources. Naturally this includes the concept that the wisest use of some areas may be to protect them as much as possible from consumption, and from varying degrees of modification by man and his activities—i.e. agriculture, dams, housing developments, etc. To borrow a phrase from my husband: conservation is applied ecology.

Education might be defined as impartation of knowledge—communication of knowledge gained from past experience as well as provision of tools and equipment for survival and hopefully for advancement. Education includes specifics as well as what I consider more important—attitudes.

Conservation education combines the above two definitions—communication of knowledge about our natural resources and their uses, and more important, communication and inspiration of an attitude of respect for all of our natural resources. This includes recognition of what our resources are and their complexity, how they interrelate and are interdependent.

All of this is very mind-stretching and anticipates how what we do today will affect us and our present goals tomorrow. So conservation education involves not only instruction in specific techniques like contour plowing and methods of halting sheet erosion, but it also involves imparting an attitude of how the soil, water, crops, air, man, and animals are interrelated and how their relationships change with changing conditions. All the points of view and characteristics of each of the elements must be considered and respected if we are to attain the wisest use, for the longest period, for the greatest number of people.

Central to this is recognition that we are on Spaceship Earth where our resources are finite. What one of us does ultimately affects the rest. We must understand that conservation involves quality of life— not just quantity, and we must foster an attitude of respect for all resources and all peoples.

*Chairman Brower:* Our culture in this United States is a little like a fruiting body of a fungus with wide-spreading roots. Our roots spread worldwide. We are grateful for learning more about them here.

## Part Two

# ALASKA'S WILDERNESS

"Three miles up the plunging creek we suddenly came upon a magnificent lake . . . Nothing I had ever seen, Yosemite or Grand Canyon or Mount McKinley rising from Susitna, had given me such a sense of immensity as this virgin lake lying in a great cleft in the surface of the earth with mountain slopes and waterfalls tumbling from beyond the limits of visibility. We walked up the right shore among bare rocks intermingled with meadows of bright lichen . . . and four loons were singing that rich, wild music which they have added to the beautiful melodies of earth. No sight or sound or smell or feeling even remotely hinted of men or their creations. It seemed as if time had dropped away a million years and we were back in a primordial world . . . where only the laws of nature held sway."

(Loon Lake, described here, is on a tributary of the John River and close to the recently created John River Transportation Corridor which bisects the Central Brooks Range wilderness.) Quote from Robert Marshall, *Alaska Wilderness: Exploring the Central Brooks Range.*

# INTRODUCTION

*Richard A. Cooley*
Associate Professor of Geography, University of Washington

Someone once defined wilderness as a place where the hand of man has never set foot. In our modern parlance we would refer to this kind of country as de facto wilderness. These areas have remained relatively untouched by either the foot or hand of man, not because they are protected by law, but merely because they are remote from centers of population or are inaccessible because of natural barriers or lack of transportation access. Few areas of de facto wilderness remain in the conterminous United States, which is one of the main reasons why it was absolutely necessary to pass the Wilderness Act to protect and preserve some of the remaining wild and remote lands of this country before it was too late.

The Wilderness Act has been in existence now for a little over four years and much progress has been made toward its objectives in the lower 48 states. But the situation in Alaska, which is of course the subject of this session, is an altogether different breed of cat. A very large percentage of the vast and beautiful state of Alaska is today de facto wilderness, largely untouched except around the few and widely scattered centers of population—though this is changing rapidly. But this novel position in which Alaska finds itself this last third of the twentieth century is viewed quite differently by different segments of the population. There are the extreme twentieth-century developers who think of Alaska as a northern extension of the great western frontier of the nineteenth century. They wish to populate and industrialize Alaska as rapidly as possible. They envy California its crowded millions and want to create cities in Alaska like Los Angeles. To them it is manifest destiny that this should occur. This view is epitomized very well by an editorial in Alaska's largest newspaper, the *Anchorage Daily Times*, of July 31, 1962, that said: "Alaska is more than 99 percent wilderness. The threat of dissipating such a vast area by economic development must be several generations away. Shouldn't economic development be allowed to take place with as few restrictions as possible at least temporarily? Why not provide the needed protection in the other states and let this state remain in status quo at least until development has penetrated a bit further into this vast wilderness?"

53

A large number of people, including government officials, subscribe to this view of Alaska's destiny. At the other extreme are those who would like to see Alaska remain as wild and unsettled as possible. They are quick to attack any proposal for development. This group includes a growing number of young people who have moved to Alaska in search of a fresh environment where they can build a better life and a closer and perhaps more intimate relationship with nature than is possible in the other states. Aligned with them is a much larger number of people scattered throughout the United States, including many if not most people in this room today, who are concerned with and dedicated to the preservation of at least some portion of this Alaskan landscape. They believe that this goal is in the national interest.

This group would tend to subscribe to the beliefs of Robert Marshall, who participated in an historic governmental study of Alaska's resources and future development in 1937. At that time Bob Marshall disagreed strongly with the recommendation of the final report, which emphasized resource extraction and economic development. He submitted a minority report that concluded with these words: "Alaska is unique among all recreational areas belonging to the United States because Alaska is yet largely a wilderness. In the name of a balanced use of American resources, let's keep Alaska largely a wilderness!" He saw this then as being the national interest.

Somewhere between these two extreme views, the people of Alaska and of this nation must reach an agreement on the direction Alaska is going. Through hindsight we now realize that uncontrolled economic development can only lead to chaos. We need only to look around us to see that. We also know that it is unfortunately perhaps impracticable and even self-defeating to think of trying to keep Alaska largely a wilderness as Bob Marshall would have liked.

Our discussion today seeks to explore these problems. Economic development of Alaska is coming at a rapid pace and the de facto protection of wilderness is rapidly slipping away, as anyone can attest who has taken a boat trip up the inside passage in the last year or two. As yet, no lands in Alaska have been given the legal statutory protection afforded by the Wilderness Act. The time has come for decisions to be made if we are going to preserve some of this precious northern environment.

How much land for wilderness are we talking about? In what location? When should action be taken? These are the kinds of critical questions this session and this panel will address itself to because these are the questions that now face this nation with respect to Alaska's resources and Alaska's wilderness.

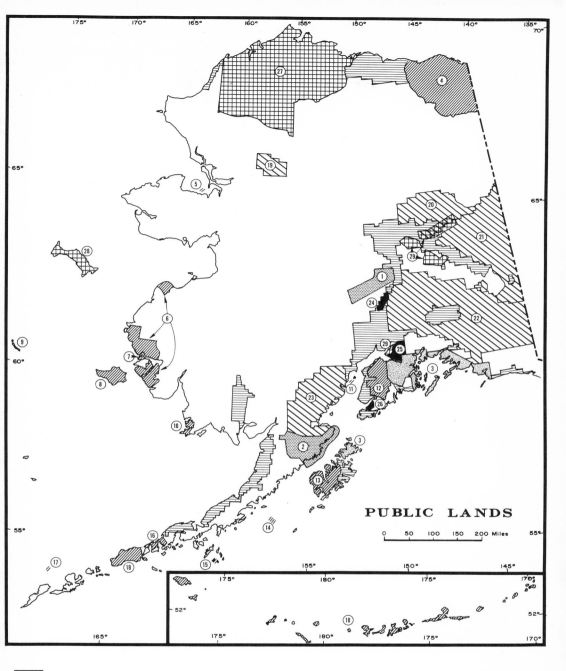

PUBLIC LANDS

National Park or Monument
1 Mt. McKinley National Park
2 Katmai National Monument

National Forest
3 Chugach

National Wildlife Refuge or Range
4 Arctic Range
5 Chamisso Refuge
6 Clarence Rhode Range
7 Hazen Bay Refuge
8 Nunivak Refuge
9 Bering Sea Refuge

10 Cape Newenham Refuge
11 Tuxedni Refuge
12 Kenai Moose Range
13 Kodiak Refuge
14 Semidi Refuge
15 Simeonof Refuge
16 Izembek Range
17 Bogoslof Refuge
18 Aleutian Islands Refuge

BLM Planning Unit
19 Bornite
20 White Mountains
21 Forty-Mile

22 Copper River
23 Iliamna

State Selected Land

Proposed State Park
24 Denali
25 Chugach
26 Kachemak

Other Public Land
27 Naval Petroleum Reserve No. 4
28 St. Lawrence Reindeer Station
29 Military Reserve

Bureau of Land Management is principal
management agency for balance of land

0   50   100   150   200 Miles

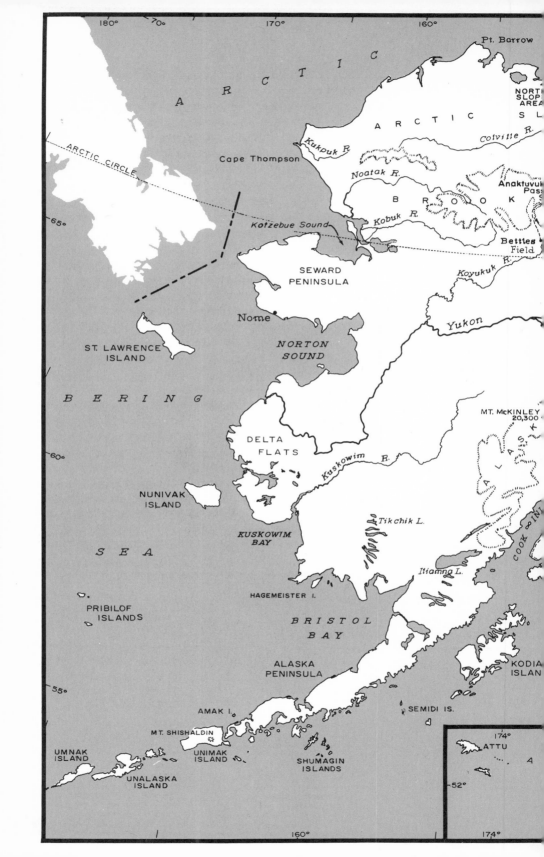

C E A N

Prudhoe Bay

E

NERAK

R   A   N   G   E

Porcupine R.

River

Birch Cr.

YUKON
FLATS

Chatanika R.

Fairbanks

Tanana R.

R A N G E

×NEUBERGER MT.

Gákona

Gulkana
Glennallen
Copper Center

WRANGELL MTS.

CHUGACH

chorage   Valdez

Copper R.

MOUNTAINS

Prince William
Sound

ENAI
NINSULA

G   U   L   F

O   F

A   L   A   S   K   A

Yakutat Bay

Juneau

CHICHAGOF
ISLAND

Sitka

BARANOF
ISLAND

PRINCE OF WALES
ISLAND

Ketchikan

# A L A S K A

0          100          200 Miles

- - - - - Roads
·········· Approximate pipeline route

140°          130°          70°          120°

65°

60°

55°

140°

178°          178°          174°

52°

B E R I N G     S E A

T I A N          I S L A N D S

MCHITKA

178°          178°          174°          170°

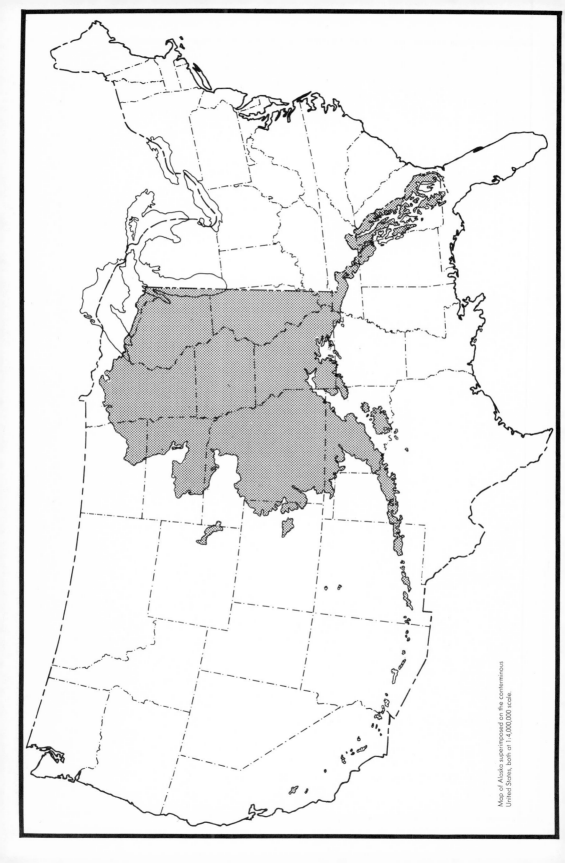

Map of Alaska superimposed on the conterminous
United States, both at 1:4,000,000 scale.

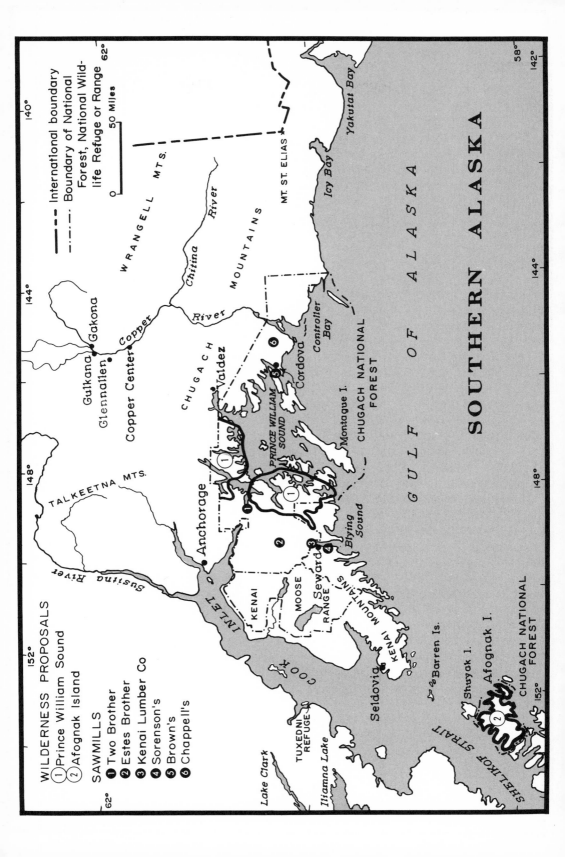

WILDERNESS PROPOSALS
① Prince William Sound
② Afognak Island

SAWMILLS
❶ Two Brother
❷ Estes Brother
❸ Kenai Lumber Co
❹ Sorenson's
❺ Brown's
❻ Chappell's

— — — International boundary
— ·· — Boundary of National
Forest, National Wild-
life Refuge or Range

0          50 Miles

SOUTHERN ALASKA

GULF OF ALASKA

WRANGELL MTS.

MOUNTAINS

MT. ST. ELIAS

Yakutat Bay

Icy Bay

Controller Bay

Cordova

CHUGACH NATIONAL FOREST

Montague I.

PRINCE WILLIAM SOUND

Blying Sound

Valdez

CHUGACH

Copper River

Chitina River

Copper Center

Glennallen

Gulkana  Gakona

Susitna River

TALKEETNA MTS.

Anchorage

COOK INLET

KENAI

MOOSE RANGE

Seward

KENAI MOUNTAINS

Seldovia

TUXEDNI REFUGE

Iliamna Lake

Lake Clark

Barren Is.

Shuyak I.

Afognak I.

CHUGACH NATIONAL FOREST

SHELIKOF STRAIT

152°    148°    144°    62°    142°    140°    58°

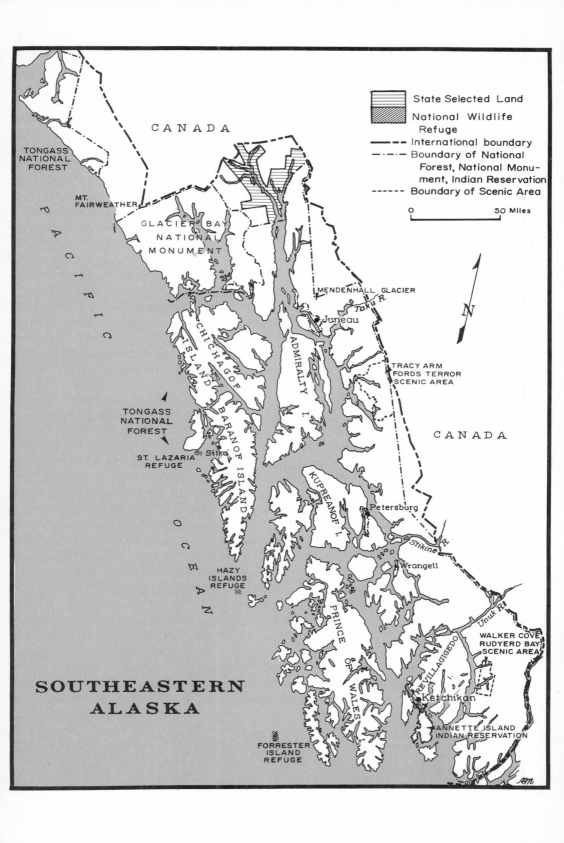

State Selected Land

National Wildlife Refuge

International boundary

Boundary of National Forest, National Monument, Indian Reservation

Boundary of Scenic Area

0          50 Miles

CANADA

TONGASS NATIONAL FOREST

MT. FAIRWEATHER

GLACIER BAY NATIONAL MONUMENT

P A C I F I C

MENDENHALL GLACIER

Taku R.

Juneau

TONGASS NATIONAL FOREST

TRACY ARM FORDS TERROR SCENIC AREA

CHICHAGOF ISLAND

ADMIRALTY I.

CANADA

ST. LAZARIA REFUGE

BARANOF ISLAND

Sitka

O C E A N

KUPREANOF I.

Petersburg

Stikine R.

Wrangell

HAZY ISLANDS REFUGE

PRINCE OF WALES

Unuk R.

REVILLAGIGEDO

WALKER COVE RUDYERD BAY SCENIC AREA

Ketchikan

SOUTHEASTERN ALASKA

FORRESTER ISLAND REFUGE

ANNETTE ISLAND INDIAN RESERVATION

N

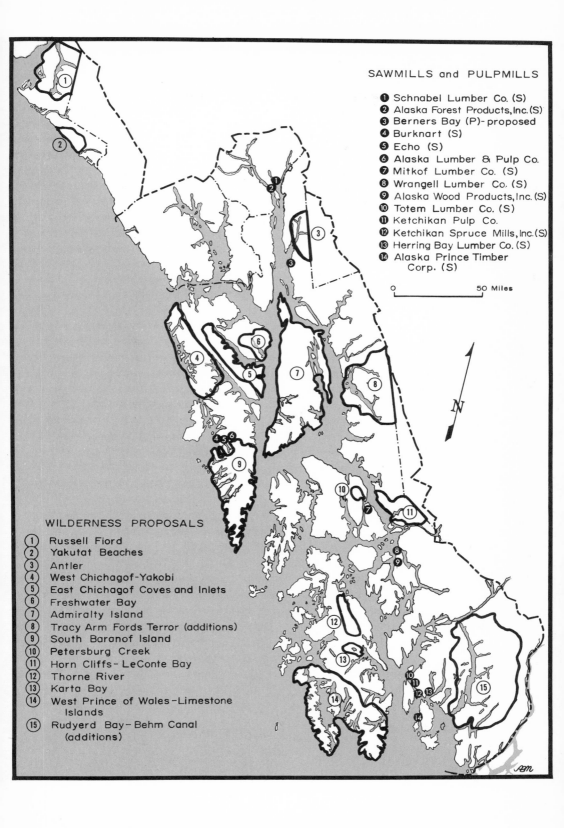

SAWMILLS and PULPMILLS

1 Schnabel Lumber Co. (S)
2 Alaska Forest Products, Inc. (S)
3 Berners Bay (P) - proposed
4 Burknart (S)
5 Echo (S)
6 Alaska Lumber & Pulp Co.
7 Mitkof Lumber Co. (S)
8 Wrangell Lumber Co. (S)
9 Alaska Wood Products, Inc. (S)
10 Totem Lumber Co. (S)
11 Ketchikan Pulp Co.
12 Ketchikan Spruce Mills, Inc. (S)
13 Herring Bay Lumber Co. (S)
14 Alaska Prince Timber
   Corp. (S)

0        50 Miles

N

WILDERNESS PROPOSALS

1 Russell Fiord
2 Yakutat Beaches
3 Antler
4 West Chichagof-Yakobi
5 East Chichagof Coves and Inlets
6 Freshwater Bay
7 Admiralty Island
8 Tracy Arm Fords Terror (additions)
9 South Baranof Island
10 Petersburg Creek
11 Horn Cliffs- LeConte Bay
12 Thorne River
13 Karta Bay
14 West Prince of Wales-Limestone
   Islands
15 Rudyerd Bay- Behm Canal
   (additions)

# ALASKA'S WILDERNESS: A GEOGRAPHIC APPRAISAL

*Douglas R. Powell*

Acting Instructor,* Department of Geography, University of California at Berkeley

With the purchase of Alaska from Russia in 1867 the United States acquired its last large land unit. And large Alaska is—586,400 square miles or 365 million acres. It is one-sixth the total area of the United States, and greater in size than the combined land areas of Texas, California, and Montana. In the interest of perspective, however, it should be pointed out that Canada's Quebec province is a little larger than Alaska, and its Northwest Territories is more than twice the size.

Little known and widely derided in the Seward's Folly tradition at the time of purchase, Alaska remained an obscure northern outpost until the beginning of the twentieth century. By this time important gold strikes at Nome and Fairbanks and in the Klondike of adjacent Canada, the growing exploitation of wildlife resources such as salmon and furs, and the publication of numerous geological and geographical reconnaissance surveys—all these did much to direct attention to Alaska.

Nearly all of Alaska can be currently considered as de facto wilderness, land not permanently inhabited and relatively untouched by man. Only 0.2 percent of the total area was in private ownership at the time of statehood in 1959; that figure has increased only slightly since. The various agencies administering the public lands, particularly the Bureau of Land Management, the Forest Service, the National Park Service, and the state of Alaska's Division of Lands,

* Mr. Powell is now associate in geography at the University of California at Berkeley.

are presently engaged in classifying much of this land for future use. By 1969, however, almost none had yet been officially designated as wilderness in formal or administrative terms.

An important element in American attitudes toward land since earliest nonnative settlement has been the concept of untamed wilderness awaiting development by the persistent, arduous, and noble work of the hardy pioneer. By 1900 just about all of conterminous United States had fallen to his ax, plow, or shovel. The remaining unknown and unused land was Alaska, an image still retained. In recent years, however, a different approach to wilderness has been gaining acceptance—preserving and maintaining wilderness for its own sake. Regardless of the point of view, Alaska contains by far the largest area of actual wilderness left in the United States.

The extent of Alaska can be explained with figures. Longitudinally, it extends from 130 degrees west longitude (the southeast corner) to 172½ degrees east longitude (Cape Wrangell, Attu Island, last of the Aleutian Islands). Theoretically it encompasses four time zones. Obviously Alaska is the westernmost portion of the United States but from a technical standpoint it might be argued that Alaska is also the easternmost portion. This last fact has very little relevance to an understanding of Alaskan wilderness but is unmistakably a fine ploy to be used at social gatherings. So too is the fact that the great arc of the Aleutians sweeps so far west that it lies about 800 miles under the Asian continent. If the international date line were not dislodged westward to keep from slicing through the Aleutians (near Amchitka Island), the last 340 miles would be tomorrow.

Latitudinally, Alaska extends from 51 degrees north latitude (the southernmost point in the curve of the Aleutian Islands) to 71 degrees north latitude at Point Barrow. This entire extent is farther north than the conterminous or adjacent United States, which has a northern boundary of 49 degrees. It should be noted also that most of Scandinavia is located in similar latitudes, and that Moscow is a few miles north of the latitude of Ketchikan. Alaska's northern location has wide ramifications for its vegetation, wildlife, and climate.

Another way to depict the extent of Alaska is by superimposing it on a map of the conterminous United States. The southwestern tip of the Aleutian Islands would be at San Luis Obispo, California; the southeastern Panhandle would extend all the way to Charleston, South Carolina; and Point Barrow in the far north would be at the Minnesota-Canada border. Alaska's configuration and its tremendous west-east extent is a cartographer's nightmare. In order to depict it on some workable scale, it is the eternal fate of the Aleutian Islands always to be represented on a small inset.

Most of Alaska has been above sea level continuously since mid-Jurassic and Cretaceous periods, approximately 150-100 million years ago. During the Pleistocene epoch (also called Ice Age) of roughly the last three million years, glaciers accumulated to such an extent that the level of the oceans sometimes fell as much as 350 feet below present levels. Because most of eastern Siberia and much of the great Alaskan plateau were not glaciated in spite of their coldness, Bering Straits became a land bridge in the form of a plain perhaps up to 1,000 miles in width and 50 miles across as sea level dropped. It is probable this happened at least twice, permitting the migration of plants, animals, and human beings. The last land bridge was exposed during the final advance of glaciation, called the Wisconsin stage, between 25,000 and 12,000 years ago. Under present conditions a drop of sea level of 150 feet would expose a land bridge between the two continents.

The predominately Precambrian, Paleozoic, and Mesozoic sediments, with some younger terrestrial deposits inland and younger marine deposits in south coastal areas, have been intruded in many regions, especially in the mountain ranges of the southern coast, by granitic rocks similar to intrusives farther south along western North America to Baja California. Extrusive lavas are common in Alaska, and most of the higher summits south of the Brooks Range consist of granitics or lava. Intense and recent tectonic activity characterizes the southern portions of the state; the earthquake of March 27, 1964, centered in Prince William Sound, was the strongest yet measured by precise instruments in North America. Reflecting this tectonic activity are some 75 volcanoes, about 35 of which are presently active.

Physiographically, Alaska is generally mountainous with fringing coastal plains in the north and west, some limited alluvial covered structural basins inland, and a major delta in the west formed by the Yukon and Kuskokwim rivers. Two major physiographic provinces found in western conterminous United States and western Canada are continued in Alaska; from south to north these are the North American Cordillera and the Interior Plains.

In Alaska the North American Cordillera may be subdivided into three parts. Farthest south is the Pacific Mountain System, consisting of two more or less continuous ranges with a zone of intervening lowlands. In more detail, the outer ridge consists of a mountain range from the island of Kodiak up through the Kenai Peninsula along the Chugach Range and then joining into the massive St. Elias Range and continuing southward through the islands of the Alexander Archipelago. There is a small zone of intermediate lowlands that are represented by Cook Inlet and the Copper River drainage, and also a fault trough on the inside passage along Lynn Canal and Chatham Strait. The second series of ranges consists of the Aleutian Range joining the Alaskan Range, then merging into the St. Elias Range and joining the coastal border range which divides southeastern Alaska from the province of British Columbia. The general alignment of these topographic features is in arcuate belts parallel to the Pacific coastline, and they constitute an effective barrier to easy transportation into the interior from the Gulf of Alaska, the courses of the Copper and Susitna rivers being the only significant penetrations. This is the zone of spectacular alpine terrain, culminating in Mt. McKinley in the Alaska Range, 20,320 feet, highest in North America. This area has a larger span of glaciation than any other region on earth outside of Greenland and the continent of Antarctica. It contains innumerable massive glaciers, some of which discharge directly into the Pacific, and steep-sided coastal fiords, partly clothed by dense coniferous forest.

North of and parallel to this Pacific Mountain System is a zone of intermontane plateaus and a heterogeneous assemblage of low mountains somewhat comparable to the Great Basin of western United States. In general, this area slopes gently to the west and the southwest, and is drained by the two largest rivers in Alaska, the Yukon and the Kuskokwim. This region is often called the interior and is regarded by many as the heart of Alaska. The third and northernmost zone of the cordillera is the Brooks Range, an Alaskan continuation of the Rocky Mountain System. Various local names are applied to discrete segments of this 600-mile-long, 80 to 100-mile-wide belt of mountains reaching a maximum elevation of slightly over 9,000 feet in the northeast. Both north and south flanks rise abruptly above adjacent lowlands. A few small cirque glaciers still exist, and most of the area was extensively mantled by earlier Pleistocene glaciers, whereas the intermontane plateau was largely free of glacier ice at all times during the Pleistocene, probably because of inadequate snowfall. Bedrock is overwhelmingly sedimentary or metamorphic, and the stratified appearance of the erosion patterns is markedly different from the configuration of granitic and volcanic mountains to the south.

From the northern base of the Brooks Range to the Arctic shoreline is the Alaskan prolongation of the interior plains province of western North America. The Arctic coastal plain is a remarkably smooth plain rising imperceptibly from the Arctic Ocean to a maximum altitude of 600 feet at its southern margin. Coastal cliffs are nearly nonexistent. The surface is marshy during the brief summer and dotted by innumerable ponds and lakes. In this area occurred the recent major oil discovery at Prudhoe Bay. The terms "Arctic Slope" or "North Slope" are often used in referring to this extensive plain as well as the north-facing portion of the Brooks Range.

Ever since Alaska became known to Americans, its reputed climate has been notoriously and widely misunderstood. Major influences on the region are the Japan Current, a relatively warm flow of Pacific waters which moderates both summer and winter temperatures along the entire southern coast; the persistent low pressure area (called the Aleutian low) over the Aleutian Islands and the Gulf of Alaska during most of the year, which results in the passage of numerous storm fronts across southern Alaska; a very strong high pressure system with accompanying low temperatures which often forms over interior Alaska during the winter months; and great topographic diversity that causes vast differences in temperature and precipitation in short horizontal distances.

Moreover, in an area as large as Alaska there will be major climatic differences independent of topographic diversity. For convenience, four general climatic zones can be described. First is one of dominant marine influences extending along the immediate coast from the southeastern Panhandle to the Aleutian Islands. This is a region washed by the Japan Current, of relatively mild winters with temperatures much above those of corresponding latitude on the east coasts of North America and Asia, of cool summers, and of much cloudiness and high precipitation with maximum amounts during the fall of the year. Annual averages often exceed 100 inches. Inland from the coast is a second transition zone, occurring along the intervening lowlands of the Pacific Mountain System and the terrain adjacent to the Bering Sea, differing from the preceding zone by greater extremes of temperature in winter and summer and by significantly less precipitation with a maximum in late summer. Third is the continental zone between the Alaska Range and the Brooks Range with long, cold winters and brief, warm summers. Much of the light annual moisture of 10 to 20 inches comes in the form of warm season convectional showers. This is the climate most people imagine when thinking of Alaska. Fourth is the Arctic Zone, from the Brooks Range north, a region of long cold winters but with less temperature variation in winter than in the continental zone and of very cool, often foggy, summers with temperatures too low for tree growth. Precipitation is very light, often less than five inches annually, with most of it occurring in summer. In general, this zone would be considered the most unpleasant for human occupance, especially with the additional factor of long winter nights.

A striking feature of climate throughout Alaska, particularly to a resident of California or the Southwest, is the high incidence of cloudiness in the summer half of the year. Deep sunburned countenances are infrequent in the Alaskan population, except on glacier travelers; skin cancer is also infrequent. Portions of the coastal mountains in the southeast receive annual snow accumulations comparable to the highest totals anywhere on earth, but elsewhere snowfall is relatively light, much less than that of the Cascade or Sierra Nevada ranges. Temperature extremes have ranged from 100 degrees above to 78 degrees below zero, both occurring in the continental zone at stations only a few miles apart. Annual precipitation averages vary from less than five inches along the Arctic coast to over 250 inches along the southeastern coast.

A large part of Alaska north of the Pacific Mountain System is underlain at shallow depths of a few feet or less by perennially frozen ground, or permafrost. From the Brooks Range north, permafrost is nearly continuous. Many intricate and complex problems result from construction of buildings or roads over permafrost, which tends to melt unevenly with disturbance by humans. Drainage is also a massive problem. Few social gatherings in interior or northern Alaska do not discuss plumbing difficulties at some point.

The climate impinges upon the consciousness of Alaskan residents or visitors in much sharper fashion than is general in the rest of the United States. A larger proportion of human activity and cost of living is directly related to the impact of climate, whether in town or wilderness. There is a widespread feeling of accomplishment in dealing with the climate, both by town-dweller and wilderness traveler.

Almost one-third of the natural surface runoff of the United States occurs in Alaska. The Yukon River system, originating in Canada, is the fifth largest in North America. Since local water demands for agriculture, hydroelectric power, and municipal use are, as yet, well below one percent of the total runoff, there is an abundance of untamed rivers. A superb attraction of Alaska's wilderness is the phenomenon of rivers flowing out to sea unused by man except for a minimum navigation.

With the exception of man-induced fire, particularly in the dry interior, human controlled grazing by domestic reindeer on grassland and tundra in the west and the interior, and increasing logging on the southeast coast, the natural vegetation of Alaska is relatively little disturbed by man compared to other areas of the United States. There are three basic types of natural vegetation in the state:

1) The coastal forest is a continuation of the coniferous forest extending along the margin of the Pacific from California north and west to about Kodiak Island. In the southeast this forest often consists of large trees with growth rates sometimes similar to the high values found farther south in the Pacific Northwest. Western hemlock comprises about two-thirds of this forest, with Sitka spruce, western red cedar, and mountain hemlock as other important species. Total forest area of this type is about 16 million acres. The two national forests in Alaska, the Tongass and the Chugach, are found along the southeastern and south central coast.

2) The interior forest occupies about 125 million acres of inland Alaska south of the Brooks Range. Important species are white spruce, black spruce, white birch, balsam, poplar, aspen, and various willows. This forest (also called taiga) continues in a broad belt across North America to the Atlantic seaboard, and a very similar forest is continuous at comparable latitudes across the entire Eurasian continent. Fire, of natural origin and to a rapidly increasing extent in recent years of human origin, plays a significant role in vegetation succession in this region, often subject to extended summer droughts. There is also a fascinating succession from invading shrubs through a sequence of particular species of trees along the shifting and often braided courses of major rivers, like the Yukon, where habitats are constantly changing because of continual erosion and deposition occurring along the floodplains. Tree size is smaller and growth rates much less in this forest than along the coast.

3) Treeless areas are found from the south slope of the Brooks Range to the Arctic, in much of the west coastal area, and above timberline, 3,000 feet as a general maximum in southern Alaska. Grasslands occupy much of southwestern Alaska and the Aleutians. Some shrubs and low mat-like herbs and lichens collectively called tundra cover the rest of this zone, except for about six percent of the total state area which is ice-covered or barren bedrock. This vegetation type is extremely susceptible to man-caused interference. Growing seasons are short, growth rates very slow, and scars remain much longer than in the forest regions. Differences in the severity of winter temperatures and to some extent the amount of precipitation seem to mark the boundary between coastal and interior forests. Summer temperatures appear to be critical in differentiating either forest from the treeless areas. Where average monthly temperatures in summer drop below 50 degrees F., trees, other than small poplars or willows, cease to grow.

Important features of Alaskan wildlife are the abundance of big mammals, especially moose, caribou, Dall sheep, mountain goat, and various species of bear; predators like wolf, wolverine, and lynx; and large populations of migratory waterfowl, which breed in Alaska during the summer months. To many wilderness travelers scenery is sterile without the invigorating presence of wildlife. This is especially true in Mt. McKinley National Park where a persistent cloud cover frequently obscures views of the main peak, and observations of the wildlife are often the most valuable wilderness experience in the park.

Presently there are about 275,000 people in Alaska, and over half of those are concentrated in the two main urban centers of Anchorage and Fairbanks. This represents a density of .47 persons per square mile for the entire state as compared to 55 for the United States as a whole. This exceedingly low density, superimposed upon the geographic scene described above, means Alaska's de facto wilderness is a vast open space of great attractiveness to lovers of wilderness. However, much of Alaskan wilderness is not as unique as often portrayed in American statements and literature. The immense glaciated mountains, like McKinley, are distinctive, but a similar flora and fauna occur over more extensive areas in Canada and the Union of Soviet Socialist Republics. Population densities are as low as .02 persons per square mile in Canada's Northwest Territories. Canadians must often wonder at American hyperbole in discussing Alaskan wilderness. Nevertheless, political boundaries do focus attention on areas within them, and Alaska is the great remaining wilderness of the United States. It has an outstanding array of physical and biotic features, relatively undisturbed, and it is for Americans to decide its future use.

An obvious problem in such decisions is the irritation many residents of the state feel toward what are considered unwarranted efforts by outsiders to manage Alaskan affairs. Much of the drive for statehood, achieved in 1959, was stimulated by desire of Alaskans to mitigate outside influence. Delicate and sensitive issues are involved here, but wilderness is the concern of people from all 50 states, though that interest may best be expressed by advice rather than compulsion. Wilderness advocates in Alaska generally need all the support from outside sources that can be mustered, and it should be kept in mind that even after present legally determined land exchanges are made to the state by the United States government, over two-thirds of Alaska will still be in federal ownership.

Statehood brought a significant change in the economy from one of basic federal support, much of it military, to one based on the state's resources, such as salmon, oil and gas, timber, and tourism—in all of which Alaska is in competition with other states. The transition period has been accompanied by financial difficulties which have evoked an understandable, though often regrettable, desire to realize the greatest possible income from natural resources, a situation apt to be detrimental to wilderness preservation. Below are listed briefly some of the major problems affecting wilderness preservation in Alaska— areas where the thrust of the 1970's will be felt.

Under terms of the Statehood Act, Alaska is entitled to claim 104 million acres, an area slightly larger than California, from federal ownership by 1984. There is unparalleled opportunity here for intelligent land planning by the state, including the formal establishment of wilderness; there is also much temptation to repeat the same mistakes made earlier in the lower 48.

The native population of Alaska—Eskimo, Aleut, Indian, about one-fifth of the total—is pressing claims to as much as 80 percent of Alaska's land area. Pending a settlement of such claims, the Department of the Interior in 1967 declared a moratorium on land exchanges in the state, which has been extended into 1970. This is a complicated and delicate issue to be determined on the basis of human rights, rather than on wilderness values. In general, settlements favorable to the natives would also be favorable to the preservation of de facto wilderness.

Oil and gas have been produced successfully for some years in the Kenai Peninsula-Cook Inlet area, and much of the Arctic Slope has been known as oil potential country for decades. In 1968 there was discovered at Prudhoe Bay on the central Arctic coast what will quite probably become the largest oil field in North America, possibly the world. Of obvious great interest to Alaskan wilderness problems are the great temptations to the state to encourage maximum production from this and other possible Arctic Slope fields with the resultant billions of dollars of income to bolster the state's heretofore shaky financial condition, and the questions of transportation of oil, men, and equipment in the extremely sensitive tundra environment.

The abundance of surface water runoff leads to various plans for damming major rivers for hydroelectric power development or for possible water transport to Canada and the western two-thirds of the United States. Thus far, no such major project has been inaugurated, though the proposed Rampart Dam on the Yukon River, which would have flooded an area the size of Lake Erie, has received wide consideration. This, and other hydro proposals, have been stalled largely on economic grounds—power can be produced at competitive costs much nearer the centers of population in the United States and the increasing use of nuclear power will likely be a further barrier to massive hydro power projects in Alaska. But pressure will most probably mount in the seventies for the damming of major rivers like the Yukon, Tanana, Kuskokwim, and Copper to provide water for transport to western United States, plus supplemental hydroelectric power.

Lumbering, mostly for pulp, is increasing along the southeast coast. There is some question whether cutting schedules being negotiated by the Forest Service are actually sustained yield plans. Much of the timber to be cut is on the islands framing Alaska's famed inside passage, and most of it grows within two to three miles of tidewater. An immediate wilderness problem in Alaska is the preservation of a significant area of coastal forest in the southeast before it is submitted to contracts. A particular economic thrust affecting Alaskan forests, and other natural resources, such as many minerals is the desire of Japan to find materials for its rapidly expanding economy in relatively nearby areas.

Present cropland acreage in Alaska is a miniscule 20,000 acres. Estimates range up to one to three million acres of potential cropland, eight million for grazing—both probably much too high. The combination of a climate too wet or cold, of terrain too steep or rocky, and of soils of limited fertility is a significant physical constraint to agricultural expansion. Economic barriers are also most important. A paradox of Alaskan agriculture is that as the local market has expanded with population growth, it has become more attractive to outside competition, which with present transportation costs can often undersell the Alaskan producer. Cropland area will most likely increase very slowly and be largely restricted to those regions currently in production—the Kenai Peninsula and the Matanuska and Tanana valleys. Grazing may well eventually expand in the southwest and the Aleutian Islands, though no extensive immediate growth is in prospect.

The very existence of open space with sparse populations in Alaska is a lure to agencies desiring room for testing. The Atomic Energy Commission dropped plans for testing massive earth excavation by nuclear explosions near Point Hope in northwest Alaska only after spirited objection from Eskimos in the area and a few interested persons pointing out the deleterious ecological impact of such tests. Current plans for testing underground nuclear devices at Amchitka Island in the Aleutians, part of a National Wildlife Refuge, raise serious questions as to compatibility of such testing with wilderness values.

Much has been said and written of Alaska's supposedly hostile physical environment. For example, the climate is too rigorous or the terrain too rough for back country travel. Some of this type of language is simply a mask for special interest which would like to develop a specific area for its own material gain.

Much of Alaska does indeed present a more formidable physical environment than what wilderness travelers are accustomed to throughout the rest of the United States. But it is a challenging, stimulating environment, and one certainly not invulnerable to human entrance and appreciation. Wilderness lovers, though some may deny it, most certainly use the products of technology—down sleeping bags, wind- and water-resistant tents, insulating clothing, freeze-dried food—to adapt to supposed harsh environments when a large portion of Alaska in midsummer is scarcely harsh. Wilderness trips in Alaska may require more equipment, more expense, and more planning than trips elsewhere in the United States, but they are definitely feasible, even to residents of such professed mild, benign regions as Florida or southern California.

In earlier years Alaska was regarded primarily as a howling wilderness, to be subdued and conquered when the necessary capital and energy were available. More and more of Alaska is now being thought of as a "singing wilderness," to be appreciated for its own sake.

# ALASKA, THE LAST GREAT OPPORTUNITY

*Burton W. Silcock*
Alaska State Director, Bureau of Land Management

Alaska has a popular label—"The Last Frontier." This title today is more appropriate than ever before; the forty-ninth state is indeed a frontier for arctic and subarctic research and technology, for advances in techniques in fisheries, mineral extraction, and forestry. It is also the one remaining large area of the nation where we can—with careful planning—avoid some of the environmental mistakes made elsewhere.

Alaska is blessed with an abundance of resources—40 percent of the nation's fresh water, 34 percent of the undeveloped waterpower, nearly 50 percent of its seaward coastline, 65 percent of the outer continental shelf—oil, coal, natural gas, minerals, and timber yet to be measured, and in an area greater than 21 of the smaller states combined.

Alaska is strategic to the nation for its natural resources and for its location in terms of national defense. Among the many federal agencies concerned with Alaska, the Bureau of Land Management of the Department of the Interior is perhaps most extensively involved—with some 80 percent of the land area under our jurisdiction.

Two hundred years ago, aboriginal Aleuts called it "Alyeska"—the great land. One hundred years ago, people called it "Seward's Folly." Seventy years ago, it was the scene of the last great gold stampede. Ten years ago, it became the forty-ninth state. Today, it's still a great land.

Alaska is a great land in many ways—from the forests of the interior, to the towering peaks of some of the most impressive mountain ranges of North America, to the tundra extending far to the north and west to the shores of the Bering Sea.

Alaska is still land of opportunity, and one of the last largely undeveloped areas within reach of most Americans. This word "opportunity" has many meanings for many people. For some of you, it might mean wilderness, a vast untouched region where we have an opportunity to refresh the soul, and cleanse the spirit. For some others, concerned with supplying the fuel needs of a nation, it might mean opportunity to develop the oil resources of the Arctic. And for those interested in harvesting the renewable natural resources, it could mean an opportunity to build an industry based on the forests of this great land.

Historically, the growth of this nation has rested on a generous endowment of natural resources. Not until the early years of this century did we awaken to the fact that these resources are not unlimited; they can run out. Renewable though they may be, they can be abused.

With Alaska's abundance, the nation has a second chance. Alaska is the conspicuous national opportunity for the nation to make the wiser choices.

But with all her abundance, Alaska is a delicate ecological community governed by nature, and a complex interrelationship of the desires of individuals, local and state governments, and the federal government, which still holds most of the land.

We are standing on the threshold of a new era of growth in Alaska. Of those of us living within Alaska, some have suffered from "tunnel vision." We need the help of organizations such as the Sierra Club to broaden the focus, to see the national opportunities on the land.

Alaska is both undeveloped and underdeveloped. We have the potential for development. With forward-looking resource development plans, we can attract industry, capital, and skills, and still protect the environmental qualities that make such a unique land.

In trying to realize the potentials of Alaska, we must recognize some limitations, too. These involve both man-made laws and the harsh rules of nature in the Arctic and subarctic regions of the north.

Here's the way land status looks today in Alaska:

| | | |
|---|---|---|
| Petroleum Reserve #4 | 23 | million acres |
| Fish and Wildlife Refuges | 20 | " " |
| Rampart Withdrawal | 10 | " " |
| Military Reservations | 2 | " " |
| National Parks | 7 | " " |
| State-selected Lands | 26 | " " |
| Public Lands | 262 | " " |

Unlike the earlier laws creating public land states, the Congressional act granting statehood to Alaska provided an economically useful land base impossible under any arbitrary grant of numbered sections in every township. Alaska was given some 103 million acres, if she chose to select them. The State of Alaska has recently selected some 26 million acres.

In the past two years, long steps forward have brought the state and federal governments closer to settling century-old native land claims originating in aboriginal use and occupancy. There is every reason to believe that Congress will move forward in this session to provide equitable settlement for the natives, giving them opportunities for a better future. Settling these native claims will allow better planning for the future by all—the natives, the state government, the federal government, and private enterprise.

Late in 1968, in an effort to protect native rights until Congress provides for a settlement, the Department of the Interior withdrew unreserved lands in Alaska from further homesteading, mining, and states claims for a two-year period. Secretary of the Interior Walter J. Hickel has conditionally accepted this moratorium, with the hope that Congress will act promptly to meet the problem.

Perhaps the word "urgent" is overworked in today's world of crises; however nearly every issue in the field of conservation is an urgent one. There is an urgent necessity for gaining a balance between development and preservation.

Unwise development could destroy the very things that make Alaska great as a land to live in—the clean waters, the unscarred landscape, the virgin forests, and the wildlife that abounds from the Canadian border to the Bering Sea.

Management of resources is never simple. Pure emotion cannot resolve a problem to everyone's satisfaction. In the eyes of many, wilderness is Alaska's greatest value.

The Alaskan economy now depends in part on the extraction of natural resources, renewable and nonrenewable. Minerals are where you find them. So are the fisheries on which many people depend, mostly for salmon, shrimp, king crab—products that bring high value on the "outside" market. Many who depend on the fisheries are natives who struggle to make a living in an area where markets are limited and costs are high.

Lumber is essential to community and industrial growth, and yet is in short supply in interior Alaska. While timber is plentiful in the national forests of the southeast, in the north lack of access and basic inventories complicates the harvest.

While Alaska is one-fifth as large as all the other states combined, only a portion of this vast acreage can ever be productive in the traditional sense. Permafrost underlies vast areas of the interior and northward beyond the Brooks Range to the Arctic Ocean. This condition extends over millions of acres.

Parts of the country are bogs, thawing in summer but becoming lakes because of limited drainage. And vast areas are covered with still-active glaciers—ice fields many feet thick.

Among the economists it's a handy reference point to speak of the year 2000, when we expect twice as many people to be fed from our land. But in Alaska, with short growing seasons and other factors stretching out the recovery period for abused land, we need an even longer range view.

As a nation we have grown much more sophisticated in the last decade or two. We talk total environment; DDT in the headwaters of the Mississippi can contaminate seafood in the Gulf of Mexico. Instant communication makes us belong to just one world these days.

We in the Bureau of Land Management would like to think that mistakes of the past, the environmental blunders people have made, came not so much from greed or deliberate disregard for the future but from a lack of data and a lack of foresight into the needs of tomorrow.

Alaska possesses a priceless asset in a nation growing thirsty for clean water—a surplus yielding almost four times the water available in the 17 western states. Along with the water flowing into Alaska from Canada, the total runoff of fresh water in Alaska accounts for 40 percent of the entire fresh water supply of the United States. High-quality water is an increasingly important factor in the location of some industries. The arctic rivers of North America score close to 100 on almost any system of evaluating water quality and quantity. These water sources are dependable—far more than most of America's river systems.

Alaska's water represents outstanding fish and waterfowl habitat and production grounds, superb natural beauty and recreation, and a lifeline to remote villages dependent on water for transportation.

While water resources are a known quantity, minerals are not. Despite advanced prospecting techniques, no one knows how great is the extent of Alaska's mineral wealth.

Once Alaska was almost synonymous with gold. Today, we know that other metallic minerals can be found in this geologically young area, minerals that could unfold a multi-billion dollar industry.

What could well be the largest oil strike in this continent has brought worldwide attention to the oil and gas potential of Alaska's

Arctic. Now, the companies face gigantic problems of transportation, processing, and facilities for their labor forces. Everyone must be careful, in the rush to mine the black gold of the Arctic, that the measures necessary to safeguard the environment are not overlooked. This environment includes scenes of awesome beauty, places where one can immerse himself in wilderness, and test himself against the stern and yet exhilarating discipline of the untrampled frontier.

Recreation in the out-of-doors is one of Alaska's most priceless assets, whether in a wilderness setting or at a developed recreation area where entire families can enjoy their surroundings. How this asset is used, helter-skelter or with careful consideration for the people-carrying capacity of the land, is something we must consider even today as we make our recreation investments for tomorrow.

The vast range and quality of wildlife in Alaska make this resource of interest and concern for sportsmen and wildlife lovers throughout America. It varies from the famed Alaska brown bear to huge concentrations of migratory waterfowl, which come from all four continental flyways to Alaska's summer nesting grounds. It includes the moose, largest herbivorous game animal still found in abundance in North America. The caribou herds, along with other highly specialized animals, live only in Alaska and Canada but are in a real sense the priceless heritage of the entire continent.

The grandeur of Alaska's geography and her multitude of wild animals make the state a mecca for visitors who yearn to see a part of their nation that still contains so much of the primitive and untamed. Such resources deserve the best protection we can give. Whether one thinks of timberlands as economic units in the production of forest materials or as wilderness, no one likes to see a fire-blackened hillside. But in 1968 we lost one million acres to uncontrolled fire. The Bureau of Land Management is responsible for fire control work over most of Alaska, including millions of acres of state lands protected under cooperative contract. Most of the serious fires come from lightning, striking sometimes hundreds of miles from the nearest outpost of civilization. We have learned in this country, with its vast distances and extremely dry summer conditions, that the most effective fire suppression technique is to hit it with all we have as soon as we can get there. This means dropping fire retardant from converted bombers and dropping smoke jumpers, trained in ground attack, sometimes far north of the Arctic Circle. And we depend on the Alaska natives, among the best fire fighters in the world. At one time in the summer of 1969 we had 2,500 emergency fire fighters on duty—so many that we flew in absentee ballots to aid the state in its primary elections.

All of this is expensive in men and materials. Sometimes we have to make bitter choices when the available resources won't stretch to cover all fires.

These are just some of the natural limitations that influence the potential development of Alaska. But there are man-made limitations, too—factors that favor some type of development while impeding others. These factors include the public land laws under which we in the Bureau of Land Management (BLM) must work. These factors also include human nature, particularly of those rare people hardy enough and daring enough to try homesteading in Alaska. The coming together of these two—the public land laws and the public in Alaska—warrants some discussion. Combined, they place at this time some restraints on resource management that must be recognized in any planning that might lead to wilderness designation.

In a series of legislative and executive actions in the 1930's, all of the public domain except that in Alaska was closed to settlement in advance of classification. Thereafter, would-be settlers had to have Uncle Sam's permission. This requirement did not apply to Alaska, and generally the public lands remained open to anyone who wished to settle. There were—and are—other laws far more effective for transferring public lands to citizens, such as the town site law under which cities like Anchorage and Fairbanks were settled.

But until recently, federal laws had placed the federal government in a passive position—sit until someone comes and asks for the land, then examine and survey it. Finally, in 1964, Congress passed the Classification and Multiple Use Act which gives BLM authority to go out and classify public lands in advance of demand.

The C&MU Act, as we call it, stipulates that we classify land either for disposal or retention for multiple use management. This law is companion to the act establishing the Public Land Law Review Commission, expiring at the same time—June 30, 1970.

In Alaska, this gives us an opportunity to make broad plans, based on local needs for expansion while protecting public resource values. If classified for retention, BLM is directed to manage the land for a variety of multiple uses as listed in the act. These uses range from mineral development to wilderness preservation.* We are guided by public hearings and by comments from grass-roots and national-level organizations. The classification process is perhaps the most forward-

---

* See Appendix D for regulations on public outdoor recreation use of Bureau of Land Management Lands including areas determined to be primitive in character. The C&MU Act allows the BLM to classify and manage public lands for wilderness preservation purposes, but the BLM refers to the lands it manages for wilderness values as "primitive areas."

looking land management tool ever devised by Congress. It gives us, and the people in the involved communities, a chance to look ahead.

Recently we completed the public review process for classifying the Copper River area, a huge basin north and east of Anchorage. This involves a large portion of the Wrangell Mountains including some of the most impressive living glaciers of the continent. The Copper River area covers some 22 million acres—by far the largest single area classified by the Bureau of Land Management. Basic economy of the area now depends largely on tourism, transportation, and communications. The big-game and sport-fishing potentials of the area are responsible for most of the development so far. About 1,200 people live in this 22-million-acre area, mostly in the towns of Glennallen, Copper Center, Gulkana, and Gakona. A third of these people are of native descent. The paved Glenn Highway, overland route from Anchorage to the Alaskan Highway, bisects the area, making it accessible to tourists and Alaskans alike.

As part of the preliminary work on the Copper River classification, BLM inventoried some of its assets. We found that about one-fifth of Alaska's moose live within this basin, along with many of America's most prized trophy animal—the Dall sheep. It includes a high proportion of Alaska's famed caribou, and numerous other game and fur-bearing animals of importance in the ecological community from the marmot to the "parka" or ground squirrel, which, for all its cuteness, is important in the food chain of other animals. These animals are of more than just local significance. In addition, the Copper River provides summer nesting grounds for about one-third of North America's entire population of trumpeter swans.

There is also the famed Alaska fishing, with whopping red salmon and grayling, just two of the many species that bring sportsmen—and sportsmen's dollars—from the lower 48.

Well, what did the classification accomplish? Did it simply assert Uncle Sam's intention of continued ownership of lakes, streams, forests and ice fields? Within the area are some 70,000 acres that are already partially settled and, except for the moratorium, would remain open to all types of claims. Another large area is state-selected. Some other lands best suited for individual development were left open for growing room. But the remainder have been closed to indiscriminate settlement and especially to claims that would block public access to the vast forests, lakes, and mountain ranges that lie remote from the highway. Perhaps, in the future, some of this land beyond the highway can be managed permanently as wilderness, protected in its natural state for future enjoyment by a nation even more in need of solitude.

What has been accomplished is only the beginning. The period of intensive study and investigation is just starting.

As land managers we have to look at a complex variety of problems. Through all of them are woven the natural limiting factors as well as operations of the public land laws. While some land uses tend to use the land lightly, often we are dealing with an extremely fragile resource. Alaska is such a land.

These are some of the problems and some of the promises of Alaska. It is a land blessed with an abundance of resources, her face shining with the newness of an untouched wilderness.

We invite you to come see us in Alaska.

# NATIONAL FOREST WILDERNESS PLANNING IN ALASKA

*W. Howard Johnson*

Regional Forester, Alaska Region, United States Forest Service

After a century of isolation, Alaska has moved dramatically from the role of a remote and forbidding subarctic possession of the United States into the mainstream of international travel, trade, and commerce. The demand for its resources in both national and international markets is growing rapidly. Its central position, both in air transportation and as Pacific rim country, places it in a dominant role for world trade. Whether we like it or not, the process of growth now started will continue at an ever-increasing pace.

Burt Silcock mentioned that the name "Alaska" is derived from the Aleut word "Alyeska" meaning "Great Land"; Alaskans like to brag just as Texans do. I have pointed out many times that this remarkable new state is larger than Denmark, Norway, Sweden, and Finland combined, and it lies in about the same latitudes. Further, if we are to understand the future of Alaska, we must look closely to both its geographical and social position in the world community.

Our coastal waters are major fishing grounds in a world that is chronically short of protein food supplies. Rising world living standards and increasing populations have expanded to the ultimate a demand for every type of fish product that we can produce. And, incidentally, 40 percent of the Pacific salmon caught off Alaskan shores are produced from national forest spawning streams. There is a growing need both in the United States and in the Orient for our timber supplies. This is pushing the state rapidly toward the full harvest of the sustained allowable yield of wood. Our oil and gas resources have received much national publicity. They are needed in

81

Hawaii, on the West Coast, and in Japan. Recent discovery on the Arctic Slope of what may be one of the largest oil reserves in the world is a tremendously exciting new development. The search for other minerals is being accelerated, and all projections of both United States and world demands versus reserves show rising needs and lower reserves.

Not commonly understood is the fact that Alaska has very decided geographic advantages that make its broad field of both renewable and nonrenewable resources unusually attractive. In the air world, it is the central point between Europe and the Orient. There is a constant two-way flow of traffic from our West Coast to Europe over the polar route. We are not more than a day away from any section of the world. Alaska looks forward to a full exploitation of this medium of transportation, for both people and commerce.

As a maritime state, Alaska is in an advantageous position at the top of the central Pacific to trade with Japan, Hawaii, and the West Coast states of the United States at favorable shipping rates. The markets which these outlets provide are more than adequate to absorb the entire resources output of the state. In short, Alaska has an advantage, not a disadvantage, in dealing with these areas.

In addition to its renewable and nonrenewable resources, Alaska has another priceless heritage—its people. We have rugged sourdoughs, cheechakos, Eskimos, Aleuts, and Indians. We have Alaska natives living often in abject poverty. On the other hand, we have large segments of the population living in cosmopolitan cities, such as Anchorage, with all of the amenities of modern society. Our people tend to be sturdy, self-reliant, aggressive, and straightforward. I can assure you that the pioneer spirit still prevails in the north.

Finally, Alaska has an abundance of space, which is rapidly becoming the most critical commodity in an overpopulated world. Our space constitutes the largest area of wilderness under the American flag. Alaska will surely be a great recreation ground of the future, not only for Americans, but for international tourists from Europe and Asia. Alaskan scenery is unparalleled. The great country offers just about everything, even for the most sophisticated outdoor recreationist.

My responsibility and my specific interest are directed toward the management of Alaska's two great national forests. The Tongass, containing some 16 million acres, embraces nearly all of southeastern Alaska, often called the Panhandle. The Chugach, with nearly five million acres, lies mainly in Prince William Sound and on portions of the Kenai Peninsula. Also included is Afognak Island, near Kodiak, which is near the beginning of the Aleutian chain. These dedicated public properties were established by presidential Executive orders between 1892 and 1911. These national forests, however, with their vast area of 21 million acres, comprise only a little more than five percent of the total acreage of the State of Alaska.

Conservation and development are not by any means antithetical concepts. In May of 1968, my friend Joseph H. FitzGerald, chairman of the Federal Field Committee in Alaska, delivered a commencement address entitled "Development and the Quality of Life" at the University of Alaska. I quote a portion of his address as an appropriate prelude to our consideration of wilderness in Alaska as a national forest resource:

> Clearly we need a development policy consistent with sound conservation practices and one that is accepted jointly by state and federal agencies with broad public support.
>
> What is such a policy?
>
> Broadly speaking, there are two areas that must be considered. First there are the uses of land traditionally associated with conservation—parks, wilderness areas, wildlife refuges, and recreation areas of many kinds. These are usually established in response to public demand in areas uniquely suited to such purposes.
>
> What is needed now is an identification of a statewide system of parks, wilderness areas, wildlife refuges, and recreational areas, a blueprint which all governments can follow as funds become available. The success of these efforts will have more profound effect on the future of Alaska than any other development effort that we can make.
>
> But the bulk of public lands in Alaska will not be set aside for special uses. What is the answer here?
>
> The undedicated public lands are the land bank upon which future population growth and development will draw. They will be needed for all the many uses that man makes of lands—uses that vary with time and reflect the rapid changes occurring in our civilization. Accepting, then, the premise that there will be many uses that we cannot fully foresee, it is clear that land management must be a continuing process, flexible in application, permitting present uses, accommodating to future uses, but always constraining use so that it does not become destructive.
>
> We are moving in this direction today. Land management, often under the heading of multiple use management, is the present goal of federal and state agencies. The logical progression is for us to achieve a common system of multiple land use management applied by all state and federal agencies in an agreed pattern. Our hope is that we in Alaska can develop and protect, use and conserve, enjoy in the present, and will to the future the unspoiled lands of Alaska.

I want you to know that the Forest Service has moved rapidly forward in its planned definition and management of the wilderness resources in Alaska. During the last year wilderness has been the topic of discussion at three region-wide meetings involving all of our top land managers. All of our forest supervisors have initiated special projects to study areas that can be considered for inclusion in the Wilderness Preservation System. In order to better orient our efforts, this office prepared a booklet entitled "Alaska Wilderness in Perspective" which was used as a basis for discussion at the wilderness workshop held in Juneau in February, 1969. Subsequent sections of my speech today on availability of wilderness, wilderness criteria, and wilderness management objectives are taken from this booklet.

The problem of analyzing potential areas for wilderness in Alaskan national forests is unusual in many ways. At the outset, we find that about 65 percent of the land consists of muskeg, scrub timber, rocky mountain peaks, snow, and ice. Much of this is interspersed with thousands of lakes of varying size; the entire area is broken up by 14,000 miles of saltwater shoreline and fiords. It is logical to assume that a great portion of the land will remain essentially in a primitive or pristine condition for the foreseeable future. Indeed, it will remain wilderness, almost regardless of man's future impact.

To locate lands suitable for wilderness classification seems, on the surface, an easy task. The beautiful and spectacular mountains, glaciers, bays, fiords, rivers, streams, forests, and abundant fish and wildlife— all in a relatively undeveloped state—seem to add up to unlimited areas suitable for wilderness. Yet there are suitability problems which tie directly to the very abundance of these undeveloped lands.

Road access is extremely limited. Population centers are few in number and widely scattered. Many communities are not accessible by highway. "Back country" is a rule rather than the exception. Most back country use is made possible and economically feasible only by aircraft and motorboats. Use of horses for trail travel is impractical in southeastern Alaska and in Prince William Sound. Because of inclement weather and the heavy cost of transporting camp gear, shelter cabins are widely established and used.

In light of these considerations, we are faced with the possible dilemma of creating areas of nonuse through wilderness classification. This, of course, is owing to the requirement to restrict motorized access and to eliminate developments such as shelter cabins. In this connection, the Alaska region of the Forest Service feels strongly that present wilderness standards should not be compromised.

One of the first steps in analyzing potential wilderness areas is a study of availability. It is obvious to me that the value and need of national forest land for wilderness must be conditioned on and balanced against the value and need for other uses. Following are some of the limiting conditions:

1. Some areas exist where the need for increased water production and on-site storage is vital. Here, the installation and maintenance of needed public facilities would be incompatible with wilderness classification.

2. There are many areas where wilderness classification would seriously restrict or prevent wildlife habitat management or improvement measures of significant importance. An example is the needed improvement of many salmon streams.

3. Alaska is replete with highly mineralized areas that the United States Geological Survey, Bureau of Mines and the Forest Service believe have substantial economic potential for development. In many such cases, the restrictions and controls necessary to maintain the wilderness character of the land would not be in the public interest.

4. The national forests support substantial areas of high-quality timber stands which are essential to the economic welfare of the nation and more particularly to existing dependent communities.

5. Many areas contain natural phenomena of such unique or outstanding character that public access should be provided. Examples are the internationally famous Mendenhall Glacier out of Juneau and Portage Glacier near Anchorage.

6. A good deal of land is needed to meet important long-range requirements for developed recreation areas, such as winter sports sites, campgrounds, and picnic areas.

7. Unique to Alaska are the lands needed for public recreation that are accessible only by plane, and where cabins are necessary to provide shelter and to fulfill the lands' highest use.

One or several of these conditions are often evident in areas otherwise suitable for wilderness. Two of the most serious conflicts are with minerals and timber.

Minerals are present in varying quantities throughout the region. Some of the more valuable deposits are known now and should be avoided in selecting wilderness areas. A concentrated program of more intensive study and field examination is greatly needed to identify other areas with high mineral potential.

National forest wilderness in Alaska will contain representative examples of all important forest types; however, the location of wilderness study area proposals in this region will be influenced by our plans and commitments to develop the timber resource. The harvest of national forest timber is progressing in accordance with sound long-range plans. More than $200 million has or will shortly be spent to install permanent manufacturing facilities. Three thousand workers are now directly employed by the wood-using industry. More than 20,000 people will be directly or indirectly dependent upon the manufacture of national forest wood products. Four large long-term timber sales have been consummated to help sustain this industry, which is now the principal backbone of southeastern Alaska's economy.

Values are relative, the need for the wilderness resource must be considered together with the demand for other resources. In the weighing process, it is essential to analyze separately the need for wilderness in order to establish, within definable limits, its relative value. And I can assure you this is no easy task.

We know that the demand for and use of designated wilderness will increase with expanding population levels and a growing appreciation of wilderness values. Lands that are not presently developed and that satisfy substantial back country recreation use will tend to become less available, thus sharpening the demands for wilderness. The question of how much to provide is paramount.

Some of the criteria which we in Alaska think are basic in determining whether an area is needed for wilderness are:

> 1. The location, size, type, and capacity of other wilderness in the general vicinity. This includes not only national forest, but also, classified or otherwise, the obviously true wilderness in national parks and monuments, national wildlife refuges and game ranges. In southeastern Alaska this would include Glacier Bay National Monument. On the Chugach National Forest, it would include mainly the Kenai National Moose Range and Katmai National Monument.
>
> 2. The present use of other wilderness; the trends or changing patterns of use; population expansion factors; trends toward changes in transportation; national travel patterns; and the anticipated changes in wilderness use.
>
> 3. The extent to which national forest and other lands can provide continuing opportunities for unconfined recreation, such as trail riding and hiking, fishing in alpine lakes, hunting, and back country camping.
>
> 4. How much of the Alaska wilderness needs should the national forests provide? Our two national forests comprise a very minor part of the total land package and are generally no better endowed with wilderness characteristics than many other areas of federal and state lands. Consider too, that

due to the nature of the country, most of the land will remain roadless and virtually undisturbed by man whether classified or not.

These considerations are not intended to be all-inclusive, nor are they intended to substitute for direction provided by the Wilderness Act. But we feel they are essential to an understanding of the land use planning and management problems in our Alaska Region. They reflect some of the extensive thinking that has gone into the preparation of a new set of wilderness management objectives. I know you will be interested in these:

1. The Alaska Region will recommend to the chief of the Forest Service that certain selected areas should be studied in accordance with the procedure set forth in the Wilderness Act and that recommendation as to their suitability or non-suitability for inclusion in the wilderness system be submitted to the president and to Congress. Preliminary identification of these areas will be made prior to June 30, 1970, but final review will not be completed until we can be certain that this will not interfere with Forest Service obligations in its review of primitive areas.

2. In selecting and managing wilderness in Alaska, the Forest Service will aim to maintain high quality in conformance with criteria and standards prescribed by the Wilderness Act.

3. The availability of Alaska national forest land for wilderness will be conditioned by its value and need for this resource compared to its value and need for the other phases of multiple use management.

4. The Forest Service will seek the assistance of key individuals, organizations, state officials, and other federal agencies in the consideration of proposed wilderness areas.

I reiterate that we in Alaska are working seriously and diligently to develop sound, and I hope adequate, proposals for additions to the national forest wilderness system. As these preliminary proposals are developed, they will be discussed with your people and others. And finally, we are pushing to beat the June 30, 1970, deadline.

# A CONSERVATIONIST VIEWS
# ALASKAN WILDERNESS

*Brock Evans*
Northwest Representative, Federation of Western Outdoor Clubs and Sierra Club

Those of us who consider the wilderness to be a resource of great value and wish to protect it are in serious trouble in Alaska, because another class of society—those who consider wilderness as something to conquer or do away with on the road to great riches—is doing rather well in that state.

This may sound like alarmist talk about a state that extends across 20 degrees of latitude and four time zones; but this is part of the problem. In the past it has been the remoteness and vastness of our largest state that protected it. It was an immense terra incognita of glaciers, forests, rivers, and mountains which would somehow always be there as a place of refuge and inspiration.

But things are happening fast in Alaska. What has taken 150 years to happen in Ohio, 100 years in California, or 50 years in my adopted State of Washington will probably take only a generation to accomplish in Alaska, if present trends, attitudes, and policies continue.

This is not the talk of a Cassandra; I have no intention of crying wolf. But consider these things:

Two years ago, the Arctic Slope of Alaska, together with the Brooks Range just to the south, was almost a total wilderness. No roads penetrated the mountains; the immense tundra plains of the coast were, with the exception of perhaps a half-dozen scattered tiny villages, only the home of caribou, polar bear, grizzlies, wolves, and other forms of wildlife. It would probably be exaggerating to say that the population of this region approached 5,000 human souls.

All that has changed. Culminating several years of intensive prospecting, a great oil discovery was made at Prudhoe Bay in July, 1968. A feverish rush for the new black gold has begun. Millions of acres have been leased for exploration and drilling activities which continue around the clock all winter long. A boom town atmosphere now exists in Fairbanks and Anchorage, and new airstrips have been constructed on the North Slope. Everywhere are the scars of bulldozer tracks, the litter of oil drums and the other equipment of man, and incessant noise. A winter road, later to be followed by a 48-inch oil pipeline, is being pushed across the mountains and the fragile tundra. None of this activity appears to be undertaken with the slightest thought to the environment or any other values except getting oil out. At least 10 million acres of wilderness have been lost in six months; even if the oil strike does not succeed, the land will not be what it was a year ago for many centuries to come.

Consider also the great ice-clad peaks and the dark forests sweeping down through thousands of miles of saltwater passageways and archipelagoes and rugged mainland of southeastern Alaska. This area is unique in the United States; yet, last summer we lost a million acres of it. Culminating a decade of effort on the part of the Forest Service, that agency finally offered for sale 8.75 billion board feet of southeastern Alaska's forests—and U.S. Plywood-Champion Lumber Company accepted the offer. Not all of these one million acres will be logged; but it is safe to say that nearly all of it will be within sight or sound of some work of man by the time the contract period is up—50 years from now. This loss happened at the stroke of a pen, and it is doubtful that it can be undone. It was the fourth such 50-year sale of southeastern Alaska timber in the past 15 years.

These are the reasons why it is not idle talk to say that we have lost a great deal in Alaska already. Now is the time to look at the potential of this state from the standpoint of planning to protect what remains of its wilderness before it is truly too late, and before we are doomed to repeat the experiences of wilderness protection efforts in the lower 48 states. We still have a chance, despite recent losses, to protect a good deal of some of the finest wilderness in the world.

What kind of wilderness potential remains? It is very exciting to consider what might be done, if, for the first time in our history, the concept of wilderness as a resource becomes a factor to be taken into equal account with the factors of economic development which have taken precedence everywhere else.

Of the total area of Alaska—about 375 million acres—only about 6.9 million acres, or 1.8 percent, have any truly strong protection from commercial exploitation. They are in Mt. McKinley National Park, and Katmai and Glacier Bay national monuments. Even Glacier Bay, however, is opening to mining activity, and parts of it have been severely damaged in the last year or two. Another 20 million acres receive some degree of protection in the great system of wildlife refuges and ranges. There are now 18 of these areas, protecting about 5.6 percent of the state. But these areas receive less than complete protection because they were all established by Executive order, and can be abolished the same way. All of them are open, after approval by the secretary of the interior, to mineral exploration, drilling, and mining activity.

The Bureau of Land Management has recently reclassified for multiple use management some 23 million acres in the Copper Basin area east of Anchorage, and another five million acres in the Iliamna region west of that city. These areas, also, are open to mineral activity and generally to state selection. The State of Alaska has obtained patents on about five million acres of land taken from the federal government under the Statehood Act. Less than four or five thousand acres of the total is managed for its natural values, and none of it has been classified as wilderness. The policy has been quite the opposite, as we shall see. No formally classified wilderness yet exists in the national forests in Alaska, although a scattering of very small units has been established as natural area, free from logging.

Thus, the real wilderness of Alaska—the wilderness that we know will continue to be with us, the areas that are really protected by law—is quite small. At this time, it consists only of national parks and monuments. And even these, as with the wildlife ranges, will have to go through the reclassification processes of the Wilderness Act. Not all of them are going to make it. Some, like the Kenai Moose Range, have already been severely compromised by mineral activities. Developments of various types exist in the other areas too. I estimate, however, that if the maximum wilderness were classified in these areas, it would probably amount to about 25 million out of the existing 27 million acres now under the jurisdiction of the National Park Service and the Bureau of Sport Fisheries and Wildlife.

There is potential for at least three new national parks in Alaska (totaling about six and one-half million acres) in the Gates of the Arctic, the Wrangell and St. Elias mountains, and around Lake Clark Pass, where the Aleutian and Alaska ranges meet. Another two million acres should be added to Mt. McKinley National Park to include the entire mountain for which it is named and add some caribou range on the north. Almost all of these new areas would be wilderness, about eight million acres. Glacier Bay National Monument should be made a national park to remove the mining threat.

A good dozen potential large wilderness areas, together with numerous smaller ones, exist in southeastern Alaska. They might protect adequate representative samples of the magnificent fiord and forest country. I want to stress that it is absolutely essential that substantial portions of the old growth spruce, hemlock, and cedar forests at tidewater be protected, because they are the essence of southeastern Alaska. The total acreage of wilderness here would be about four to five million acres.

At least two more refuges could be added to the wildlife refuge system. One to protect the tremendous seabird colonies in the Cape Thompson-Kukpuk River region of about one million acres of northwest Alaska; and the other, about three million acres in the Yukon River flats, which would be flooded by the Rampart Dam. The existing wildlife ranges should be confirmed by Congress, and their wilderness sections added to the wilderness system.

When the state land selection process is finished, well over 100 million acres of federal land will remain under the jurisdiction of the Bureau of Land Management in Alaska. Much of it will qualify as wilderness, particularly in the Copper River Basin, Iliamna region, and Brooks Range. The bureau, showing a great interest in protecting wilderness, should be encouraged to proceed.

The state-owned area with the most outstanding potential for wilderness protection is the Wood River-Tikchik Lakes region which was once proposed for national park status. Unfortunately, it was selected by the state to keep it out of the hands of the Park Service. If the present frontier attitudes of the State of Alaska persist, this area will probably be ruined in every way that provides any economic gain. One of the first acts of the state, after the land was selected, was an attempt to set up a commercial fishery in the lakes. There are about two million acres of potential wilderness here. Another million or so acres in the Chugach Mountains east of Anchorage could be so classified. That has also been selected by the state for recreation purposes.

A category that has been little discussed is the many large, wild, and beautiful rivers in the state. Some rivers, like the Yukon, are already well used by recreationists. Perhaps 2,000 miles of river could be classified under the Wild and Scenic Rivers Act: Porcupine, Golkana, Kenai, Sheenjek, Yukon, Kobuk, Koyukuk, Chena, Chatanika, Stikine, Wood, Willow, Birch Creek, and many others. Many thousand more miles would remain available for the state's economic development.

When all this is added up—both wilderness in the existing areas already set aside in some category, and the potential for more—there could be about 50 million acres in Alaska to be added to the wilderness system—not even counting the future classifications under the Bureau of Land Management. This is more wilderness than is possible in all the rest of the United States put together.

All this is a nice dream, and something fun to talk about; but is it going to happen? I return again to the beginning of my talk. These are only dreams; they are only measures of what could happen if we plan correctly and, for the first time in our history, consider that wilderness is a resource of an equal or higher value than all the other resources. But it isn't going to happen unless conservationists in the rest of America realize that Alaska belongs to all of the country, not just to the promoters, the fast-buck operators, and the local chambers of commerce—to those who see the land only as a way to get rich quick. We need to help our brother conservationists in Alaska; fortunately, they are a strong and devoted band.

It is doubtful that much wilderness will be so classified in Alaska if present trends and attitudes continue. Probably, after great effort, most of the wilderness in the existing national parks and monuments can be reclassified, but mining in Glacier Bay National Monument, without change of status, is going to remain a threat. Another threat to the wilderness of the existing National Park Service areas could come from our new secretary of the interior, Walter J. Hickel. During his confirmation hearings, Secretary Hickel urged protection for the national park system, but insisted again and again that Alaskan national parks are somehow "different." These parks, he seemed to feel, needed more capital improvements to open them up to the public. He cited, especially, Glacier Bay National Monument. What he meant is unclear, but a capital improvements program usually means more roads, lodges, and other mass recreation facilities.

Given this attitude, I think it doubtful that any proposals for new national parks will be favorably received by either the secretary of the interior or the Alaska Congressional delegation unless the political situation in Alaska changes. There will be great resistance to wilderness classification on the refuges or to the creation of new ones. Pressure to open up the nine-million-acre Arctic Wildlife Range for prospecting and oil drilling came from then-Governor Hickel as well as from many other Alaskans. As governor, he also advocated opening up still more portions of the 1.7-million-acre Kenai Moose Range to oil drilling. What he will do as interior secretary remains to be seen.

One of the greatest barriers to wilderness protection of areas other than barren mountaintops is the attitude of the state government, most Alaska politicians and the news media. Some state legislators and officials understand wilderness values. But the feeling in the state is generally characterized by the well-known frontier mentality—cries of "inexhaustible wealth for the taking" and "a vast treasure house"— phrases common in chamber of commerce parlance. This would perhaps not be such a great problem if most of Alaska were to remain under federal control. But, unfortunately for the cause of wilderness, under the Statehood Act the state is entitled to select 103 million acres for iself. This unusually large grant—nearly one-third of the entire state—was deemed necessary to provide the state an adequate economic survival base, and that may be true. But it was intended also that the state set up a planning system for land use which could be a model to avoid the mistakes made in other states. The thinking envisaged that all selected lands would first go through a careful allocation process to ensure retention of enough land for purposes such as recreation, and not be disposed of wholesale as happened in so many other states. So far, the performance of the state has not been encouraging. Nearly all of the state agencies, with perhaps the exception of the State Parks Department, seem preoccupied with putting the land they select into private hands as fast as possible. The main cry of the state seems to be more and bigger economic development at any cost, if the pronouncements of many public officials are to be taken at face value.

So it is this reason—the frontier attitude of the state itself, and its right to 103 million acres of what will surely be the most habitable and hospitable parts of the state—that makes me feel that at least that much wilderness is in great trouble, unless something changes. The state is certain to select not only oil-bearing lands along the coast, but river valleys, and probably many of the great interior forests on the assumption that they can be logged. It seems doubtful that wilderness values will be much considered in all of this rush. Because the state land selection process is now being held up pending resolution of the Indian claims problem, there perhaps is a chance to change attitudes before it is too late.

My opinion, shared by many Alaska conservationists, is that the most serious and immediate threat to Alaska's wilderness lies in the southeastern Panhandle with its heavily forested islands, bays, inlets, and tremendous chain of glacier-clad peaks rising, in many cases, literally out of the water.

The threat there is logging, and there are fears that we may already be too late. The blame for the situation is with the Forest Service which manages nearly the entire area. I am sorry to say this, particularly with my old friend, Howard Johnson, here sharing the same platform. But the situation does exist. And it appears that Forest Service land management planning in southeast Alaska has been made with one primary goal—to get that timber out.

All other resources, particularly wilderness, have so far at least taken a very distant back seat to this goal. While the agency has made a few hesitant and tentative steps in the direction of some protection of the magnificent natural environments of the Panhandle, the steps have been grossly inadequate and minimal.

The result has been strong efforts by the agency to sell the maximum amount of timber that was considered to be available for cutting. A strenuous attempt has been made to attract pulp mills into the region; the lure for inducing their establishment in the southeastern section has been long-term contracts for huge quantities of timber at highly reduced (perhaps subsidized) prices.

To further this goal, the Forest Service has conducted at least five major sales of this type since 1954:

### LONG-TERM ALASKA TIMBER SALES

| Date of Sale | Years | Name of Company | Total Acres | Volume Sold in Board Feet |
|---|---|---|---|---|
| 1954 | 50 | Ketchikan Pulp | 786,000 | 8.2 billion |
| 1959 | 50 | Alaska Lumber & Pulp | 1,600,000 | 5.2 " |
| 1960 | 50 | Pacific Northern Co. | 450,000 | 3.0 " |
| 1968 | 50 | U.S. Plywood-Champion | 1,000,000 | 8.8 " |
| 1968 | 15 | Perenosa | 120,000 | .5 " |

Thus, in 15 years the Forest Service has contracted nearly 26 billion board feet of the choicest forests of southeast Alaska on what are known as allotment areas covering an area of 4,150,000 acres. These sales cover only a part of all the logging being done there, for a normal timber sale program to smaller purchasers is going on at the same time. Of course, not all of the 4.15 million acres will be logged; but it seems certain that all the accessible areas will be.

The most serious concern about any land management agency engaging in such long-term contracts is that it is impossible to predict social patterns, desires, and needs 20 years hence, much less 50. Contracts of this type, which commit immense areas of scenic and wilderness lands to a single use—logging—have left the agency little freedom of action. And they have left us, the great majority of the American public—not logging-oriented, not benefiting from logging because most of this timber goes to Japan, but owning the national forests—holding the bag. To my knowledge no hearings were ever held on this procedure. There was no real consultation with our organizations. The protests that we were able to muster were brushed aside.

Unfortunately, the contracts are only the beginning, and I feel that in the future we will be in even graver trouble. These contracts permit a mill to become established with a certain capacity and demand— that is, appetite—for timber. The mill is entitled to a certain amount over a 50-year period; but at the end of that time, it cannot go back to recut the first acres it cut 50 years earlier, because the rotation cycle is 100 years—twice the contract period. The mill will have to obtain other timber, or people will be thrown out of work. You know the answer: it will get other timber, on other acres, in other forests on other coves, bays, and inlets. We have committed all the forests in 4.15 million acres—26 billion board feet—to logging in the next 50 years; if the present contracts are renewed (the Perenosa sale will be renewed about six times) we will be cutting another 29 billion board feet on almost five million more acres during the second 50 years of the 100-year rotation. This means that one century from now at the end of the first rotation, at least 55 billion board feet on nine million acres of southeast Alaska will have been promised and committed to and cut by the loggers. Of course, the other timber sales programs will have continued cutting perhaps equal volumes and probably on the same aggregate amount of area.

Another problem with this kind of contract is that the mill opera- tors, once lured into southeast Alaska and promised large quantities of timber, know a good thing when they see it. They expand their capacity beyond that required by the sale, as both the Sitka and Ketchikan mills have done. Sitka conservationists tell me the Alaska Lumber and Pulp Company mill has doubled its capacity since 1959, and the Georgia-Pacific Corporation mill in Ketchikan is close to that. These mills are, of course, buying many of the independent sales offered, but it seems plain that their appetite will expand when the time comes to renew the long-term contracts.

Another matter may be even more potentially serious than all the above put together: the volumes of timber available within areas allotted to the large-scale contracts may have been greatly overesti- mated. It is rumored in Sitka that this is the case within the area allotted to the Alaska Lumber and Pulp Company, and that the company will have to go outside its area for its timber if it hopes to stay in business for a 50-year period. A high official at the Georgia- Pacific mill in Ketchikan, in a press statement of April, 1967, stated the same thing for part of his mill's allotment area, and indicated that volumes might have been overestimated by as much as 20 percent.

If this is true, taxpayers will either have to pay penalties when the contract volumes cannot be fulfilled within the allotment areas, or will have to sacrifice what remains of our forests in southeast Alaska to fulfill contracts outside of the allotment areas. This is an unhappy situation.

We can see that a great deal of planning has been done for utilization of the timber resource in the national forests of southeast Alaska. What planning has been done for the wilderness resource, which is unparalleled anywhere in the United States? Keep in mind that when we speak of wilderness, we are not just talking about gross acres. There is much rock and ice in southeast Alaska. Although these beautiful areas will probably be safe for a good period of time to come, they should have the protection of the Wilderness Act.

What is threatened is the very thing that makes southeast Alaska's wilderness unique. Think of the great spruce and hemlock forests growing next to the beach around thousands of tiny coves, inlets, and islands, along miles and miles of incredibly beautiful and sheltered fiords and passageways. Scenic and beautiful in themselves, they also furnish the setting for the combination of water, glaciers, and great mountains that makes this entire area qualified for national park status. The scenery is like a hundred North Cascades—all at tidewater—probably unmatched anywhere on this planet.

What sort of planning has been done for this scenic and wilderness resource? The Forest Service did take the step of proposing a wilderness area in the Walker Cove-Rudyerd Bay region in the mid-1950's, and that is much to their credit. Because of strong local opposition the classification did not proceed. Now the territory is managed as a scenic area which is at least an attempt to protect it. The same management is accorded to the Tracy Arm-Ford's Terror region farther north. We are glad for the existence of these areas; but it is only fair to point out that while extremely scenic, they contain little of the great old-growth forests that are the essence of the southeast; the total amount of commercial forest barely amounts to as much as 1.5 percent of both of these areas combined. But even these areas can be logged, for the scenic area restriction is not a complete restriction against timber cutting. Present administrative policies are against timber cutting, but there are no guarantees that this will continue to be so.

The Forest Service has set aside another 17,000 acres in four small natural areas, of which less than one-fourth represents old-growth forests. There are other zones like water influence zones to protect some of the tourist routes of the inside passage. But even these zones can be logged, although at a much slower rate, and they sometimes are cut.

So it appears that in an area the size of the State of Indiana, possessing a unique wilderness resource, there has been little protection, but a great deal of timber management.

The Forest Service is making studies aimed at recommending a system of wilderness areas in the southeast. While we are very glad for this, and want to encourage and help the regional forester, we know that probably recommendations for wilderness will not be made in areas already allotted to long-term timber sales contracts.

I think it's fair to say the Forest Service would think that we cannot now consider for wilderness protection the entire west coast of Admiralty Island, which boasts a tremendous, sweeping expanse of forest which rises from the blue waters of its bays and straits to cover the sides of the beautiful mountains in the island's center.

We may not be able to consider West Chichagof Island, which is probably the only opportunity in all of the southeast to protect an entire large unified island wilderness complex which typifies all that southeastern Alaska used to be.

We will not be able to consider for wilderness protection the easily accessible island-studded bays and passageways of northern Baranof Island or the east side of Prince of Wales Island.

All of these areas probably will be omitted from the Forest Service recommendations. What about the rest? Timber considerations will have to be uppermost in Forest Service planning and recommendations because of long-term contracts and overcalculation of volume.

Although we are glad that some steps have been taken so far, we find the attitudes of the agency discouraging. A strong negative tone runs through two recent Forest Service publications. The first is "Alaska Wilderness in Perspective," and the second, "Assessing Benefits and Costs for Alaska National Forest Wilderness Proposals." Both are dated February, 1969, and both were presented to the first all-Alaska wilderness conference held in Juneau during February, 1969. Mr. Johnson's paper, given today, includes quotations from them.

These items from the first publication are cited as factors in deciding how much, if any, wilderness shall be reserved in southeast Alaska—with my analyses:

1) "A great deal (14.6 percent) of Alaskan national forests has already been set aside." This total was arrived at by including three million acres of the Glacier Bay National Monument and Kenai National Moose Range as areas "withdrawn" from the national forests, and therefore to be included in national forest totals.

2) "The fact of previous commitments to timber management," the situation that I have already discussed.

3) Analysis of "needs," seeming always to be expressed in terms of "use" or "recreation."

4) A feeling that perhaps Alaska's national forests don't need to provide much wilderness, as in the following statement on page seven: "Our two national forests comprise a very minor part of the total land package and are generally no better endowed with wilderness characteristics than many other areas of federal and state land."

5) A requirement "that lands to be classified are to be free of present or foreseeable conflicts." In other words, don't waste time on areas which have other values.

6) A number of references and statements conveying the probability that "wilderness classification will hinder wildlife management programs and damage the salmon industry, because we cannot practice stream habitat improvement programs."

7) A number of statements that "more tourists would be attracted if there were more access roads in an area."

The true attitude, I think, is epitomized by this statement on page three of the second document: "How much would timber growing within an area contribute to a national and local economy that has made the wilderness system possible?"

All these statements put together have a distinct negative tone which harks back to the frontier philosophy that wilderness is a genuine detriment. We are told that very little or no wilderness will be recommended for protection if any commercial resource of any magnitude is involved, or if there is any possible conflict with other recreational uses. That this will be the result of the studies has been indicated by an elaborate effort to discredit a recent proposal made by Sitka-area citizens for a West Chichagof Island wilderness area. The discrediting effort was centered around the above reasons, despite the fact that the island is one of the most accessible of all potential wildernesses in southeastern Alaska.

Based on all the above considerations, the future for strong wilderness proposals in southeastern Alaska is bleak. I predict that a number of rock, ice, and barren areas and noncommercial forests will be recommended; but the essence of the Panhandle will not be. That will be gone unless something is done by citizen groups.

There are some things that we can do for southeastern Alaska and for all the state:

1) We must give strong support to the growing conservation movement within Alaska. Despite the frontier mentality, there are many

Alaskans who live there because they love its wilderness, its vastness, and its beauty. These people are now organized in the Alaska Wilderness Council, the Alaska Conservation Society, and the Alaska Chapter of the Sierra Club. They need our financial and moral support as well as our help on the national scene. We also can help educate other Alaskans as to the value of these organizations. Alaska's population is still small enough so that dedicated groups of individuals can make a real difference in the political climate.

2) I propose a freeze on all state land selections, not only until the native claims question is settled, but also until the state puts into practice the plans established by farsighted men 10 years ago. The Alaska legislature and state government still operate in a somewhat frontier fashion, and have little real concern for the wilderness environment that makes the state unique. Policies should not be directed so completely toward land disposal and exploitation. The only time to control this is when land is still in the hands of the federal government, before state selection. We should not permit the selection of regions like Wood River-Tikchik Lakes country without guarantees and safeguards that they will be managed with consideration for their natural values.

3) We must seek congressional confirmation of the existing wildlife ranges, and the change of Glacier Bay from national monument to national park status.

4) A scenic resources review commission must be established to investigate immediately the situation in the southeast, and to make recommendations on early protection of scenic and wilderness areas. The president is now appointing blue-ribbon commissions to investigate the housing shortage and timber supply; as a corollary to this, he should appoint a blue-ribbon commission to investigate the loss of scenic resources in southeastern Alaska.

5) Congress should investigate the entire timber sale procedure, particularly in southeastern Alaska. The long-term contracts, which stimulate demand and appetite for Alaskan timber and commit land resources to a single use for long periods of time, should be carefully examined. The uncertain question of available volumes should also be studied. Such an investigation would tie in with the scenic resources review.

6) Conservation organizations should consider legal action to halt any activity under the long-term contract to U.S. Plywood-Champion. The mill is not yet built and cutting has not started. Once the mill starts operating, and if volumes are overestimated as rumored, we will have lost the chance for most of the forested-inlet-bay wilderness in

southeastern Alaska. This development should be withheld until the entire situation is reevaluated.*

7) We must give strong support to those agencies which show an interest in protecting Alaska's wilderness resources. The political climate in Alaska, while improving, is not generally favorable to this concept, and the agencies that really care need our support at all times.

I urge that this program be undertaken immediately because we cannot hope to protect Alaska's wilderness properly without it.

Think back in time. What would our country be like today if we had been able to attend a conference in 1800 to discuss the future of wilderness in Ohio and Michigan; in 1900 to take positive steps to protect California's beaches and redwoods; in 1920 to protect the Colorado and Columbia rivers; or in the 1930's to protect the great fir forests of Oregon?

All these assets are nearly gone; we were not strong enough earlier, and did not have the opportunity. But we do have the opportunity for Alaska and today we are much stronger. There is still a chance to do in Alaska what we did not accomplish anywhere else. I hope that we do so.

* On February 10, 1970, the Sierra Club and the Sitka Conservation Society filed a lawsuit in Federal District Court in Anchorage to prevent construction of the new pulp and lumber mill on Berners Bay near Juneau that would be built by U.S. Plywood-Champion Papers, Inc. The action against the secretary of agriculture, the chief of the Forest Service, and the regional forester seeks to enjoin cutting under a 50-year timber sale contract that would provide timber for the proposed plant.—Editor.

# DISCUSSION

*John L. Hall, director of field studies, The Wilderness Society\*:*

Today I will talk about the Alaskans, the people of this "Great Land," specifically the Alaskan conservationists. We have heard the challenges: the Bureau of Land Management classification opportunities, National Park Service and Bureau of Sport Fisheries and Wildlife opportunities in wilderness classification, and the Forest Service's forward-looking wilderness proposals that Howard Johnson mentioned. They are great. However, I think we must go back in history to the visionaries of the past to see where all of this thinking has evolved from.

It was Henry Gannett of the Geological Survey who stated in 1904 that Alaska's greatest resource was the scenic and wilderness resource. Many of you know of Olaus Murie's and Bob Marshall's work in the interior of the state, and of Benton MacKaye, the national planner. They have all had a great feeling for the wilderness movement in Alaska and in the nation. Olaus, Bob Marshall, and Benton were among the founders of the Wilderness Society. Mardy Murie is continuing this work today in trying to preserve Alaskan wilderness.

Let us review the recent losses in wilderness. In a six-month period in the interior of Alaska we lost nine million acres of wilderness that never can be reclaimed.

Regarding wildlife, we heard this morning about the wolves—they will be gone from Alaska if blind progress continues. I know from the experiences I had in southeastern Alaska since I first arrived in 1950 that the conflicts there are between brown bears and man. At one

\* Since September, 1969, Mr. Hall has been special assistant to W. Howard Johnson, regional forester, Alaska Region, U.S. Forest Service.

101

logging camp in Eliza Harbor on Admiralty Island, in one season 13 Alaska brown bears were lost because they were a threat to the loggers.

We know the timber sale program in southeastern Alaska has resulted in land use conflicts between timber and potential recreation, fisheries, wildlife, and wilderness resources. The battles to have other land values recognized and statutory wilderness designated are going to be tremendous, as the people in Alaska now realize.

Also, some of the 104 million acres of lands that can be selected by the state will be available for open entry for filing by individuals. The old-type homestead and other land entries can be located in potential wilderness areas.

The environmental threats from the oil exploration and development that face Cook Inlet are real when compared with the recent blowout near Santa Barbara, California. In 1964 Alaska suffered a severe earthquake, and there have been many others. Think what can happen in the oil fields and to the pipeline and at the terminal facilities. An earthquake could cause the 48-inch pipeline to rupture. Dr. Weeden mentioned that one-half million gallons of oil per mile would spill out of that pipeline onto the tundra and into the Arctic Ocean.

In 1968 not one winter road 450 miles long, but two were built from the Fairbanks area up into the Prudhoe Bay area. That land is gone forever as wilderness designation. When the snow and ice melt, it is said, erosion and damaged streams will result.

We must also look at the opportunities that people have lost—opportunities for land and resource decisions. While it is encouraging to see so many young people attending this conference, the truth is that the opportunity for the adults of tomorrow to make decisions in land use and land management planning is being taken away from youth today at a very fast rate.

However, a very encouraging sign is the strong emergence of the Alaska conservationist. This year I analyzed The Wilderness Society membership throughout the nation. I found out that Alaska has the highest percentage of members—850 per million population. I congratulate the Alaskans and the great work of the Alaska Conservation Society and the Alaska Chapter of the Sierra Club. The productive wilderness workshop, held in Juneau in February, 1969, was under the auspices of the Forest Service, the Bureau of Sport Fisheries and Wildlife, the Alaska Conservation Society, and the Sierra Club. A lot of good came out of that workshop and more will come. Things are moving; the people are concerned and becoming effective. We are dealing in the democratic process, and when we see it in action, as at this conference, we become believers. I am a believer after working a year and a half on wilderness legislation both at the grass roots level and in Washington, D.C.

Now, as people from the "Outside" (that is what Alaskans call those of us who live in the other 49 states) we must strongly support the Alaskans. I say "we" as conservationists. I include the agency people and citizen conservationists. We must support the Alaskans with men, money, research, and education. We must do so through the agencies and also through the national conservation organizations. The opportunity is tremendous: the wilderness potential in Alaska amounts to over half the potential wilderness in the United States. Also important is that the 375 million acres receive "tender loving care." The Alaskans have demonstrated their concern for wilderness by the high percentage of membership in The Wilderness Society. I think the Sierra Club membership statistics are somewhat the same.

There is room in Alaska for staff people from all the national conservation organizations: the National Audubon Society, the Sierra Club, The Izaak Walton League, the National Wildlife Federation, Defenders of Wildlife, Trout Unlimited, The Wilderness Society, and any other organizations interested in a quality environment. These staff people must be Alaskans—they must be there, living and residing in the state. They, and the membership of their organizations, are a tremendous political force. The challenges are there. Here is an example of what the Alaskans face: in the last state legislature in Juneau, there were 20 registered lobbyists for the oil industry. Twenty! There was one part-time lobbyist for the citizen conservationists. This is why I strongly urge the national conservation organizations to put money and top staff people in Alaska.

There are top people available: young conservationists, those who have the degrees and the intense interest. All of us are working hard to preserve a quality environment for this world, for our nation, and for the great State of Alaska. We must work together nationally, striving for better coordination and cooperation between national conservation groups. One way to achieve this cooperation is similar to the political process: at the grass roots level with grass roots support. I appeal to all conservationists in every field to support the Alaskans and work with them for a quality environment in Alaska.

*William B. Lord, director, Center for Resource Policy Studies and Programs, School of Natural Resources, University of Wisconsin:*

Alaska is a geographically huge state. Its land area is almost seven times that of my own State of Wisconsin. At the same time it is socially a very small state. There are fewer than 300,000 Alaskans, fewer people than live in my own county in Wisconsin. Alaska's economy is in many ways that of an underdeveloped country. It is highly dependent upon a very few export-oriented extractive industries for its income and, because it is too small to produce most of its needs efficiently, it is highly dependent upon imports to supply the goods and services demanded by its residents. Almost everything is costly in Alaska, whether it is consumer needs, industrial inputs, transportation, or basic social services provided by government.

Alaska is also a young state, with relatively little political influence in Washington and a heritage of paternal control by a large remote federal government. Many Alaskans feel that their problems are almost unique and that they are neither fully understood nor adequately appreciated by the rest of us. There is sound historical basis and even a good bit of current foundation for this feeling.

Earlier speakers have described the unparalleled scenic, wildlife, and wilderness resources of Alaska. They have not described the grave fiscal difficulties faced by a young, sparsely populated, and economically disadvantaged state as it attempts to build the social capital (the transportation, health, education, and other systems) necessary for it to attain the self-sufficiency and independence appropriate to a member state within our federal system. With few people to draw upon and little capital to employ, Alaskans have looked, of necessity, to the land and its associated natural resources as the first and most important foundation for the economic development that many so desperately desire.

A special word must be said for the needs of native Alaskans, the Eskimo, Aleut, Athapaskan, Tlingit, Haida, and Tsimshian peoples who constitute about one-fifth of the state's population. These native peoples have for centuries depended upon the environment in quite different and more intimate ways than have the more recent arrivals who have claimed title to their land. The concepts of property indigenous to the native cultures were quite different from our own, and we have not recognized native rights to their own land by treaty or any other formal means, save in a very few specific cases. These original Alaskans are now undergoing the terribly difficult cultural changes necessary to adapt to a space age civilization within just a few generations, something which has taken the rest of us centuries and which some would say we still have not done well.

Out of all of this has come what I call the notion of land magic. Native Alaskans are preoccupied with land because it has been the traditional basis for their subsistence economy and because we do not recognize their rights in that land. The government of the State of Alaska is preoccupied with land because it is the only important source of the revenues which are needed to finance basic social services and to build the infrastructure upon which development depends. Businessmen are preoccupied with land because it is the basic source of profits in an extractive economy. Most Alaskans are preoccupied with land because, paradoxically, they have so little of it. Prior to statehood, over 99 percent of Alaska's land was owned by the federal government. Today, the vast bulk of the land remains in federal ownership, even though the state is entitled to select about one-third of the state's total land area and has selected an appreciable acreage. Private holdings remain small. Land is seen by many as the answer to all problems, a frontier attitude which has been powerfully reinforced by the recent oil strikes.

Actually, what native Alaskans need is not land but income, education, housing, health services, transportation, and the opportunity to participate meaningfully in economic and political institutions. The State of Alaska needs money, not land. Businessmen need markets, capital, trained labor, and security of expectations, not land. And all of Alaska's citizens, with all of us and our children, need the magnificent scenery, wildlife, and wilderness that is Alaska, not divided up into a few acres for each of us to do with as he will, but protected, preserved, and managed for all of us for all time.

No one can doubt that there will be great problems to solve if we are to safeguard major areas of wilderness in Alaska. The land magic notion must be put down; no easy task with multimillion-dollar oil revenues in prospect. Federal government actions must respect and involve Alaskan interests more adequately than in the past. (Many Alaskans bitterly and properly resent the unilateral federal withdrawals which have set aside Navy Petroleum Reserve Number Four, the Arctic Game Range, and other large areas without extensive public debate and participation.) These actions in the past were partly responsible for the fact that wilderness is such a dirty word to many Alaskans. An attempt by the Forest Service to establish a small Tracy Arm-Fords Terror wilderness area was shouted down only a few years ago. Federal and state agencies must be adequately authorized and funded to undertake the detailed information-gathering and dissemination which is essential to land use planning.

Several specific problems standing in the way of an adequate wilderness policy for Alaska deserve discussion. The first is state land selection. Under the terms of the Statehood Act, Alaska may select over 100 million acres of public domain lands in the state without federal approval. It then classifies selected lands for state retention and management or for sale, as appropriate. Given the orientation of the state government towards revenue and development and the lack of power in the federal government to prevent selection of lands deemed to be of overriding national importance, this law can only be seen as dangerously inimical to the long-range interests of both the nation and the State of Alaska in wilderness protection and preservation.

The Bureau of Land Management (BLM), which is the custodian of the vast public domain lands which still constitute by far the largest ownership category in Alaska, is inadequately staffed and inadequately empowered to protect the public interest in the lands entrusted to it. Much of the bureau's statutory authority dates from an earlier era when its mission, or that of its forerunners, was to dispose of the public domain as expeditiously as possible. Its most enlightened authority, under the Multiple Use and Classification Act of 1964, is only temporary. Even land classified as wilderness by BLM cannot now receive the statutory protection of the Wilderness Act because BLM was not included under the provisions of that legislation. And the bureau staff, many of whom are capable, dedicated, and enlightened public servants, are spread so thinly that their effectiveness cannot but be impaired. The agency lacks both the authority and the political support to effectively regulate and control such uses of the public domain as those which will be associated with North Slope oil development and transportation.

Most of the distinctive coastal forest of southeastern and south-central Alaska is managed by the United States Forest Service. This agency has the legislative authority, the appropriations, and the capable professional staff necessary to serve the public interest well. Unfortunately, it has not demonstrated its determination to discover that public interest through seeking broad public involvement in its planning and decision-making process. Whether because of a misguided professionalism which results in a "father knows best" attitude or too great sensitivity to the desires of the forest products industry, the Forest Service has not developed a planning process which gives adequate attention to wilderness considerations. It has now concluded long-term sales contracts with a few industrial firms which seriously conflict with desirable wilderness proposals in southeastern Alaska and which will inhibit the agency's already feeble initiatives in this regard for years to come. The Forest Service must be pressed soon and pressed hard to establish a comprehensive land use planning program which provides for continual and broadly based public participation in decision-making.

In conclusion, achieving an adequate wilderness policy for Alaska is both crucial and extremely difficult. Creative thinking will be required to devise ways of meeting the legitimate and deeply felt needs of Alaska's native peoples and its state government, and to relieve the hostility and distrust with which some Alaskans view the actions of their federal government. A satisfactory wilderness policy cannot be achieved until these obstacles are removed, for our political system will not tolerate riding roughshod over sincere local objections, even in the name of a worthy cause.

Once the necessary atmosphere of confidence is established, the next step is to declare Alaska's great de facto wilderness to be de jure wilderness, pending careful and considered land use classification and planning. By this, I mean that the policy on all federal lands should be one of no further development until it can be responsibly established that such development is in the public interest. This will require a well-funded land classification program and one which is able to respond quickly by examining without delay those areas for which development is proposed. It will also require that the program be oriented as much or more toward wilderness and other so-called environmental considerations as toward development, so that all sides of the story are fairly and fully presented for public consideration. Anyone familiar with water resource, forest management, and other kinds of natural resource planning as they have been conducted in this country, will appreciate that this has been far from the case in the past. Finally, the land classification program must recognize the importance of, and provide for, broad public involvement in the process of making land use decisions. The Multiple Use and Classification Act under which the Bureau of Land Management now operates could well serve as the model for this planning program but the program must cover all federal lands in Alaska, not just the public domain now managed by BLM.

One implication of the planning program which I have proposed is that no further state land selections could take place prior to classification, and that only lands classified as appropriate for state ownership and management, or for disposition to private owners, could be selected by the state subsequent to classification. For this to be appropriate, it would be essential that the state participate in the planning process and that its interest be fully recognized. Another implication is that no further unilateral federal withdrawals be permitted, and that no federal withdrawals occur prior to classification, however laudatory the purpose might be. Yet another implication would be that the Homestead Act and other laws permitting unilateral private appropriation of public lands be repealed and replaced by provisions for orderly disposition of public lands to private parties in accordance with the classification and planning program and in such ways that the public interest in environmental protection, in public land access, and in just recovery of economic values be preserved.

The conceptual foundation of my proposal clearly is the avoidance of irreversible decisions made in haste and without adequate information or public participation. We face many irreversible decisions with respect to Alaska's often fragile environment. The most pressing concerns oil development on the North Slope. To place a moratorium on such development until we know oil is needed and how to go about extracting it with minimal environmental damage involves only the cost of waiting. The oil will still be there when, how, and if we decide to develop it. If we go ahead now, however, we risk permanent and pervasive environmental damage. The oil will always be there but the wilderness may not.

Those of us in what Alaskans call the lower 48 have good reason to appreciate the irreversibility of some land use decisions. In my own Midwest our prairies and our virgin forests are long since gone. More recently we have lost one of our Great Lakes. When we visit the less developed western states, and particularly Alaska, we realize the enormity of our loss. We also see now that we do not need all our prairies for growing corn, all our forests for producing lumber, or all our Great Lakes as receptacles for sewage, industrial wastes, and the nutrients, fertilizers, and pesticides flowing from our farms. But now it is too late for us to protect these resources or to set aside more than a few small areas of wilderness. We must act quickly, wisely, generously, and understandingly to help Alaskans avoid the mistakes that we have made; mistakes which if repeated will destroy this last great wilderness which belongs to all of us and yet to none of us.

R. W. Behan, assistant professor,* School of Forestry, University of Montana:

For my part of this afternoon's discussion, I would like to talk about souls and shirts in Alaska—some funny words I will explain in a few minutes.

In 1899 John Muir went to Alaska with the Harriman expedition. Another participant was Henry Gannett, the redoubtable chief geographer of the Geological Survey. In his 1904 report on the expedition, Gannett wrote:

> There is one other asset of the territory not yet enumerated; imponderable and difficult to appraise . . . This is the scenery. There are glaciers, mountains, fiords elsewhere, but nowhere else on earth is there such abundance and magnificence of mountain, fiord and glacier scenery. For thousands of miles the coast is a continuous panorama. For one Yosemite of

* Dr. Behan is now associate professor.

California, Alaska has hundreds. The mountains and glaciers of the Cascade Range are duplicated and a thousandfold exceeded in Alaska. The Alaska coast is to become the showplace of the entire earth . . . [its] value measured by direct returns in money from tourists will be enormous; *measured in health and pleasure it will be incalculable.*

This passage is taken from Richard A. Cooley's *Alaska: A Challenge in Conservation,* 1967. I think Gannett might have been implying here that Alaskan landforms can do something for men's souls; and if he didn't, I will attempt to do so today.

Doing something for men's souls is a fairly mushy and sentimental piece of business: I will admit to this, too, and face the issue of emotionalism a little later.

Alaska, to phrase an understated cliché, is immense. Its natural resources—forests, fisheries, minerals, scenery, space—are at least abundant and in many cases redundant. Finely tuned, detailed land use planning is probably impossible at this time, if indeed appropriate. We are in the framing stage, and we need 16-penny spikes, not finishing nails. I will be speaking, consequently, in broadly generalized terms, for the techniques of planning and management in Alaska have been and will be necessarily crude for a long time to come.

One time in Ketchikan, for example, we took a forest fire report from the pilot of a Pan American jet. He did his best and reported its location—in approximate coordinates of latitude and longitude, which is to say plus or minus about 300 miles. We didn't know whether the fire was in Alaska, and hence within our jurisdiction, or somewhere in British Columbia. We did know it had to be a big one, because the jet flew at 34,000 feet, and we knew we would have to take a look.

I chartered a Grumman Goose and went for one of the most fantastic flights in my memory. Let me describe it now briefly, for in retrospect I saw a series of zones.

We took off from Ketchikan, the pilot and I, and saw first what I would like to call now the Living Zone. There is a dense, lush timber resource that supports a thriving forest products industry. There is a rich fisheries resource that sustains a major investment in fishing boats and canneries, and all the people dependent upon them. This is a rather gentle landscape where, in a general way, natural resources and human activities interact successfully and tolerably well. And there is lots of color: the greens and browns of the gentle mountains, the robust blue of healthy salt water, and the variegated hues of the town itself.

We fly toward the mainland, over Punchbowl Cove, where a granite face rises out of the salt water 3,000 almost-vertical feet. The topography is much more rugged now; we have entered the Transition Zone. There is no sign of either human habitation or human industry; the forest resource here is sparse and stunted, the slopes are precipitous, and there appears a well-defined timberline. There are clear subalpine lakes—literally choked with native trout. There are deer, mountain goats, and grizzly bear, and there is scenery by the cubic mile. But there is a little less color; we have seen the last of the undulating brown and yellow muskeg characteristic of the gentler terrain in the Living Zone. And the robust blue of deep salt water has given way to the startling azure or turquoise of glacial colloids in suspension. Though we sense that commodity values in this zone are much lower, still it is extremely attractive; the lakes are pure, there is yet a great deal of vegetation, wildlife, and natural beauty. It is altogether an amenable landscape.

We fly on, northeast, until the coast is far behind. The characteristics of the Transition Zone gradually become harsher and far less hospitable. We enter now what I can only call a Zone of Nameless Immensity. From horizon to horizon the region is devoid of life, it is devoid of color, and it is nearly devoid of motion. There are only grays and blacks and whites here; each valley contains a bleak and dirty glacier, the rubble.of the lateral and terminal moraines, and a silky-soupy-mucky stream of meltwater and silt. There is not a trace of green or a hint of animal life. This is raw country and savage, and I am consciously pleased that the Grumman Goose is a stout twin-engine aircraft. We fly on for perhaps another half hour, past naked, jagged peaks and tortuous icefalls, one stark nameless canyon after another, and there is no color, no life. Finally the obvious, stupendous, and utterly simple reality occurs to me: it has been nearly an hour since we last saw a shred of combustible vegetation. There is simply no fuel in sight to support a wildfire. That means the fire has to be in Canada. We bank and fly to Ketchikan, out of the Nameless Immensity, over the sparkling Transition Zone, back into the Living Zone once more. It is good to be home.

Professor Kenneth P. Davis at Yale recently sent me a new edition of Benton MacKaye's book, *The New Exploration, a Philosophy of Regional Planning*. I began to share Professor Davis's enthusiasm for the book when I read such good stuff as this:

> Man, when boiled down to lowest terms, seems to consist of three things: his soul, his body, and his shirt. I speak not in jest: the shirt is a symbol and a sample of the artificially

supplied, though inevitable needs of physical man. A civilization consists of the respective equivalents: the thoughts of men; the bodies of men; the material equipment or effects of men.

It seems to me that Alaska uniquely can present us with physiographic analogues to MacKaye's three concepts of body, soul, and shirt.

The Living Zone corresponds obviously to the shirt—the "material equipment or effects of men." This is where resource development ought to be concentrated—and happily it is.

And in the same way that a mathematical function defines a curve, access in this zone will define resources; perhaps indeed the resources of the Living Zone are a function of access, and development planning might well progress accordingly.

The Transition Zone, the amenable environment of scenic and recreational resources, can do some fine and noble things for man's body—his physiology. It is here that designated wilderness areas ought to be staked out and managed in a more or less conventional manner. There are some special problems of getting there and back, and some real needs for developed shelter, but by and large the wilderness areas in Alaska will not be different in kind from those in the lower 48. I agree with Dean John Zivnuska, who said in the September, 1968, *American Forests*, that capital-intensive management should be applied to these areas to maintain safe and high-quality recreation experiences.

Both the "shirt zone" and the "body zone" are recognized, with other labels, in the planning of state and federal agencies in Alaska, and I think those efforts are generally good. I might add, however, a hearty endorsement to Michael McCloskey's plea (in the *Denver Law Journal*, 1968) for a landscape policy to be built into the planning effort. The Ketchikan city dump—a not-so-sanitary landfill—used to be, at least, almost adjacent to the ferry terminal, and I personally helped design some logging operations that strike me now as unconscionably crude. We need to manage, in other words, the body zone and the shirt zone with sense, discretion, and good taste.

Now then, what shall we do with the Nameless Immensity and what can it do for the soul, the "thoughts of men" that MacKaye speaks about?

The conference program contains a quote from Thoreau that neatly implies an answer:

> We need the tonic of wildness . . . At the same time that we are earnest to explore and learn all things, we require that all things be mysterious and unexplorable, that land and sea be infinitely wild, unsurveyed and unfathomed . . .

Could it be that the soul of each of us, and collectively the thoughts of men, need a limitlessness to ponder, to think about, to imagine? I don't really know, of course, but I do know this: if we need a land-to-imagine, only in Alaska can we give it a physical embodiment. There are no other Nameless Immensities in the United States, and if there are others in the world they are politically inaccessible. Only in Alaska does our culture have a realistic opportunity to make a quantum jump in land use policy, to proceed from conventional, managed, prepared wilderness areas to establish in fact what Robert Service called The Land of Beyond:

> Thank God! there is always a Land of Beyond
>   For us who are true to the trail;
> A vision to seek, a beckoning peak,
>   A fairness that never will fail;
> A pride in our soul that mocks at a goal,
>   A manhood that irks at a bond,
> And try how we will, unattainable still,
>   Behold it, our Land of Beyond!

Now that is about as mushy and sentimental as a forestry professor dares to get, and the time has come to make my defense of emotionalism.

There is no immortal imperative that I know of to intellectualize all human and social affairs. On the contrary, I think there is no way to establish goals or objectives other than simply wanting to do something. Once we establish a goal, then we can invoke an unemotional, no-nonsense scheme of decision-making, choosing the best alternative to achieve it. Means, in other words, can be selected rationally, but ends must be asserted. They are nonrational. They are preeminently emotional.

So let us talk about a goal of a designated, delineated Land of Beyond. It will be absolutely undeveloped. There will be no trails, no bridges, no access roads to the edge of it, no facilities, no management, and perhaps, virtually no physical use. The boundary will not enclose anything; it will be an exclosure, with the body zone and the shirt zone on the outside. This is land for the soul and the thoughts of men and its benefits are primarily psychic.

Does all this sound really screwball? I do not want to foreclose the possibility that it just might be, and yet I know it can be done if the determination is there. The Nameless Immensity is a physiographic fact. The Statehood Act of 1958 and Article VIII of the Alaska Constitution are legal facts, providing for state selection and classification of 104 million acres of federal lands. Designating a Land of Beyond, therefore, is simply a matter of political will.

The opportunity costs of making the selection are probably negative, for as Cooley says in his previously cited book, fewer than 40 million acres of the total land grant of 104 million acres are economically worthy of selection. If there were some gain in designating a Land of Beyond, and zero impact on economic land selection, the net opportunity cost of making the selection would be negative. The opportunity costs of the land itself would be, almost by definition, zero.

But this comes perilously close to justifying intellectually a Land of Beyond, and that is not my intention at all. Instead, let me conclude with a question: what do we want to do? There are shirt zones all over the country, and some fine body zones, too—but only in Alaska can we find land that is "infinitely wild, unsurveyed and unfathomed . . ."

*Session Chairman Richard A. Cooley:* We will start this part of the discussion with questions from the audience for Howard Johnson. Is there any commercial timber in the Prince William Sound study area? Also, what other areas are actually being studied for wilderness status?

*W. Howard Johnson:* The figures indicate that we have 26,000 acres of typical coastal, mature, spruce and hemlock timber in the Prince William Sound study area. Also there is a total of 615 million board feet involved. I believe this was evident in the 20 slides of the area just shown. With respect to southeast Alaska, there are other areas under consideration, including expansion of the Tracy Arm area south of Juneau, and the Granite Fiords area on Behm Canal east of Ketchikan, plus two additional large study areas. We have approached this broad study from the standpoint of looking at all the 16 million acres that we have on the Tongass National Forest to define what best suits the provisions of the Wilderness Act. We will have these recommendations in shape to present to the chief of the Forest Service and the secretary of agriculture prior to the end of June, 1970. We hope to beat this schedule quite a bit.

I would like to add that if we had a negative attitude toward wilderness I certainly would not be here today.

*Chairman Cooley:* How much area as a percentage of the total land the Forest Service manages in Alaska do you think will be submitted under the Wilderness Act before the 1970 deadline?

*Mr. Johnson:* It is premature to make even a guess. I know we will have several more substantial areas, perhaps similar, maybe more or maybe less in individual acreage than the one that we unveiled this afternoon.

*Chairman Cooley:* Would you comment on the widely accepted notion that the conservation movement in this country would not have evolved but as a reaction to economic development?

*Mr. Johnson:* I guess that I will have to remind the group here that the United States Forest Service actually started what we know today as the wilderness movement in 1924 with the Gila Wilderness designation. And most certainly we, with that early start, should get credit for the millions of acres that are in this category now, something like eight percent of all national forest acreage. Possibly I answered the question in reverse, but the interest in wilderness and primitive area classification dates back a long time. I want to mention also that one of my predecessors, my dear departed friend, B. Frank Heintzleman, former governor and regional forester of Alaska, in 1939 was one of the prime movers in contributing to the Glacier Bay National Monument from national forest status 905,000 acres of land. In this 905,000 acres, incidentally, there are over three billion board feet of coastal type timber.

*Chairman Cooley:* What is the Forest Service's present view on the Chichagof-Yakobi Island proposal for wilderness?

*Mr. Johnson:* I do not know whether it is fortunate or unfortunate, but the entire area proposed for wilderness by a citizens' group is included within the boundaries of the timber sale area contracted to the Alaska Lumber and Pulp Company at Sitka, and we have no unilateral right to change that. We do have a study of the area. This is not the only problem with respect to wilderness classification of West Chichagof-Yakobi. There is a whole shirttail full of conflicts—mining claims, timber-cutting areas, areas that have been cut over, various uses of Forest Service cabins at lakes, and this sort of thing. We are going to talk in detail about this within the next month or two with the Sitka Conservation Society and other interested people at Juneau.*

*Chairman Cooley:* Are any provisions made for the control of pollution by pulp mills in southeast Alaska? How can we be assured that enticement for establishment of these mills does not include ignoring the pollution problem?

---

* The meeting was held May 13, 1969, and was primarily a talk session; no additional formal written presentation was made. The west coast section of this area has been studied intensively for several months by North Tongass National Forest personnel. They are preparing special plans for management with emphasis on recreation use and aesthetic protection.

*Mr. Johnson:* In the first place we have laws that relate to pollution—or the avoidance of pollution, I should say. This is particularly true with respect to the effluent that comes from the milling process. We have both state and federal laws. The companies are required to comply with these laws, and I should mention that prior to the time the Sitka pulp plant was constructed the most comprehensive study of pollution control factors in the history of the industry to that date was made. So far as we know there have not been any serious problems. I will say that U.S. Plywood-Champion is extremely aware of this problem. It just simply has to be prevented and they intend to prevent any possible pollution. Another factor is possible siltation of streams. With 15 to 16 years of experience we feel that we have enough knowledge to adequately protect the streams.

*Chairman Cooley:* We can now turn to a few questions on Bureau of Land Management policy regarding its Alaskan lands. Mr. Silcock, when will the BLM establish a wilderness policy for Alaska? If one exists, what is it generally?

*Burton W. Silcock:* The Classification and Multiple Use Act (Public Law 88-607) provides a classification for wilderness as one of the multiple use management principles. Also in January of this year regulations were issued that provide for designation of primitive areas, and these sorts of things. We are getting into that field at the present time.

*Chairman Cooley:* Has there been much opposition to the BLM's proposals for retention of lands in public ownership?

*Mr. Silcock:* In Alaska we have run into some opposition and I am sure we will run into more. But basically after the opponents have found out what we are talking about and what we are trying to do, the problem has been cleared up. Some of the homesteaders, for example in the Copper River area, were quite concerned over the fact that the area was being closed for public studies. In our proposal, we are leaving open 70,000 acres, which are quite a few homesteads at around 80 acres each. Also we are leaving open additional areas which would allow what we call trade and manufacturing sites, home sites, and headquarter sites—which are five-acre sites—for filing so that they could go into some areas that are already partially settled. The moratorium on settlement will be lifted after December, 1971.

*Chairman Cooley:* I thought we squelched Rampart Dam. What is the status of the project?

*Mr. Silcock:* The present status of Rampart Dam is that the withdrawal order is still on the records. But as far as the position of the Department of Interior is concerned, the project is delayed at this time. But the withdrawal is still there and it is of such a size that I felt it is important to include some 10 million acres on the land status list.

*Chairman Cooley:* It is now Brock Evans's turn on the firing line. Do you feel that conservationists should become revolutionaries?

*Brock Evans:* I have a split feeling whether we should or not. Keep in mind that we are talking about the land, the air, the water, every-thing around. We are talking about the source, in other words, of our material and spiritual substance. We have tried working the legislative process for a long time now to do something about the situation that has been facing us for the last few years. We have made some gains in this way but not many of them are very great. I personally want to continue to try this political process. But so far our experience has been that gains in the legislative process have been compromise gains. They are called necessary compromises—but they are compromises with the land. And every time there is a compromise with the land, in my opinion we lose because it is not a real compromise.

Now we are getting to the point where we are starting to try the courts for relief too. We are getting into this as a next step. The Forest Service told me yesterday in Oregon that they are going to log one of the last, free remaining untouched valleys in Oregon, and I think this should be taken to court. This is what we are faced with in the Northwest and everywhere else. If politicians won't protect the land, perhaps the courts will. Then after that I do not know. I started out this job mad about the North Cascades, and I am getting angrier all the time when I see what is happening to us. Some decisions we cannot accept. If Kennecott Copper Company decides to have an open pit mine in the North Cascades, I cannot accept that and I am not sure what I am going to do. If they finally do decide to log that valley in Oregon, I cannot accept that, either. Lots of things I do not feel I can accept. That is about what my frame of thinking is right now and I am sorry I do not have an idea where that is going to end some day— that is how I feel.

*Chairman Cooley:* Why should the classification of wilderness areas in Alaska national forests be set by multiple use timber cutters—the Forest Service?

*Mr. Evans:* That is not my word now. I realize that the Forest Service has many responsibilities; but we asked that same question in the North Cascades: why should wilderness classification be done by an agency which appeared to us at that time, 12 years ago, to be concerned mostly with timber cutting? We are asking it again in Oregon too. I think our position is we do not care who sets the classification as long as the approach is made with an open mind. I know the Forest Service has other concerns and they have a lot of problems. Everybody talks about balance as far as wilderness goes, but we need a *real* balance. Trees need to be in these areas too. With regard to what Howard Johnson said earlier, that is fine about 26,000 acres in the Prince William Sound study area. But I am waiting to see how many acres of commercial timber remain when the area is proposed for wilderness.* And I am waiting to see what is going to happen to the bays, the coves, and inlets in the southeast where the trees are too. If there is a lot proposed, if there is an adequate amount of timber to preserve the sense of vastness of the wilderness forest—that will be wonderful and I will be the first to say so. But I frankly doubt that the Forest Service will do this. Right now we are waiting to see what classifications are proposed. If they are adequate then the Forest Service will have done a good job and we will approve it. If they are not, somebody else should do it.

*Chairman Cooley:* The last question asks Mr. Evans to comment on the statement that it appears your remarks indicate a collision between the economic laws and the growth economy and the ecological principles of a fertile life-support system.

*Mr. Evans:* I am not sure in the case of southeast Alaska if there were any economic laws operating at all because I do not think the mills would have come unless there were substantial inducements offered to them in the form of lower timber prices. So my remarks do in a sense indicate a conflict; it is the same conflict we face all over the world, all over the country. We are indeed destroying our life-support systems in the southeast—the fishing streams, the watershed, the estuaries, the wildlife—for what is still called "growth." I say this is growth in the same sense that cancer is growth. I think I would go back to what Dave Brower said, let's develop that 90 percent or so of the world we developed already and leave the 10 percent untouched right now. I think we can do this and have a decent world to live in.

* I learned from a trip in that area the summer of 1969 that almost all of the good commercial timber is in the de facto wilderness to the north of and outside of the study area. The Forest Service is *not* studying this timber.

*Part Three*

# BANQUET

# THE MOST GLARING GAP IN EDUCATION

*Elvis J. Stahr*
President, National Audubon Society

As one of the newest though scarcely one of the youngest recruits to the conservation movement, I want to say that I am proud to participate in the program of this great conference. I am proud that John James Audubon was not only an artist of genius but probably the first American to decry the rape of the forests, as was mentioned this morning by Dr. Nash. And I am proud that my own first conservation fight was a successful one to help save a matchless piece of wilderness in my native State of Kentucky. I am proud too that the National Audubon Society has been in the vanguard of the fight to save one of the greatest remaining wildernesses, the Everglades. I noticed in the morning paper that another rather new recruit to the movement, Secretary of the Interior Walter J. Hickel, visited there yesterday in behalf of the beleaguered alligator. However, may I say that we won't really save the alligator until you and I, and our fellow citizens, stop buying things made out of his hide.

I have been a lawyer, a professor, a government official, and a university administrator, and I enjoyed them all—most of the time. But in all sincerity I believe I am now in the most thoroughly fascinating and crucially important work in which any man could be engaged— conservation. The objective as I see it is very simply to bring man's very considerable but unpredictable intelligence to bear on preserving and producing on planet Earth an environment habitable for man and his fellow creatures; to bring man into control over his ever-expanding appetites and technical abilities that are combining to pollute, deface, degrade, and destroy the quality of life for himself, his fellow creatures, and his posterity.

Having been an educator as well as a concerned citizen, I am convinced that there is a big job that must be done, almost on a crash basis, a job that involves both education and conservation. And it is a job, with very few. exceptions, that America's educational system today is simply failing to recognize. I shall therefore talk tonight not about wildernesses I have known, like the jungles of Southeast Asia, the deserts of north Africa, the mountain fastnesses of the China-Tibet border, not about Alaska, though I have seen it from Point Barrow to Kodiak, from Shemya to Juneau and loved it, and not even about wilderness as such. Rather I shall explore the reason that we have so much trouble preserving any wilderness—whether it is in Kentucky or Florida or Alaska or wherever—or solving the many other environmental problems. The reason is that there is a major gap in the education our people have been and are being given.

That gap, that failure if you will, is perhaps mostly the result of specialization, which has virtually taken us over. One evidence is that chemists, sociologists, lawyers, and even biologists, doctors, engineers, and teachers—like all of the rest of us—do not know and are not learning or trying to learn enough about where even their own specialized discipline or profession fits into the intricate patterns of nature and man's relations to the natural world. We study the environmental sciences piecemeal; we break nature into little pieces: geology, botany, zoology, ornithology, bacteriology, ichthyology, climatology, astronomy, physics, chemistry, biophysics, biochemistry, genetics, soil dynamics, and so on. We fail to realize how delicately the pieces fit together; we lose sight of the big picture. We solve very challenging yet very narrowly defined problems triumphantly, while in the very process exacerbating broader, deeper, and more important problems.

There is nothing new in deploring fragmentation, or specialization. For years among doctors there has been concern that many of our vaunted gains in the science of medicine, achieved through very highly developed specialization, may have been offset by the loss of the old-fashioned family doctor who practiced the art of healing, who tried to look at the whole man, not just at one part or another of a complicated collection of separate organs and chemical reactions. In this light the recent move by the medical profession to recognize the family doctor as being fully respectable by calling him a specialist, is a step in the right direction.

The engineers have a useful term—systems engineering. By this they mean that at Cape Kennedy, say, it is not just whether a thousand and one subcomponents will test out separately; what really counts is whether they will all work together and put the space capsule into orbit and bring it back safely. In education, topics of research have a way of splitting apart on us as fast as we try to weave them together. Let me not be misunderstood: specialization in education and in vocations up to a point has been and can be very useful. The tragedy is that almost everybody is studying and teaching pieces and stopping there; hardly anyone is teaching and very few are even studying how the pieces relate to one another, and fewer still relate them to man and his total environment. This piecemeal approach is a tragic example of what I call the education gap in conservation; it has frighteningly important implications to the future of man on earth. It is ironic that during the decades when millions have been agonizing about the potential sudden destruction of man's earthly environment through atomic warfare, those same millions have been gradually but actually destroying and degrading that environment themselves.

If anyone thinks I am going overboard in saying that the future of human life on earth depends on conservation, it is probably because he and I define conservation differently. In the National Audubon Society we think conservation is concerned with wise use of all natural resources, not just the rationing of our timber and oil and such, not just the protection of wildlife and wilderness. Our definition encompasses concern for: the air we breathe, the water we drink, and the sheer space on this planet for homes, industry, recreation, agriculture, transportation, and wilderness; the problems created by man's continuing population growth; the threat to the quality of life, which is so dependent on the quality of environment; and underlying all, the incredibly complex yet systematic web of natural life forces and cycles that we can call the balance of nature. It has always been and remains the only source of life we know of in the universe. The National Audubon Society began 65 years ago for the purpose of protecting endangered species of wildlife. Its members have now recognized that the stakes are even higher; if man pollutes and upsets nature, man is an endangered species too.

The conservation education gap affects every element of society. To overcome it we must educate our citizens to recognize that their own and their children's long-term best interests lie in a habitable environment, and they must fight for it. At the top we need leadership educated beyond a narrow specialty to the broad concept of conservation as I have defined it.

What is the present attitude of the ordinary citizen? Recently there was a TV documentary on urban sprawl, a man-in-the-street interview sequence in which several residents of an area were asked about plans to tear down a block of small buildings and erect a giant office skyscraper. To a man they regretted to see this coming: "It will bring too much traffic . . . we need more parks, not more buildings . . . they are putting it in the wrong part of town," and so on. But—and this is my point—not only had not one of them raised a word of protest, they somehow did not think the building was a mistake. They had a vague idea that putting up any big building is progress, that it is wrong to buck progress, and therefore they should resign themselves to it.

Shouldn't even the high school graduate of today, through the sum total of his social studies and general sciences, have learned that unplanned urban crowding is not progress, but rather is one of the nation's major headaches? That true progress involves not just better offices and bigger factories but better houses, less crowding, faster transportation, cleaner air, purer water, and more green space? Probably the most neglected, yet most fundamentally important field of study of all is urban ecology. The one environment that man has influenced the most is the one that is the worst.

For a different kind of example of citizen reaction I would like to point, with a good deal of pride, to the way our Santa Barbara Audubon Society reacted to the oil spill in January, 1968. If it had not been for the quick thinking and fast action of that group, along with the Sierra Club, certain types of detergents would have been used far more widely in the effort at oil cleanup, and damage to wildlife and ecology would have been even more extensive and lasting. The last I heard, Mrs. E. A. Parkinson, president of Santa Barbara Audubon, was talking to our good friends in the Environmental Defense Fund (EDF) about the possibility of a law suit* that would help throw the fear of God into future offshore oil drillers, and meanwhile a flood of mail from California and all over is pouring into the Congress where three separate congressional investigations into the spill have been launched.

Speaking of EDF, the Environmental Defense Fund was mentioned this morning by Dr. Talbot as the group that is carrying to the forums of the law the fight against persistent pesticides in Wisconsin. It is building there a scientific record that will be vital to the fight on other fronts. EDF has received much of its financial support from the Rachel Carson Fund of the National Audubon Society, which was started by a lady at this head table, Mrs. Nathaniel Owings.

The enormities of oil on our beaches, smog over our cities, poison in our oceans, and filth in our rivers are examples of technology-gone-wrong that almost anyone can see. I think everyone is beginning to understand how much is really lost when a stream or the air is polluted; but the public hasn't yet learned how to protect itself from

* After study this idea was found to be unpromising and dropped.—*Editor.*

the polluters. It will learn, one assumes, but will it be in time to do the most good—or even enough good? How long do we wait—how close do we approach the point of no return? Do we even know where that point is? How much more carbon dioxide in the air blanket could be absorbed without melting the polar ice caps, for example? Do we want to find out the hard way?

I am equally concerned about the more subtle effects and interactions of modern man's way of life upon our environment. For example, in the December 29, 1967, issue of C. F. Letter, the Conservation Foundation published a paper on noise pollution, which revealed how the psychology of noise allows a man to watch a pile driver at a construction site and not mind the pounding, but just let the bathroom faucet drip at night when he can't sleep! There are hidden costs when workers perform poorly because of fatigue from high noise levels, or when accidents occur because the warning shout was not heard above the din. In addition, there is evidence that excess noise causes physical damage to the ear as well as stress-induced damage to the mind.

A moment ago I deplored the limitations of specialized training of doctors. I would like to go a step further in discussing the need for doctors to treat the whole man by asserting that physicians should be equally concerned about the toll in public health being taken by many aspects of our civilization today, including noise pollution. If the physician's job is to keep the patient (the whole man) healthy, should not the medical profession be joining the conservation movement in questioning whether such noise producers as the supersonic transport, with its trailing sonic boom, can be tolerated?

Another subtle, deleterious effect on man from his own interference in the balance of nature is revealed by recent reports that there may be an actual chemical connection between human irritability and some components of automobile exhaust in our smog-laden urban atmosphere. Again, should not the medical profession, in its concern for human health, be concerned about reducing traffic problems through better mass transit and possibly electric cars as a remedy to the decline in physical, emotional, and mental health?

I cannot help but add one more medical example—the success that has been reported in treating mental patients merely by exposing them to the peace, quiet, and beauty of an unspoiled natural area. Should not doctors be very much concerned about wilderness? What kind of world would it be if no wilderness were left at all? However, I recognize hastily that if everybody descended at once on a wilderness, it would not last long.

But my point is that if things like noise, smog, and natural beauty are in their different ways important to the health of the American people, then our medical schools should be teaching our future doctors and even our present doctors about them. I do not say that nothing is being done in this regard now—my charge is that what is being done is patently inadequate.

I do not, of course, mean to pick just on doctors or medical schools and ignore others. I have merely used them as an illustration of the gap in education. The sad fact is that I could just as well have taken almost any other profession or group. Is the farmer, for example, whose job it is to provide food and in order to do so uses pesticides and fertilizers, giving us more food from his field only at the cost of destroying other food sources in lakes, rivers, and oceans? May not the persistent pesticides be endangering even more than that? Is the highway engineer merely robbing Peter to pay Paul when he rips up community A to put a highway through for the convenience of community B? And of course you know what's going to happen to B when B gets so crowded people start moving out to C.

My larger point then is that if our fragmented approach to the natural environment is a major problem of our times, then it must follow as a matter of course that a curriculum to meet this need should be a major effort of our entire educational system. The sad truth is that, with a few happy exceptions, environmental training today tends to be only an occasional class or course tacked on as an afterthought, if at all, and is not an integral part of the student's experience. And that is because it is not an integral part of the professor's experience.

I am much too fresh from the academic community to want to let all the blame lie there. To an important extent schools and colleges must and do reflect the feelings, the needs, and even the shortcomings of the rest of society.

In two vital areas of government, we also find far too much fragmentation, specialization, and lack of coordination. At the federal level the need for cohesion in our environmental policies simply must make itself felt in Washington, where a staggering number of government agencies is making important environmental decisions with little administrative machinery for full exchange of information, let alone thorough coordination of policy. But it does not stop there. Decisions and actions having immense impact on the environment are taken almost daily, mostly without serious or competent efforts at planning, by a staggering conglomeration of state agencies and by countless local authorities, who have all too little understanding of ecology. In addition, private developers and chambers of commerce across the land are almost frenetically active in altering the natural environment for short-term objectives, very frequently heedless of long-range impact.

To top it all, there is much too little recognition that "nature" and "nation" are very different words, that this planet, this biosphere, is really a single, unpartitionable ecosystem, that air, water, wildlife, and increasingly even soil and people are not divided into tightly closed and separately manageable compartments marked by invisible national boundaries. Thus an international approach to many conservation problems is ultimately going to have to be taken. How much more damage to the balance of nature can man tolerate before he sets about a global effort in earnest?

Let me conclude by returning home. In addition to government, and to the formal education system, there is another major group concerned with conservation: ourselves, the conservation organizations. We are not free of shortcomings either. We, too, are plagued by problems of fragmentation and lack of coordination, both within our own organizations and in our joint efforts toward conservation goals.

I can assure you that we of the National Audubon Society are a long way from any self-delusions of perfection. We are in the midst of a major reorganization, establishing regional offices, trying to strengthen weak areas—that is to say, build more and stronger local chapters in geographical areas where we are not as effective as we would like to be, or ought to be. We are trying to weld ourselves into a nationwide grass roots organization with communications and coordination up and down the line and sideways, effective at the local, state, and national levels.

We think that is what we have to be to do our job, and it is a pretty overwhelming order. We are tackling it. But you do not have to worry about our feeling smug, and I doubt we have to worry about complacency in any other conservation organization.

But if just organizing and administering our own activities is becoming a bigger and bigger job for each separate group, then certainly to bring effective strength and unity to the conservation movement is going to be a continuing task that none of us can afford to neglect.

It even becomes more difficult in terms of basic ecological decisions, as the matters we deal with become more technical and complex. There was a day when the basic needs were relatively clear; there was no question about the need to halt wanton lumbering, or uncontrolled slaughter of wildlife; no question about the need to set aside some areas of great natural beauty as national parks. They had plenty of other problems in those days, of course, but on major issues there wasn't much doubt about what had to be done. In some cases that is still true, but often today it is not so clear, even to us, what the right decision is. Substitute the atomic power plant for the coal-burning one and we cut air pollution but we step not only into problems of possible thermal pollution but into the unknowns of disposal of radio-active waste. Turn to electric cars to beat the exhaust-smog problem, but what about all the added power plants that would be needed to charge the batteries of the electric cars? We will have no choice on cooperation; we will have to put all our talents together to come up with wise answers. I believe the answers can be found, for a species that can fly to the moon and back should be able to tend wisely its own native habitat and control its own technology.

Another problem of the conservation movement today is sheer numbers of organizations. The more problems that come up, the more organizations we seem to create to try to solve them. Certainly diversity can be — and has been — a source of strength to us. Some persons are simply more willing to give their time and their money to help wildlife, others to protect places of natural beauty, others to fight for clean air, and so on. All are useful. But sheer weight of numbers of separate groups can be stultifying, too. We have to be on guard against endless committees going nowhere, and against the other extreme, which is the temptation, after looking at how many organizations there are in the *Conservation Directory* that one ought to coordinate with, to decide to forget it—even unnecessary duplication could not be as bad as all that talk.

Difficult job though it is, we must all work together. We have to be effective and we have to move faster. After all, we have voluntarily taken on the job of providing leadership in conservation for our nation. As leaders we must be increasingly not only evangelical but ecumenical; we must stand together to encourage, to teach, to needle, to advise, sometimes to alarm, and always, as best we can, to point the way. If I may be a "voice in the wilderness," we must enlist more people in our cause: more from the city (for that is where the people are), more from minorities, more young people. Those who have the most to gain from true conservation are the very ones so far who seem to know the least about our message. Education is one of the most important means of pointing the way.

The way is clear. From kindergarten through graduate study, our schools, colleges, and universities must make the environmental message an integral part of education. We must feed environmental science into every course we can, all along the line. America can no longer afford to turn out engineering graduates who think only in terms of more highways and runways to handle more cars and planes.

We need imaginative engineers who will give us the best transportation and flood control with the least destruction of air, water, open spaces, natural beauty, and recreation potential. We can no longer afford agricultural school graduates who do not appreciate what pesticides and fertilizers are doing to the world beyond the farmer's fence; we can no longer afford humanists, social scientists, and civic leaders who do not realize how much the quality of people's lives depends on the quality of their environment. We must also mount a mighty effort in the field of adult education—through radio and television, the press, word of mouth, our churches, and civic groups. And we must keep at it.

Each man, after all, lives in three dimensions: with himself, his fellowman, and nature. It is ironic that he used to know a great deal about nature when he lived closer to it, and relatively little of himself and his fellowman. Today he studies himself, his fellowman, and their interrelationships through such disciplines as psychology, sociology, economics, and government and so on, while, as I said, he merely breaks the study of nature into little pieces, which he does not put back together, and does not see what they mean to him.

This must be set right. Many kinds of people—leaders in industry and government, experts in specialized fields, alert citizens—must work together to bring our lives into balance with our environment. We need to keep the big picture in focus, to remember that highways, dams, factories, pesticides, and all the rest are but means to an end. That end is very clear: it is simply to provide the best life we can, materially and spiritually, for the people of this planet. Or, as we like to put it, "a decent world to live in."

If we can plug the gaps not only in our governmental structure and in our own efforts in the conservation movement but also in our educational system, our children may yet have a chance to live in a decent world.

# THE EMPTY HORN OF PLENTY

*Richard L. Ottinger*
United States Congressman from New York

As a Sierra Club member and as a federal legislator, I have been privileged to have played a role in some of the epic conservation battles of this decade, and looking back now, I think we can view many of our accomplishments with real pride.

Largely as a result of Sierra Club leadership, a major effort to desecrate the Grand Canyon has been decisively repelled. We have seen the formation of a Redwood National Park to preserve these unique and awe-inspiring trees. In cooperation with other conservation groups we have fought the battles of the Land and Water Conservation Fund and wilderness preservation. We have seen the first steps toward establishing a meaningful wild rivers system. Perhaps the most important advance was the law that was made in the Storm King Mountain case. The ruling of the Second Circuit Court supporting the Scenic Hudson Preservation Conference's right to intervene in the case before the Federal Power Commission established that the concerned public has a defensible interest in the disposition of a natural resource. It was also established that the government agencies have an affirmative responsibility to protect that interest.

As a result of all of these efforts the Sierra Club has become a national force and one that is highly respected on Capitol Hill. Perhaps more important, because of the prestige this club has earned, conservation issues themselves have gotten the wider public attention they so desperately deserve.

Now I think I should make one thing clear. I am aware that by describing the recent successes in the conservation effort in terms

128

of "battles"—and more specifically, by the particular battles I have mentioned—I am stepping right into the midst of a controversy which is very much alive: is battling the proper function of a conservation group? Frankly, I am taking this step intentionally.

To use a phrase that you won't hear very much in conservation circles these days—I didn't come here to pour oil on troubled waters. We haven't got the time to temporize; the issues are too alive, the stakes too high.

Take the now-celebrated case of the Grand Canyon dams. I suppose reasonable men can differ over the advisability of damming and flooding this magnificent gorge. I must say that I am biased, but I am willing to admit the possibility that there may be an argument on the other side; but if you opposed this project—if you genuinely felt that it was important to protect this irreplaceable national asset which had been left in our stewardship—then you have no alternative but to wage an aggressive, hard-hitting campaign.

Even with the campaign that the Sierra Club conducted—and it was perhaps the most effective public campaign in my experience— even with this campaign, it was a very near thing. Powerful forces with substantial economic interests were allied behind the proposal. In fact, at the opening of the Ninetieth Congress it would not be too much to say that the odds were 100 to one against the opponents of the Grand Canyon dams.

The thing to remember is that this type of conservation battle is important because what you are fighting over has value and is important. If it didn't there wouldn't be any fight.

If the Grand Canyon has immeasurable cultural and aesthetic value for Americans, it also has a tremendous economic potential. The pursuit of this economic potential has attracted and will continue to attract a very powerful and a very effective constituency for development and exploitation. Unless some group is willing and able to mobilize a public constituency for conservation—for the preservation and enhancement of the environment—we are going to lose.

The redwoods offer another excellent example. I don't know how you would have come out if you had relied exclusively on efforts with your governor and the lumber companies that were involved. Your governor must be blessed with extraordinary perspicacity since he can comprehend all redwoods merely by seeing one. So perhaps you would have done better. But speaking as a legislator, I can tell you how things stood in Congress. You would never have had a Redwood National Park—a park approved by Congress—at all if it had not been for the aggressive, hard-hitting Sierra Club campaign that backed up the efforts of the distinguished California congressman, Jeffery Cohelan, and all the rest of us who were concerned with the conservation of these magnificent trees.

The oil crisis off Santa Barbara offers an interesting contrast. It is a case in which the people who were concerned and who could have made a difference bowed to pressure, accepted compromise and did not fight.

You should understand that it was not only the citizens of Santa Barbara who objected to the oil drilling in the channel. Two of the top officials of the Interior Department wrote comprehensive memoranda opposing the granting of the oil drilling leases.

I see no point in identifying who these men were. They were, and are, excellent public servants, both of whom have fought the good fight in other areas. But here they stood alone. The conservation community that should have been concerned did not rally to their support. Their memoranda were rejected by the office of the secretary of the interior. They were ordered withdrawn and rewritten. And the result? The disastrous drilling at Santa Barbara went ahead without hindrance.

This same unequal contest has plagued our efforts to deal with such crises as water pollution and air pollution.

We tried in the Air Quality Act and the Clean Waters Restoration Act to come to grips with these problems that threaten to strangle our civilization in the waste that results from our own affluence.

But we must face the fact that we have been largely unsuccessful.

We failed because the public—the people—have not been galvanized into the effective constituency that is needed to repel the exploiters. We have compromised and temporized and because of that we have fallen far short of our goal.

Not long ago I was discussing the problem of cleaning up the Hudson River with an engineer who specializes in pollution abatement. One by one we went over the sources of pollution. We estimated the cost that was involved in correcting each problem. We finally came up with the total of nearly $12.5 billion, more than the total authorization for all pollution abatement in the United States for the next 10 years. As we went along adding up the figures we also discussed the political realities of compelling the industries and the municipalities to take the steps that were necessary. Finally my engineering friend sat back and said, "You know, from both an engineering and a political point of view it would be cheaper and simpler to move the river." Of course, that is a little extreme but in some ways it is realistic. Unless an outraged public meets and overcomes the objection from the economic interests, we may very well be faced with a situation in which it would be simpler to move the river. I hope the Santa Barbara problem on the Pacific coast never reaches that proportion.

In the five years that I have been in Congress I have seen the conservation effort—the individuals concerned with the preservation and enhancement of our environment—grow from a rather small voice calling in the wilderness into an increasingly effective force for dealing with the most crucial problems facing our civilization. The Sierra Club and the battles that it has waged have played an important role in this and I am heartened to see that our club has now broadened its area of concern to touch more closely on those environmental issues involved in our increasingly urbanized society.

It may seem strange that an organization dedicated to preservation of wilderness areas should be compelled to get involved in these urban problems. It shouldn't. In the first place, the environmental pollution generated by urbanization has a very direct effect upon the natural resources that have been the traditional objects of conservation concern. I doubt if there is any park, refuge or wildlife preserve that has not felt the impact in some way.

It may come in a direct way from the growing volume of water pollution and air pollution. It may come from the effects of highways, power lines, industrial encroachment, or just plain "people pollution." However slight the effect at the moment, the trend is evident and the message clear. At the most elementary level we simply do not have the buffer between the city and wilderness that made it possible for us to concentrate our attention only on wilderness in the past. This is justification enough for turning our attention to the wise conservation of urban resources and the institution of effective measures to protect our environment.

In the long run, however, there is an even stronger justification for turning our attention to the wise conservation of urban resources: very simply stated, it is survival.

We have to face the fact now that we live in a finite environment. Perhaps there was a time when we had so much elbowroom that we could ignore the limits of our resources. But now, our growing population and the tremendous technological development that is necessary to support it, are demanding so much of our environment that the end is, if not in sight, at least in mind. Not only is our environmental system finite, but it is also complex and its factors are closely interrelated. Everything we do can have a significant and unexpected impact on crucial environmental factors—often an adverse impact.

We hear a lot these days about the dangers of the "finger on the nuclear trigger" and its potential for the cataclysmic destruction of life on this planet. It is a very real danger and one that deserves a lot of attention. But I would point out that a nuclear catastrophe requires a positive, deliberate action—a decision to destroy. Today, man has his finger on an "environmental trigger" which is, in the long run, no less real, no less dangerous to our survival than the nuclear trigger. And the environmental trigger can be pulled by accident, by indifference, or by merely continuing to do the things we have always done in the same careless way. Each resource we squander, each infusion of pollution that we dump into our environment, brings the apocalyptic day of reckoning closer.

Take an everyday urban phenomenon like transportation. One of the keys to making an urban complex work is the development of an efficient transportation system. Why should this be a conservation concern? Because our traditional approach to transportation, the highway, is rapidly assuming major proportions as an environmental threat. In fact, at the rate we are going, there will soon be justification for making the cloverleaf our national flower.

We are caught in a vicious cycle. The more highways we build, the more we rely on cars, trucks and buses. The more we rely on cars, trucks and buses, the more highways we need to keep pace with our growing population. In many areas, the citizenry already finds itself locked in mortal combat with this highway monster that would disrupt and even destroy scenery, air, water, home, and settled communities. In our cities the public health is seriously threatened by pollution from the internal combustion engine which accounts for two-thirds of the poison we dump in our air. Even the most optimistic view of the effectiveness of abatement devices indicates that we would barely manage to maintain this unhealthy status quo if we stopped growing right now. The highway syndrome is a direct and serious threat to the air needed to support life, but the dangers don't stop there. Highways, for example, have a real, if unheralded, impact on water resources, not just in runoff pollution but through actual curtailment of supply. An important source of fresh water is the aquifer, the underground supply that is replenished largely by rain seeping into the ground. However, a growing amount of rain never gets there. It falls on highways, pavements, or other runoff areas, is collected in sewers and carried directly into streams and rivers to be lost forever in the oceans. Major United States highways alone are estimated to cost us well over 335 billion gallons of water per year and the highways that are to be built by the year 2000 will cost another 1.5 trillion gallons per year.

Viewed in light of the Water Resources Council's predictions of water shortages in its report to the president, this highway issue takes on new long-range significance. The council warned that by the year 2010 the demand for fresh water will match the total available national supply. We will then be able to expand our resources only by desalinization, by a massive conservation effort, and by recycling and reuse.

The alternative to this highway madness is the development of clean, fast, efficient mass transit. Yet today under pressure from the highway lobby we allocate $2.5 billion to urban highways and only seven percent as much, $175 million, to mass transit.

The lengths to which the modern highwaymen will go just to keep building are amazing and sometimes ridiculous. In some cities we are building highways over highways, and in my own Westchester County the state highwaymen, having run out of space on land, now propose to pave a substantial stretch of the Hudson River. Perhaps the ultimate absurdity was reported in a news item in the *New York Times* three months ago which reads:

> Trenton—December 13. New Jersey's Department of Transportation is constructing an inter-state highway link that could wind up under water if the state's Department of Conservation and Economic Development goes ahead with its present plans to build a dam on the Passaic River.
>
>         \*     \*     \*
>
> A spokesman for the Transportation Department said its engineers had completed the designs for highway two years ago. Conservation officials countered that plans for the development of the Passaic Valley (dam) had been under consideration for 35 years.
>
>         \*     \*     \*
>
> (The) Commissioner of Transportation said that he was not completely familiar with the plans for the reservoir but "it seems there will be a substantial impact on present and planned highway construction especially on Routes 78, 80 and 280."
>
> (The) Conservation Commissioner . . . could not be reached for comment.

Isn't it grand? For the first time, it's the dam builders versus the highwaymen, and the mind boggles at the consequences. Fish ladders for the commuters? Spillways for the evening rush hour? In the words of the late Henry Ford, "Let's you and him go fight."

Make no mistake about it. The highwaymen are no more than a modern version of the ruthless exploiters who would have already ravaged our forests and stripped our land in the name of economic progress if they had not been resisted by earlier conservationists.

Today we fight the same battle, this time in a complex new urban environment and for even higher stakes.

Of course, highways are not the only, nor even the worst, threat to our urban environment. Power plants, transmission lines, ill-considered land use planning, industrial development and hundreds of other actions all pose challenges to the quality of environment that are at least equally serious.

But highways are illuminating in that they do provide a good example of the way thoughtless development that seems merely irritating can eventually result in quite important environmental conflicts.

Even the very actions we take to protect our environment can themselves be perverted to environmental threats in the new highly complex urban experience.

Take waste treatment, for example. The main thrust of our waste treatment effort has been to reduce raw sewage to a level of purity such that it could be accommodated by the natural cleansing actions of our waterways. The rub is that the process produces water that is rich in nutrients but deficient in the oxygen that is essential to keeping our waterways alive. The cumulative effect of this effluent—treated as best we know how—could well be to kill our rivers and eventually to turn them into noxious breeding grounds for algae. In some areas the fumes from decaying algae have been so corrosive as to take the paint off houses and cars.

The simple fact of the matter is that the demands of urban life are so great that we are continually embarking on small projects which taken by themselves have only minimal effect, but which taken as a whole add up to major environmental assaults.

Through its insatiable appetite for electric power, the urban society will be reaching into the very heart of the wilderness. Over the next 20 years, the most conservative estimates foresee a tripling of our demand for power. To meet that demand the planners predict the construction of 250 giant nuclear power plants along our waterways, each in the 2,000- to 3,000-megawatt range. Eventually 20 percent of the fresh water in the nation—one gallon out of every five—will be used in the generation of steam to run these plants.

The potential effect of this kind of development upon the environment is staggering. There is a company having the slogan "Progress is our most important product." At the rate we are going, it may be our only product by the end of this century unless we, in the meantime, perfect an effective angry advocacy for the environment.

It's interesting how each example of the issues presented by this new urban conservation reveals significant parallels with the experience of traditional conservation. The key to the success of the earlier effort was convincing the general public that our resources were not limitless and that only through the wise husbanding of those left in our stewardship could we assure abundance for the future. Step by painful step, a legal structure was enacted to protect timber, land, recreation and scenic assets, wildlife, and the other resources that could be identified as finite and threatened. Considering the American so-called frontier psychology of viewing such resources as pouring forth from a never-ending horn of plenty for the express purpose of exploitation and development by man, this was no mean achievement. Can you imagine trying to persuade a frontiersman of the early nineteenth century to practice selective harvesting of resources or leave some areas "forever wild"?

We are in much the same position today with regard to the developers and the essentials of our urban environment. Obviously we face a tremendous educational effort; but, in my opinion, our most important priority is to create a new legal structure that can provide the new protections that we need. Unfortunately, this is easier said than done.

In the first place, there is a great need for more knowledge and better dissemination of knowledge about the new threats to our urban environment that are being discovered by the scientific community. To achieve this end, I recently joined with 90 congressmen and 97 leading environmental scientists in the formation of an ad hoc committee on the environment. It is my hope that this committee will give the scientific community the opportunity to evaluate each new legislative proposal and to alert lawmakers to possible adverse environmental consequences. The committee will also prove an effective vehicle through which lawmakers can be informed of environmental issues that require legislative action.

Already this program has made significant contributions. As a result of the advice from the scientific community, Senator Edward Kennedy, Congressman John Moss, and I recently introduced legislation proposing a major revision of the Federal Power Act which we believe proposes the first effective and comprehensive environmental protections in the important area of power generation and transmission. One provision of this new legislation sets forth a new concept in government. It creates a National Council on the Environment to act as devil's advocate on behalf of natural resources in Federal Power Commission proceedings. You might call it an ombudsman for the environment. The council would consist of five representatives of the scientific and conservation communities appointed by the president with the advice and consent of the Senate, and would be fully independent of the Federal Power Commission. It would have its own expert staff and independent funding. It would have the authority to suspend power commission actions if it finds they have an adverse effect on the environment. If, in the end, it is overruled by the commission, it would have standing in court to challenge the commission's decision.

As incorporated in the present legislation, this council would only have authority over projects governed by the Federal Power Act. However, I plan also to introduce legislation that would expand its power to include review of the procedures of all federal agencies insofar as they affect the environment. This would not be an advisory body as has been proposed before.[1] It would have effective and enforceable police powers. Such a council could make a substantial contribution to the preservation and enhancement of our environment but it certainly would not provide the final answer.

One of the major problems of governmental structure with respect to protection of the environment today is that none of the agencies having power to affect the environment has any environmental constituency. While legislation may be drafted to give the Federal Power Commission environmental responsibilities, the agency lacks the expertise to fulfill these responsibilities, and more importantly, a constituency to provide the incentive to regard this as one of its major responsibilities. The Federal Power Commission's constituency is the power companies. The Bureau of Public Roads' is the highway builders, the Interstate Commerce Commission's is the railroads, etc., and each of these agencies has the tendency to become the captive of the industry it is supposd to regulate. The Interior Department has perhaps the most varied constituency of all. At times it is the oilmen, at times the timber industry, and at times the power industry. Only very occasionally is it the environment—and then only when there is little dispute or when the agency is compelled to act by public outcry.

To meet this problem, an intervenor is required, the sole concern and constituency of which is the environment. The national council established in the Electric Reliability Act is intended as the first step.

Beyond such an intervenor, however, what is needed, in my opinion, is a broad new statement of national policy establishing the protection of environmental quality as a prime national priority. Environmental protection needs the same kind of mandate as was given to the protection of individual rights over and above the rest of our legal structure in the Bill of Rights.

To achieve this further goal, I have proposed an amendment to the

[1] Since enacted into law in the Environmental Policy Act of 1969.

federal Constitution which has come to be known as the "Conservation Bill of Rights."* Personally, I think it would be more accurately described as the "Environmental Bill of Rights." But by whatever name it is called, I believe that such a broad mandate of national policy is an essential element needed to meet the environmental challenge of the future. The proposal is not complicated. It merely recognizes the established and undeniable national interest in preserving and protecting the essential elements of our environment. It defines this interest as an individual right no less important than our rights of free speech, free assembly, and due process. By declaring this as national policy, we are providing the most effective protection within our power. Each law, each governmental action, would be subject to test against this standard: does it diminish the common interest in a livable environment? Any action which would endanger the individual's interest in such essentials as breathable air, drinkable water or any other natural resource would be against national policy and subject to the same legal challenge as any abridgment of our other constitutional rights.

No legislative or constitutional answer alone will assure us success. No matter how sophisticated our legal structure becomes, it will still work only when it responds to public demand—when the voice of an organized and angry citizenry is heard in the land. Of course, it would be nice if we did not have to fight, if we could simply reason together and arrive at an effective compromise, but history shows we cannot. We have to fight and I believe it is more than worth the candle.

One of our leading biologists has recently reminded us that, of all the forms of life that existed on this earth, 99 percent are now extinct and—to take literary license with the imperatives of evolutionary theory—they were all *trying* to survive.

Man alone of all the species has the capacity to exercise control over his environment. Yet, as Dr. Ernst Mayer, director of the Harvard Museum of Comparative Zoology, recently noted, "Almost everything we do is harmful to the species and works against our survival."

Whether we pull the environmental trigger; whether we follow the well-traveled road to extinction or blaze a new trail to a better world through the enhancement and preservation of our great environmental assets is entirely up to us.

In closing, I quote the words of the late Robert Kennedy that were repeated by his brother Ted at his funeral. While they are directed at perhaps an even broader subject matter than our concerns about the environment, I feel very strongly that they apply equally because they

* See Appendix E for text of the proposed amendment.

direct themselves to the power that we have as individuals to change the life around us if only we will act.

Few will have the greatness to bend history itself, but each of us can work to change a small portion of events. And in the total of all those acts will be the history of this generation. Each time a man stands for an ideal, or acts to improve the lot of others, or strikes out against injustice, he sends forth a tiny ripple of hope. And crossing each other from a million centers of energy and daring, those ripples build a current that can sweep down the mightiest walls of oppression and resistance.

Like it or not, we live in times of danger and uncertainty, but they are also more opened to the creative energy of men than any other time in history. All of us will ultimately be judged, and as the years pass we will surely judge ourselves, on the effort we have contributed to build a new world society and the extent to which our ideals and goals have shaped that event. Our future may lie beyond our vision, but it is not completely beyond our control. It is the shaping impulse of America that neither faith or nature nor the irresistible tides of history, but the work of our own hands matched to reason and principle will determine our destiny. Some men see things as they are and say why. I dream of things that never were and say why not.

# CLOSING REMARKS BY
# MASTER OF CEREMONIES

*Norman B. Livermore, Jr., Secretary of Resources, State of California:* I certainly agree with Congressman Ottinger's comments on transportation, and I was amused by his simile on water shortages. Speaking of water without naming organizations, names, or valleys, I can say this much to all my friends present: In one of the biggest problems currently on my desk, you might be amused to know that flood control benefits of some $36,000 per year are being claimed for a valley that a certain project will place permanently under some 200 feet of water. This is, indeed, hard for a layman to understand.

This project is one that is being proposed for construction in northern Mendocino County. If approved, a beautiful valley would be flooded, a group of Indians forced off their ancestral lands, a town destroyed; and all this promoted largely under the guise of claimed benefits for flood control that seem to me to be highly questionable. This proposition is to permanently flood by inundation a valley of some 14,500 acres of irrigable lands in order to occasionally protect some 20,500 acres of lower valley lands. Not only is this basic reason economically questionable but, as noted above, there are even benefits claimed for flood protection of a valley that would be obliterated!

It seems to me that we have reached a point, in projects of this type, where the protection of environmental, cultural, historical, and social values, even though these values cannot be accurately measured (or measured at all) in dollars and cents, should be weighted equally with material values.

Turning to another subject, I feel obliged to set the record straight as to the congressman's reference to California's governor and the Redwood National Park. While I do not for one moment intend to minimize the aggressive and successful efforts of the Sierra Club and the yeoman efforts of many congressmen in this important cause, there is an inference that the governor and his administration were not important partners in this outstanding conservation accomplishment. A check with President Edgar Wayburn and with Congressman Wayne Aspinall, who chaired the committee which passed out the park bill, would reveal that Governor Reagan's administration had a great deal to do with the successful passage of the redwood park legislation.

Although I have not yet made up my mind on this project, I can assure you that I will weigh carefully these nonmaterialistic values before recommending a state position on a project of this magnitude.*

* Secretary Livermore refers to the high Dos Rios dam project for the Middle Fork of the Eel River, a proposal by the Army Corps of Engineers that included drowning Round Valley. In May, 1969, Governor Ronald Reagan announced that he would not approve this project, and instructed Secretary Livermore to submit a detailed report of alternative plans that would not flood Round Valley.—Editor.

## Part Four

# ALASKA'S
# WILDERNESS
# WILDLIFE

"When we were . . . very near the ice,
a large white bear passed us in the water;
but made for the ice at a great rate. In half
an hour, we saw multitudes of them upon the
ice, making to the eastward, when we observed
the sea-cows, as the bears approached them,
flying like sheep pursued by dogs."
                    John Ledyard, 1778

"Not a breath of air fanned the glassy surface
of the sea, which was only broken by the wake
of the steamer and the circling ripples from
the breasts of thousands of waterfowl. About
the ship whirred and circled auks, gulls, and
fulmars, as we moved through the pass of Akutan
to Unalaska Harbor."
                    Edward W. Nelson, 1877-81

# ALASKA IN TRANSITION: WILDERNESS AND DEVELOPMENT

*George W. Rogers*
Professor of Economics, University of Alaska

The form and content of this talk emerged almost unbidden from three sets of "givens" in the problem presented by its composition. The originally assigned title was an act of desperation on the part of the conference chairman, caught between publicity deadlines and an elusive, fast traveling speaker. Second, the talk was to be addressed to a conference with the theme "Wilderness, the Edge of Knowledge" which should be taken into account. Finally, I am an economist laboring, not at the center of our known universe of development theory and practice, but at its frontier or the edge of its wilderness. Following university graduation my career choice, made in the spirit of this conference's theme, was to seek knowledge and insight into the phenomena of economic change in remote regions where reality and the ideal present clear cutting edges. Everything I write or say is now conditioned by this experience. To combine these three elements, the title only needs the three-word subtitle, "Wilderness and Development." I will attempt to explain why I used "and" rather than "or" in the subtitle, and will review Alaska's transitional experience and aspirations to shed some light on or suggest new ways of looking at the meanings of these words.

As an opener, let us consider the two words in the most obvious and elementary terms. Wilderness might simply be called what is left over, after human occupation and physical use of the land and sea have been defined. To some these are the desert lands which the farmer's plow cannot break or from which the rancher's cattle turn back. To others this is wasteland awaiting the magic touch of reclamation projects. In classical times and in Elizabethan plays, undesirable citizens or wrongly deposed dukes and their beautiful daughters were exiled to it from the human community. Wilderness was the desert to which saints, sages and shamans retired to gain spiritual renewal and insight, and to which contemporary urban man looks for similar aids to survival.

Development also has many meanings, underlying all being some notion of change, sometimes referred to as progress. As used here it will be a process over which man has some significant degree of control or conscious direction, although this sense of control seems in danger of being surrendered to nonhuman man-made devices, and direction left to the blind forces of scientific and market research. Its objectives might ideally be defined as improvement of the human condition and measured precisely but inadequately in such bookkeeping concepts as increased per capita national or regional income, or less precisely but more meaningfully in terms of distribution of income or population-income balance. The process comes in a wide range and variety. It involves exploitation of nonrenewable and harvesting of renewable natural resources, which can be done wastefully and destructively for short-run gain, or rationally with maximization of long-run benefits, the two extremes commonly being identified as exploitation or conservation. Development is further modified by where man lives or aspires to live—the objectives and process differing as the mover and beneficiary, man, lives in huge urban concentrations, in modest-sized rural communities, or in the socio-economic unit of the family farm.

Alaska's past development can be generalized in terms of three major turning points or transitional jumps from one form of economic and social organization to another, from one set of objectives of development to another, and from one set of attitudes or conceptions of wilderness to another. We will not attempt to go back to the first human inhabitants of Alaska, but start with the Eskimo, Aleut, Athapaskan, Tlingit, and Haida variations of the human animal in residence at the time of the first European-American contacts (circa 1740). Each of these named groupings of the estimated 75,000 aboriginal inhabitants of Alaska represented differing social, economic, and cultural systems.

The basic differences between each arose from the limitations imposed and the opportunities offered by the physical environment and the natural resource base which could be harvested. The coastal areas from the Arctic around to the south-central part were inhabited by

Eskimo and Aleut hunters who lived primarily off the sea, although some turned landward. The southeastern Panhandle area was an extension of the culture of the Indians of the Pacific Northwest into the far north. In the interior of Alaska the Athapaskan Indians wandered about following a hunting, woodland culture. There are differences between each of these groups which were determined by the physical environment and the natural resource endowment and how people responded to these. But underlining all of these groups, from what we can determine from talking to the older people and our understanding of other primitive societies, there were certain very common notions. For example, there could not possibly have been any concept of wilderness in the sense that we think of it. To the Indian and Eskimo, man was not separate from nature but was part of nature. The other living things were all his brothers. They might prey upon one another in the struggle for survival, but they all shared a broad kinship of the living. The Tlingit hunter would beg forgiveness of his brother the bear for taking his life in order to provide food, or if seeking something else might ask permission of his brother the bear to pass unmolested through the bear's fishing territory. A contemporary Tlingit hunter and sometimes guide assured me this was why he was successful in the conduct of his business enterprise, having had a record of good luck in the hunt and not yet having lost a single tourist.

There were no uninhabited places on or under the land and the sea and in the air. Regions we would classify as uninhabited teemed with spirits and supernatural forces, good and evil, which had to be avoided, thanked, appealed to, or appeased. In this there was no meaningful distinction between man and the natural environment, between inhabited space and wilderness. All was unity and the rituals of man's life reminded him of this.

Development or progress, as we think of those terms, had no meaning. Change had taken place and continued to take place, but the change was so gradual over such a long period of time that within the memory of living man for all practical purposes things stood still. Man operated or reacted as an opportunist, adapting to seasonal changes in the physical environment and changes in the annual yield of the resource base. Success was measured in survival; failure to adapt, in death. These were the givens in the life of man. Man was not the manipulator, the changer.

Starting in the mid-eighteenth century and accelerating toward the end of the nineteenth and beginning of the twentieth century, Alaska's aboriginal, self-sufficient, and limited stage of economic development was disrupted and in many regions overthrown by outside forces of colonial development for the benefit of distant, non-resident interests. The 1867 change in "ownership" of Alaska really changed nothing else. After the purchase, the United States merely increased and expanded the Russian colonial period of extraction and exploitation of a highly specialized, narrow range of natural resources.

A few statistics, which I have repeatedly quoted before, sum up this whole period better than volumes of words. In the decade 1931-40, immediately before World War II, average annual value of all out-shipments from Alaska totalled $58.8 million, of which canned salmon accounted for 55.1 percent, gold 26.6 percent, other fish products 6.4 percent, furs 4.4 percent, and miscellaneous 6.5 percent. Very prominent in this miscellaneous category were such things as scrap machinery, and cannery and mining machinery being sent outside for repairs. It was a very specialized, very narrowly based economy, one where the action was at the mill, at the cannery, or on the fishing grounds. The colonial nature of this period was further indicated by average value of in-shipments of $28.4 million, in which the three leading items were tin cans, petroleum products, and alcoholic beverages. The value of in-shipments to Alaska, about half the value of the out-shipments, tells a great deal. This looks like a favorable balance of trade, but actually it was a measure of the degree to which Alaska was being exploited.

The physical environment as well as wilderness was simply something to be totally ignored or ruthlessly subjugated if it got in the way of the cheapest and easiest means of extracting the desired resource. Development was not only a highly specialized process, but it was short-term with mining of renewable as well as nonrenewable resources. The aboriginal or indigenous people, now referred to as natives in colonial tradition, were treated in the same manner. Development was a simple linear process which ignored its impact and effect upon everything and everyone but the desires of the exploiter, or pretended there were no side effects. The colonial mentality of Alaska's post-World War II period has its contemporary counterpart in the highway engineer who believes that a straight line is not only the shortest distance between two points, but also the only route. It also carries over into a lot of the other ideas we have today of development as a single, simple gimmick that will somehow solve all the problems, that will have only the effects that we want it to have, and no side effects that we don't anticipate.

In terms of population and economic activity, this period passed its peak about the turn of the century. By the decades of the 20's and 30's, it was clear that colonial Alaska was nowhere and was going nowhere. In 1937 the National Resources Committee took a long, careful look and its report, *Alaska—Its Resources and Development*, in effect wrote it off as being of no real national significance in the foreseeable future. No forced development or even modest programs encouraging development were recommended. The committee even suggested that we not bother spending any more money on things like roads because there was nowhere for roads to go. The Departments of War and Navy, still refusing to recognize the existence of the flying machine, declared Alaska to be of no military value, but rather a distant and difficult-to-defend outpost. The only positive note was sounded by one of the staff, Robert Marshall, who declared in a special supplemental statement to the final report of the committee, "Alaska is unique among all recreational areas belonging to the United States because Alaska is yet largely a wilderness. In the name of a balanced use of American resources, let's keep Alaska largely a wilderness."

The outbreak of World War II and the discovery of Alaska's strategic importance in the defense of North America in the air age was another major turning point. The natural resources of the colonial period declined in importance, both absolutely and relatively. Defense construction and support of the defense establishment became the basic economy of Alaska, accounting directly for more than half of total employment and resident income, and indirectly much more. Space became a militarily valuable resource, second in importance only to location. Wilderness became grist for the defense mill as bombing and later missile firing ranges, training areas, or simply as a buffer zone in which invading ground forces might become lost and bogged down. Development was a by-product. The size of a defense economy increased or decreased in response to national policy decisions, technological changes, and shifts in the international situation. But within this were important developmental forces and the seeds for the next turning point. The defense establishment carried with it or attracted large numbers of people, and Alaska's population rose from 75,000 in 1940 to 228,000 in 1957. These were people from politically developed parts of our nation and they were not satisfied with the limited self-determination represented in territorial political status. The statehood movement came to life, and Alaska became a full member of the union of states.

It is open to argument whether or not statehood played a role in the launching of the present era of resource development Alaska is now experiencing, but there is no question that the political context has changed and with it the objectives of development. The political act of creating the State of Alaska carried with it the objective of creating and sustaining a level of economic and social development sufficient to keep the new ship of state afloat. Long-term and resident interests had to be considered. Elements of the old colonialism might still lurk in the Japanese investment in timber, fish, and petroleum development, and in domestic United States and British investment in petroleum development on the North Slope. But the new colonialism can no longer be overt or go its own way unchecked. Government development programs are not simply promotional efforts, but include overall planning attempting to realize the fullest potential, both direct and indirect, of any major development prospect which appears on the horizon. Controls aiming to minimize adverse effects are being devised and the real needs of native people are being discovered. All of this adds up to the necessity of some attention being paid to the interests and desires of persons residing in Alaska, and to the sort of place Alaska might become as a result of development activities. It is no longer a place to be exploited and then forgotten or discarded. Or is it?

Statehood is not the happy ending to the Alaska story, but a new beginning. We today face another transition and a crisis. Whether development is to be solely for nonresident interests or should contribute to the creation of a resident society within Alaska was at least technically answered by the granting of statehood. But the new Alaskans speak in a babel of voices when it comes to stating the direction in which this development should be pointing. The present secretary of the interior in an interview shortly after statehood announced that we were to engage in the building of a Fifth Avenue on the tundra. The followers of that path can now point with some pride to their accomplishments in at least the two major population centers of the state. A few years ago when a novelist-journalist in personal transition, Norman Mailer, was visiting Alaska, the chamber of commerce types in Anchorage made the mistake of dragging him before the local TV cameras to ask him what he thought of their beautiful city. His hosts were thrown off balance and the show hurriedly terminated by his reply that when he landed at the airport and was being driven into the downtown center he said to himself, "Hell, I've been here before, this is the American nightmare." And, indeed, it is all there with a special northern accent. Urban sprawl and slums in the subarctic present human discomfort and misery surpassing that of their counterparts in more temperate zones. Pollution of water and air is accomplished more quickly than in our tougher more southern environments. (In winter the air pollution over Fairbanks rivals that of any Californian megalopolis.) Our major centers can boast similar rates and varieties of crime, violence, ugliness, and filth typifying any major cities elsewhere. The transplant has not yet been rejected by the Alaska body politic.

The crisis is further deepened by the popular appeal of the last frontier syndrome. Many Alaskans, including political leaders, dream of themselves as heroes in a TV western. In the northern version of the last frontier, as in the western version, wilderness is to be despoiled and destroyed as valueless, a nuisance or a threat. This usually included the human beings who were already there. Unfortunately, many Alaskans hold this view without realizing it or questioning it. But the story will not be repeated in its entirety. Like the buffalo, the caribou may not vote, but unlike the Plains Indian, the Alaskan Eskimo, Aleut, and Indian are a political force to be reckoned with.

Our present crisis does not arise solely from conflicts and uncertainties within ourselves and the political boundaries of our Brave New World. New outside forces are present in the threat of the awesome power now in the hands of our technicians and their itch to demonstrate it. Shortly after the granting of statehood, the Atomic Energy Commission made a bid to convert Alaska's arctic lands into a testing ground for what they euphemistically called nuclear devices and for the demonstration of what was called, also euphemistically, the new science of engineering geography. The Corps of Engineers promoted the construction of a project at Rampart Canyon on the Yukon River which, if it had been carried through, would by the turn of the century be capable of generating only the second or third largest block of hydroelectric power, but which would have had the unchallenged distinction of creating the largest man-made lake in the world. Another technical marvel has been announced as a possible accompaniment to the development of petroleum resources on our North Slope, a $900-million pipeline across Alaska to tidewater on the Gulf of Alaska. The pipeline would have an initial capacity of 500,000 barrels per day but be designed to carry double or quadruple that amount by 1980. The pipe would be four feet in diameter and because of unstable permafrost and tundra subsoil conditions, would for much of its distance be above ground supported on a series of concrete piers or steel stilts anchored to cement blocks sunk 20 feet into permafrost.[*] In effect this would result in an ecological Berlin Wall about five feet high dissecting much of the main landmass of Alaska from the shores of the Arctic Ocean to the Gulf of Alaska,

* B. F. Sater, editor, *Preliminary Report of Symposium on Arctic and Middle North Transportation*, Arctic Institute of North America, (Montreal, 1969), p. 43.

accompanied by the threat of an inland version of Santa Barbara if leaks developed. It would indeed be a triumph of modern technology over the wilderness.

This leads to the final element in our present crisis with which I wish to deal here, the impending oil rush and boom on our North Slope. The details are well known, but unless you live in or are interested in the north, you may not be fully aware of the emotional content of these developments and their possible consequences. I have just come from participating in two development conferences both sponsored by the Arctic Institute of North America. Although their announced subjects and purposes differed, they both shared a sense of urgency and unintended dominance fostered by oil in the Alaskan and Canadian north.

The largest and the most publicized was a symposium on "Arctic and Middle North Transportation" held in the Hotel Bonaventure in Montreal and attended by over 300 representatives of industry and government listening to discussions of transportation problems that affect the development of northern resources. The reason for the large attendance (another 300 applicants were turned away because of space limitations) was oil, not transportation as such. To me the meeting presented a model of what has been happening to people in the north or those who are interested in northern development. The general air of the symposium was one of intense excitement stimulated by an urge to discover how to cash in on what looked to be the biggest thing ever to hit the north. One variation of this theme was stated in a keynote address by a senior vice-president of a Canadian bank who urged his colleagues to stake out their claims to a part of the action (in Canada) before it all was taken up by the Americans, British, Japanese and, above all, the French. The conference gave over to colonial development forces that were rampant because consideration of human factors and values, including that of physical environment, were absent. Oil was everything. This was not stated in so many words, but the meaning was clear. The oil companies are faced with the task of getting the petroleum out of the ground and to market as efficiently and economically as possible. This is their prime objective. There was no other interest represented at the meeting to exert any modifying influence. The objectives of the several Canadian and United States government transportation agencies represented and those of the private transportation lobbies appeared to be simply to see that their particular form of transport got top priority in the consideration of means of getting the product to market.

In such an atmosphere, wilderness values could only be thought of in defensive terms. But they need not have been if the model of general public values and motivations presented had included a concern for the human beings affected or involved in the development, and an appreciation of the place of wilderness in the making of the whole man. As a minimum there would have been discussion of means of regulating and controlling the transportation aspects of exploration and development activities so as to minimize damage to these values. As a maximum, there might even have been a weighing of the public interest against the limited self-interest of the industrial combinations represented and individuals seeking to draw personal gain from the impending developments. There might have been a recognition of the basic madness of a development that required the destruction of one physical environment (the North American Arctic) in order to extract petroleum from the ground for conversion into materials to be used elsewhere to despoil another physical environment through air and other forms of pollution, to say nothing of the promotion of wholesale manslaughter on the highways.

Human values as such were absent from the Montreal symposium, but they were present at the center of the conference on community development in the north at Dartmouth College. This was a working session of about 50 architects, engineers, and social scientists, most of whom had been involved or interested in the planning of new communities in response to industrial development and other needs in the northern regions of North America and Europe. The sense of urgency here was as strong as that which permeated the Montreal meeting, and it also arose from the impending petroleum boom in the north and other anticipated industrial developments. But it was a different sort of urgency based upon the participants' firsthand knowledge of what this had meant to the human condition and the environment in the past, a concern that the future efforts of the planners result in something better, and an awareness that, whether or not they did anything to improve these prospects, the industrial developments were going forward without them. As a minimum, the conference follow-up hoped to open avenues for expanded and continuing interchange and communication between engineer, architect, and social scientist to the end that the planning process take into account the whole man and his place in his environment, and to launch programs to educate or influence top decision makers in directions leading toward the ideal of new northern communities or other social units fit for human living.

I drew great hope from this meeting for it represented builders who knew that they were not engaged simply in providing shelter and sanitation, but consciously or unconsciously were engaged in creating new environments, good or bad, within which people had to live. Not only were they aware of what they were doing, but also they were motivated by a desire to promote human happiness as well as make possible the industrial developments which were the basis of their employment. The introduction of human values into the development process, of course, is not unique to that conference. In recent years it has received growing acceptance. Even the bookkeeper mentality of the professional economists has been able to accept an extended definition of natural resources that goes beyond things that enter directly into production to include physical environmental factors that indirectly condition the production process. These "amenity resources" can include wilderness values, depending upon the sort of lives people want to fashion for themselves. This awareness and desire is growing, but there is need for further education to promote wider appreciation and use of wilderness to enrich our lives.

In the concluding chapter of my book, *The Future of Alaska*, published in 1962, I made the following observations. "The process of determining broad purpose and specific goals must become much more pragmatic and realistic than it has been in recent years. Drawing analogies not with Scandinavian development, but with the experience of closer, more comparable neighbors to the west and east, I would expect the basic impetus for Alaska's future economic growth to come from industrialization which will be as selective and specialized as it has been in the past. But there will be a difference. The new industrialization will be accompanied by a filling-in process lacking in the past and resulting in a more diversified total economy. The land hunger which in the nineteenth century stimulated the settling of the West cannot be reckoned with as a force in the peopling of Alaska where land ownership, as such, is seldom productive of standards of living found elsewhere in the states today. But something akin to the same drive—in terms of a yearning for open space and remaining wilderness values—may generate a different sort of movement into the United States northland. City people, as their environment becomes more congested and their travel more prescribed by networks of monotonous highways, may look to Alaska for fulfillment of their recreational needs, and the present technological revolution in transportation is steadily bringing Alaska's scenic resources closer to them in terms of time and money. Properly recognized, conserved, and developed as the need emerges, Alaska can find in its wilderness an element which, with the state's forest and fisheries wealth and minerals and hydroelectric potential, could give it the type of balanced development we all hope for."

These observations were not put forward in a spirit of romantic idealism, but as hard-nosed realism. Unless wilderness is included within the meaning of the term "development" in Alaska, the future of Alaska will revert to simply another version of the colonial periods of the past. Beyond Alaska, wilderness and development must be brought together into such a unity if the north is to survive. In this the north and Alaska are models of the universe of all mankind.

# INTRODUCTION

*Margaret E. Murie*
Consultant
The Wilderness Society

The other evening at a friend's home in San Rafael, California, I was reading *The Natural World of San Francisco*, by Harold Gilliam. A quote appealed to me. "The human animal is doubtless venial and vicious, but he is also at times capable of splendor. He is the climax, thus far, of the great chain of life you have observed on this beach. Out of the watery chaos of the ocean, and the parasitisms of the earth, came the succession of evolving species. The sand dollar, the crab, the sea birds and finally man."

Finally? Maybe not. It does not seem likely that the immemorial process has come to an end. Maybe it is the role of man, at least contemporary man, to point the way toward some bigger, higher form of life, some greater destiny not yet conceivable. But I also then remembered a passage from Loren Eiseley's writings where he says he feels as we go about our busy business that little eyes are watching us from behind the leaves, thinking perhaps their turn will come next if we do not do too good a job on this planet.

There are two ways of looking at our subject of this morning, "Alaska's Wilderness Wildlife": the aesthetic concept and the economic. From the first point of view, the aesthetic, they are there, these creatures in Alaska, untrammeled, living their immemorial lives, living, breathing accents on a great wilderness canvas. People may travel quietly there to see and watch them—all of them, from the little furry red lemmings scurrying through the mossy runways of the tundra, to the magnificent bull caribou silhouetted against the skyline. Surely the wild ones in this concept are valuable to us beyond calculation.

154

And there is the economic point of view. Since man is on the scene in the north country, and bound to be more and more so, the mammals and birds have taken on another value. Both aspects are present. Both must be looked at and put in perspective. Hunting and bird-watching and scientific observation may and can take place on the same terrain. In some regions the aesthetic obligation takes the dominant role, as in the wilderness of Denali, the name by which I prefer to call Mt. McKinley, where the preference is given to observation and scientific study. In still other places in Alaska today, certain species are assured preservation even outside of national parks, monuments, and refuges where the aesthetic value is realized as preeminent. An example of that is the McNeil River country where the brown bears come to feed on the fish; the State of Alaska has made that a kind of sanctuary. Our hope must be for a careful study of all these aspects followed by courageous and wise regulations that recognize not only the rights of man but also the rights of animals. Since they cannot formulate a bill of rights, it seems that man must do it for them. And I am sure that no one in this gathering this morning would tolerate the thought of any Alaskan species disappearing from its natural place in that far-flung wilderness.

As Dr. Rogers indicated, Alaska is in the enviable position of being able to have its cake and eat it too. People can live there. Animals can live there also if the people so wish and so plan.

Last night, after the banquet, I received a special delivery letter from Big Lake via Bettles Field, Alaska. Inside the envelope were two letters and a hand-written note dated at Big Lake, March 13th, 1969, just two days ago. It said: "Dear Mrs. Murie: I hope the enclosed gets to you. The pilot said he would get it out today, but to be sure I am heading for Fairbanks with him as I need to check my films. My first time out in six months."

One of the enclosures was a letter addressed to the Honorable Keith Miller, governor of Alaska, dated February 15th. "Dear Governor Miller: The enclosed letter comes to you from a 12x12 foot log cabin 200 miles from Fairbanks and north of the Arctic Circle in the wilderness of the Brooks Range. About 20 copies were reproduced on a flat tin of gelatin to be flown out by the bush pilot in his small ski plane. There might be a month's discrepancy between the date of writing and the time you receive it because of irregular contact. I have been wintering in these isolated mountains as part of my sabbatical year study in human ecology. My studies here actually began in 1966 when I walked on foot into this wilderness in search of plots north of timber line where Robert Marshall had planted white spruce seeds in 1939. Hiking a hundred miles into Anaktuvuk Pass to be retrieved by plane, I stayed with the Eskimos living there, and was intrigued that these people were still a hunting culture based upon the caribou. Last year I returned to Anaktuvuk Pass to film changes in the life as part of a study in values in transition. During the summer I also backpacked into the range and planted on Bob Marshall's original wilderness plot 100 four-year-old seedlings from the Forestry Sciences Laboratory at the University of Alaska. I appreciate your response to my report on this continuing experiment. As you will gather from the enclosed commentary, I have developed a tie with this wilderness during the past few years which has taken on dimensions beyond my original study plans. With the great oil strike on the North Slope of the range a year ago this month, and the resultant threat to this great wilderness, I have resigned from my professorial teaching role and made this my field base from which to continue my studies in human ecology and speak for the preservation of this last great wilderness of the American continent. Sincerely yours, Samuel A. Wright."

The other letter was done in four pages on the gelatin, also dated February 15th. I will read only the first paragraph.

"As I write this a great caravan of heavily laden trucks is growling over a new winter road which yesterday reached the Eskimo village in Anaktuvuk Pass at the central top of the range. Yesterday wrote the end of Anaktuvuk Pass as it was—a small village of inland Eskimos still dependent upon migrating herds of caribou. It may have written the beginning of the end of the great caribou herds, majestic mountain sheep and the wolf. It was certainly the end of thousands of years of solitude as the great diesel trucks thundered up the John River Valley on their way to the North Slope and the great oil strike near Prudhoe Bay."

At the end of this letter he says: "There is no time left. If there is any natural resource which deserves our full attention it is wilderness. We must preserve any wilderness area left on this planet that we have now seen from the moon to be our home, or the opportunity is lost forever. Fortunately the Brooks Range is in the State of Alaska in the United States of America, and we can save it now. Next month, tomorrow, will be too late."

# ARCTIC OIL: ITS IMPACT ON WILDERNESS AND WILDLIFE

*Robert B. Weeden*
Alaska Conservation Society*
College, Alaska

In August of 1968, Atlantic Richfield announced discovery of oil reserves on the order of five to 10 billion barrels at Prudhoe Bay, 225 miles southeast of Point Barrow, the most northern community in the United States. Although far more oil has been flown into Prudhoe Bay than has yet been pumped out, there is no doubt that the oil strike is big. We can expect its impact on the landscape, already fantastic, to spread and intensify for years to come.

My main conclusion about Prudhoe Bay is that neither science nor government was—or is—prepared for discovery of oil in the Arctic. Science cannot predict the quantitative effects of the industry's disturbance of arctic soils and vegetation on biological communities, nor can science estimate the economic and social costs of these disturbances. Partly in consequence, government has not equipped itself with laws or funds to meet fully its responsibility to protect public values on public arctic lands.

I hope the thoughts I express here will catalyze and undergird conservationists' recognition of a few of the many problems attendant on this industrial development: maintaining a clean and productive environment within areas affected by exploration for and production of oil, maintaining wild animal populations in the face of widespread habitat change and heightened human predation, and revising our approach toward preserving wild and natural landscapes in Alaska.

* Dr. Weeden accepted a new position, Alaska representative, for the Sierra Club and The Wilderness Society in October, 1969.

*Historical Sketch of Oil Exploration in Arctic Alaska*

Acting on the basis of early geological surveys, the United States Government established the 35,000-square-mile Naval Petroleum Reserve No. 4 in the western half of Alaska's Arctic in 1923. Contractors shot seismic lines and drilled on behalf of the navy from 1944 to 1953, giving ecologists their first inkling of what to expect from oil activity on the tundra.

Shortly after the tantalizing data from Pet 4 were published, oil companies contracted with seismic surveyors to explore lands held by the Bureau of Land Management east of the Colville River. On December 7, 1960, however, Interior Secretary Fred Seaton established the Arctic National Wildlife Range in the extreme northeastern corner of Alaska, closing that nine-million-acre area to subsurface mineral exploration. Surface exploration and mineral leasing are allowed within the range, but exploration work can be done only by permit from the supervisor of Alaskan Refuges, Bureau of Sport Fisheries and Wildlife. Leasing is currently not allowed because the required land classifications in the range have not been made. Thus, the attention of oil exploration parties focused on the block of state and public domain land between the Canning and Colville rivers from the Arctic Ocean to the northern wall of the Brooks Range.

Immediately after Atlantic Richfield's discovery last summer, several Alaskan airlines prepared for what was to become one of the most ambitious private airlifts the world has ever seen. Cargo aircraft flew the 400 miles between Fairbanks and company-built airstrips in the Arctic, carrying millions of pounds of fuel oil, prefabricated buildings, drilling equipment, parts, dynamite, food, and people to Prudhoe Bay.

The airlift served the industry admirably during these early weeks of pell-mell, highly competitive jockeying for position, but experiences with frozen fog and extreme cold pointed toward the need for surface transportation. The State of Alaska responded quickly by starting on a winter haul road in December, 1968. Now completed, this trail (dubbed the "Hickel Highway" by Governor Keith Miller at celebrations in Fairbanks in March, 1969) connects Fairbanks with Prudhoe Bay via Stevens Village, Anaktuvuk Pass, and the oil camp at Sagwon on the Sagavanirktok River. The road has no protective surface and will thaw and erode each summer, requiring annual reconstruction.* Eventually the road may be surfaced and a bridge built

* By early in 1970 it had become clear that the winter haul road would be abandoned after two or at most three short seasons of use. Trans-Alaska Pipeline System plans to build a graveled road parallel to its pipline right-of-way, well east

across the Yukon River, allowing all-year traffic. The same route may be used for an extension of the Alaska Railroad to the Arctic.

*Helping the Tundra Survive*

Dr. Raymond Dasmann wrote recently[1] that the disturbance of any natural environment should not exceed the minimum needed to accomplish its rational use for worthy human goals. That thought is an excellent launching pad for my discussion of the interaction of tundra and industry. I accept the premise that taking oil from under the tundra is a worthwhile activity. I accept the fact that some disturbance of the whole organism "land" is inevitable, and that some is economically acceptable. I deny, however, that oil is the only significant arctic resource or that private industry should be allowed to degrade public values at will while it extracts oil.

The two big problems now for the ecologist and public defender are to find out exactly what damage is being done and how it is done, and to implement effective remedial or protective measures.

Biologists and soil scientists know a lot about the tundra but their work has centered on undisturbed systems. Knowledge of damaged tundras and their capacity for self-healing is woefully sparse. In my opinion one of the first things we must do is to plan and begin comprehensive studies of the effects of specific disturbances on tundra ecosystems, conducting this study with all the speed and resources government and private groups can muster. The International Biological Program may well provide a good planning vehicle for such a study, and the oil industry may support this work. A heartening interest in this type of research has been evident at the University of Alaska in recent months.

Meanwhile, we are faced with the fact that time has run out, at least for places like the lower Mackenzie River, Cook Inlet, Bristol Bay, and the central Alaskan Arctic. Those few men in resource agencies who monitor the oil industry have to know right now whether to issue a permit for a seismic operation on a specific piece of tidal marsh or upland tundra (if indeed they are lucky enough to have any choice).

With regard to the preservation of arctic landscapes, two facts are of prime importance. First, vegetative cover is thin and easily destroyed.

---

of the original Hickel Highway. This construction road is to be turned over to the state as a permanent highway to the Arctic when the pipline project is completed.

[1] R. F. Dasmann, *An Environment Fit for People.* Public Affairs Pamphlet No. 421. (New York: Public Affairs Committee, 1968).

When bare earth is exposed, it thaws more deeply, slumps, and erodes. The healing process is very slow. Second, any debris, organic or inorganic, takes far longer to decompose in the Arctic than in warmer areas.

The fragility of vegetative cover is a matter of common knowledge in the north. To cite but one example, wildlife biologist John Burns (Alaska Department of Fish and Game, Nome) demonstrated[2] an unexpected consequence of the use of tracked vehicles on thawed tundra. He observed that on the tundra of the Yukon-Kuskokwim delta, tracked vehicles commonly skirted the margins of lakes in traversing the country during summer seismic work. The resulting thawing, slumping, flooding, and freezing destroyed the favored denning sites of mink and muskrats. The mink of this area, incidentally, is probably the fur trade's most valuable wild mink.

I once heard it said that of the thousands of oil drums left in Pet 4, 20 years ago, half still hold water; the other half have been shot at. Apocryphal or not, that comment illustrates the dismaying longevity of discarded objects in the arctic environment. Orange peelings last months, paper lasts years, wood scraps last decades, and metal and plastic are almost immortal in the cold, dry northern climate. Furthermore, there probably is no other landscape in the world, except for warm deserts, so poorly designed for hiding debris. The only solution I see is a rigid program involving, as appropriate, central collection, incineration, burial, and backhaul to land fills in forested country.

Assuming that we know or can quickly learn how to protect tundra from unnecessary damage, how do we translate this knowledge into effective action? What can we expect the industry to do voluntarily? What can we work for by way of government action?

I think it would be naive to expect much of the industry itself during the exploratory phase of their operations. With billions of dollars of future revenue at stake and with millions invested in exploration, is it likely that a company would voluntarily issue strict orders about the use of vehicles and tractors on thawed ground, if its road-building operations were slowed down? Is it likely that competing companies would tell each other what they found during seismic work, simply to reduce the number of miles of shot holes and trails for aesthetic reasons? Could we expect cooperative use of airstrips, roads, and camps under the conditions of haste and secrecy that surround the Prudhoe Bay activity now?

The chances for accomplishing needed protective measures would

[2] J. Burns, "Of Oil and Fur." Alaska Conservation Society *News Bulletin*, III, No. 1 (January 1962), p. 8. College, Alaska.

appear much higher if uniform operational standards were set and enforced by land-holding agencies. Presently four such agencies are involved in the Alaskan Arctic: the navy on Naval Petroleum Reserve No. 4, the Bureau of Sport Fisheries and Wildlife in the Arctic Wildlife Range, the Bureau of Land Management on public domain, and the Alaska Department of Natural Resources on state-selected lands.

At this time the navy does not allow private exploration or drilling on Pet 4. There are very great pressures to open this area, however, and no one would be surprised to find seismic crews there in a few months. There is some question as to whether the Bureau of Land Management or the navy is prime guardian of land surface values on Pet 4.

The Bureau of Sport Fisheries and Wildlife has had some success in protecting surface and aesthetic values on its lands in Alaska where oil exploration and development have occurred. Alaska's first producing field was at Swanson River in the Kenai National Moose Range. There, in a situation where the industry is told exactly what it is expected to do to preserve soil and vegetation, to protect wild animals, and to repair damages; and where these instructions have been backed by daily surveillance by the bureau, cooperation by the industry has been good. A short flight from the Kenai Moose Range to Trading Bay across Cook Inlet quickly demonstrates the effectiveness of the bureau's control in comparison to the relatively free-wheeling activities on state land outside the range.

As mentioned earlier, the Bureau of Sport Fisheries and Wildlife prohibits seismic explorations in the Arctic National Wildlife Range and does not permit use of land vehicles in that area. But regulations as restrictive as those obviously are justified only where wildlife, scenic, and wilderness values have been given top priority in land management plans. Where surface values are not exceptional, and where geological reconnaissance points to the possibility of commercial mineral or oil deposits, it is unreasonable to prohibit exploration and subsequent leasing and development. Land controlled by the Bureau of Land Management (BLM) and the Alaska Department of Natural Resources in the central Alaskan arctic plain is in that latter category. The main goal of land managers in those areas is to allow orderly development of mineral resources with minimum damage to surface values.

In 1967 the secretary of the interior established regulations affecting geophysical explorations on BLM lands. These regulations require an operator to file a notice of intent to explore on specific townships, and allow a BLM district manager to specify detailed protective stipulations which the operator must follow. The stipulations themselves are not part of the regulation, but are in fact simply guidelines drawn up by the industry, the State of Alaska, and the Department of the Interior. The effectiveness of these guidelines depends heavily on cooperation from the oil and gas industry. It depends also on the ability of BLM to maintain constant surveillance, and that, quite frankly, is something the present Fairbanks district budget does not allow.

The state's authority and control in this matter is, if anything, weaker than that of the Bureau of Land Management. The only restrictions placed on the industry during oil explorations prior to leasing have been those written by biologists of the Alaska Department of Fish and Game. That agency recently began issuing seismic permits to operators referred to them by the Department of Natural Resources. The permits read as though written by a man who bellies up to a steak dinner, only to recall that he left his false teeth at home. The reason is that the authority for writing the permits derives from the state's Anadromous Fish Act, which only by strenuous use of imagination can be said to apply to arctic uplands.

In January, 1969, the Division of Lands, Department of Natural Resources, proposed an addition to Title II of the State Laws of Alaska, prescribing regulations for minimizing surface damage during mineral exploration before leasing. These proposed regulations are very similar to the guidelines issued by the Bureau of Land Management, except that they would have the force and effect of law. There will be opposition to these regulations, and some weakening of them is likely before they are adopted.* After leasing, the operator is now bound by stipulations written into lease permits. Currently these restrictions are very broadly written; they contain none of the detail of the newly proposed regulations covering prelease exploration. This is a matter of real concern because the most intensive seismic work is done after leasing.

To summarize: we need to learn a lot more about the ecology of damage on the tundra, but on the basis of what is known now managers can, if allowed, provide reasonable protection to vegetation, soil, water, and wildlife. I am skeptical about the amount of self-

* The regulations were adopted on January 1, 1970. They require everyone who travels in a vehicle across state lands (about eight percent of the land in Alaska) to take steps to prevent unnecessary damage to soil and vegetation. However, no permits are required except when earth-moving equipment and explosives are to be used. There seems little hope that the state will be able to enforce these regulations adequately.

policing the industry would do if left to its own devices. The alternative is a sliding scale of regulatory restrictions placed on the industry's activities, the most stringent (perhaps completely prohibitive) measures to be applied in areas where wilderness or wildlife values are exceptional, and less stringent (but still effective) ones to cover all other public lands. The state and federal governments now appear to be testing approaches to this problem via proposed regulations (state) or guidelines (federal). On-site inspection will be a key factor in the success of these programs, but state and federal budgets are currently completely inadequate to do the job.

## Maintaining Wildlife Populations

Wildlife managers in Alaska once had the comfortable feeling that terrestrial arctic lands and their animal populations were virtually unaffected by man. This comfortable attitude is gone. Now direct and indirect habitat losses are a fact of arctic life, and increased hunting pressure is a certainty for tomorrow.

Every new camp, road, airstrip, and drilling pad obliterates another piece of tundra. So few acres are affected as yet, in comparison to the millions of acres of similar habitat remaining, that we could consider these losses insignificant. Nevertheless, these "insignificant" losses, multiplied by the number of years the industry expects to be in the Arctic, could become of serious proportions. I should make it clear, too, that some species are crowded into very small parts of the Arctic— the Ross's goose is a good example—so that even localized habitat changes could be disastrous.

There are other ways in which wildlife habitat can be degraded. First, with huge volumes of oil being pumped, refined, stored, and transported, some inevitably will escape. (The specter of a pipeline break is frightening: a 48-inch pipe holds 496,000 gallons per mile.) The problems spilled oil can cause for animals and their habitat are familiar to all of us.* Second, the presence of men and machinery undoubtedly will cause some species like caribou and large carnivores to avoid areas that still could provide food and shelter, but are simply too close to people.

Pipelines are a unique problem. The oil industry presently plans to build one line out of Prudhoe Bay south across Alaska to a terminus on salt water and has considered another pipeline east to the Mackenzie

---

* We had a preview of what to expect in February and March, 1970, when crude oil from legal or illegal ballast-pumping washed ashore along 1,000 miles of beach on Kodiak Island. An estimated 10,000 seabirds were washed up along with the oil; a federal biologist believed that the total mortality was closer to 100,000 birds.

River and south to Edmonton. The pipelines would be about 48 inches in diameter. If laid on top of the ground in the Arctic, these pipes would be a serious barrier to migrating caribou. There are two herds of caribou in arctic Alaska, totaling about 400,000 animals, that occupy generally distinct ranges but mingle at times in the vicinity of Anaktuvuk Pass. These caribou are not nomadic just for fun: migrations are an integral part of their lives. Although we do not know what would happen if caribou movements were suddenly restricted, few biologists would care to run the risk of finding out—especially with hundreds of people depending on the caribou for food. Currently no plans have been released by the industry covering the routing or specifications of the trans-Alaska pipeline. Unofficially, pipeline engineers favor buried pipes wherever possible.

Until now northern Alaskan tundra animals have been harvested mainly by subsistence hunters. Beginning this year, biologists will have to assess the impact of large numbers of fairly wealthy people in the Arctic, using sophisticated techniques for finding and killing animals far from where the people live.

The first severe problems will be with grizzlies, wolves, and wolverines. All are highly prized trophies. All are easily seen in the open landscapes of the Arctic. The grizzlies will get themselves in trouble around camps and garbage dumps. The country is easily traversed by snowmobiles which are now so powerful that they can overhaul any mammal in practically any part of the plains. These factors point to the rapid development of managerial problems.

Fundamentally, however, these problems are less serious than the outright loss and degradation of habitat. This is partly because animal populations are quite forgiving of management mistakes if the mistakes are corrected in time. Partly, too, it is because man as predator can be controlled with appropriate action by the state and federal fish and game agencies. The important thing is for these agencies to recognize the size and urgency of the problems and to get enough men and money to do the job. Losses of habitat, on the other hand, cannot be prevented if oil is to be taken out of the ground.

*Implications for Wilderness Preservation*

Since long before statehood, Alaskan conservationists have been aware of the progressive loss of the wilderness character of parts of the state, but the vastness of de facto wilderness has lulled them into feeling that there was plenty of time to choose and protect undisturbed natural areas.

I am convinced that the discovery of oil has telescoped the margin of time for wilderness preservation in Alaska into a very few years.

There is no private industry, other than the petroleum giants, with similar ability to amass huge amounts of capital, and move men and equipment to remote parts of the earth. There is no other industry that changes the appearance of the landscape over such large areas merely in the process of looking for a resource. Surface transportation systems follow swiftly after oil discovery, as exemplified today in the North American Arctic; these roads and railroads quickly make other resource extraction and use economically feasible. Geology is favorable for commercial oil deposits under about half of Alaska, including most of the treeless areas from the Alaska Peninsula north and east to the Canadian border. Finally, consider that in the space of a few months oil explorations have destroyed the wilderness character of an area in northern Alaska bigger than the State of Massachusetts. I, for one, do not give our huge de facto wilderness long to survive.

## A Program for Conservationists

I have outlined some of the things taking place in the Arctic that concern every ecologist, natural resource manager, and conservationist. It is time to look at what can be done to minimize long-term environmental degradation and to protect selected areas from defacement. The action I will suggest cannot be done by one person, one agency, or one level of government. It requires the understanding and will to act of private industry, citizen conservationists, resource administrators, and legislators in both state and federal governments, and in Canada.

I propose a five-point program for arctic resource conservationists:

### 1) Legislation and Regulation

My impression is that oil companies will operate under any reasonable land-protective regulations. The Kenai National Moose Range has shown this conclusively. It is the agencies and the elected officials who control them, who are sensitive to any suggestion that oil companies will "go elsewhere" if regulated too severely, and who are reluctant to speak strongly as advocates of public values. Conservationists must urge the Department of the Interior to change its "guidelines" into regulations, to strengthen them in the specifics of how and when seismic and other activities can be conducted, and to extend them to new situations as during the search for suitable pipeline routes, such as crews are now engaged in north of Fairbanks. On the state side, the Anadromous Fish Act needs improving so that it effectively protects all significant fish resources in all Alaskan waters. The newly-proposed regulations of the Division of Lands, covering seismic work before leasing, should be passed. The existing regulations for seismic operations after leasing need improvement, too, although basic outlines for workable control are there. Finally, all agencies need public support for funds to commit to the expanding task of surveillance and regulation enforcement.

## 2) Wilderness Preservation

I am convinced that eventually, through the pressures of public opinion and governmental regulation, the oil industry will be operating in a manner that will cause minimal and generally acceptable damage to the land and its surface values. The one land use that is totally unable to coexist with oil or any other industrial development is wilderness. This means that whatever wilderness Americans want in Alaska must be identified and set aside, at least for study, *before* any permanent scars are made on the land. In the Arctic this means parts of the Arctic Wildlife Range, Pet 4, and the Brooks Range massif. Conservationists should immediately begin pressing for studies—and should do some research themselves—that will quickly lead to recognition of potential areas, for our National Wilderness Preservation System.

## 3) Research and Inventory

Money and manpower must begin to focus immediately on the broad problem of human disturbance of the tundra biome. This research must be of wide applicability but also must be specific to the kinds of disturbances to soil, water, vegetation and wildlife experienced during current methods of oil exploration and development. The research should identify activities causing the most serious ecological problems and should lead to suggestions for remedial action or prevention. Fish and wildlife populations and their annual rates of productivity—biological capital and interest rates, in other words—need full inventory and careful study as a basis for any harvest or habitat protection regulations needed in the future.

## 4) Communication

Canada and the United States should jointly convene an Arctic conservation conference within the next 18 months to discuss the new relationships of environment and man, new competitions for resources, and new problems of resource preservation and use in subarctic and arctic North America. By the summer of 1969 there should be a formal means of communication among all federal and state agencies, citizen conservation groups, and industry to discuss ecologic and economic problems in the north and to set guidelines for mutual cooperative action.

5) *Moratorium on Exploration:*

I propose that the United States government and the State of Alaska jointly declare a moratorium on oil exploration in Alaska except for areas within oil structures of known commercial quantity. This moratorium should last at least three years. In that time government and industry should pool resources to develop exploration techniques that will have much less visible effect on land and vegetation than present methods. Intensive research on damaged ecology should be begun. Regulations should be strengthened so that public values are given better protection on public lands when exploration begins again. Funds and men should be obtained by federal and state governments to enforce these regulations. And, lastly, areas of exceptional scenic, recreational, scientific or wildlife values should be identified and protected pending Congressional action.

In closing, I will simply reiterate that we haven't much time to act. In mid-February, 1969, the Alaska Sierra Club and the Alaska Conservation Society convened a workshop on wilderness. It was Alaska's first such meeting. It took conservationists three months to plan the conference. In that time, over 10 million pounds of equipment and supplies were flown into the central Alaskan Arctic. Hundreds of miles of seismic lines were run, and the winter trail was bulldozed 250 miles into the wilderness. The lesson is abundantly clear.

# ALASKAN WILDERNESS
# WILDLIFE TODAY

*Urban C. Nelson*
Conservation Consultant, The Nature Conservancy and
Alaska Sportsmen's Council, Juneau, Alaska

Sierra Club members and its friends, although I speak without any portfolio, I think that it behooves someone from this Alaska panel to acknowledge our appreciation for your interest in Alaska. I know that not all Alaskans would be grateful for the Sierra Club interest. Nonetheless, for those of us who will look to the future, and for those of us who are in Alaska, I want to assure you that your interest is appreciated and your compensation must be the satisfaction similar to those in the East 100 years ago who helped foster the creation and the establishment of the parks in the West.

The Sierra Club earns commendation for placing the procreation of the human being in proper perspective on the program with the keynote address by Paul Ehrlich. Conservationists who have assembled through the years to worry about the plight of fish, waterfowl, forest, wild rivers, wilderness, or environmental pollution might better weigh the target of the population bomb and spend their time on approaches to deflect an otherwise perfect blast-off. It always reminds me of the story of the stag party, when on the first beer, someone says, "Shall we talk about women now or wait until we get around to it?"

It is good to be in a big city, infrequently, to better appreciate my home in Alaska. Dr. Weeden suggested that I get up early to hear the birds cough. This city, like all, is too far away from anything. Often I am jolted by the question, "Why live in that God-forsaken country?" Ironically and regrettably, too many questioners fail to

168

comprehend that the urban areas are the forsaken country. Yet, Alaska is fast developing into the forsaken 50.

Paraphrasing Theodore Roosevelt's famous statement about the fate of the nation's resources, no other state than Alaska has been so richly endowed with such an abundance and such a variety of resources, and no state has so rapidly exploited them. The exploitation of the sea otter first, followed by fur seal, whales, gold, copper, salmon, halibut, crab, and now oil and timber has been less than prudent. But to those who would despair, let them study these challenges, note the successes, and let these failures be a lesson and a guide.

The term "wilderness wildlife" is really a transitory one. To the pilgrim, all wildlife was wilderness wildlife. Earlier in this century the term excluded farm game—quail, rabbit, and pheasant. The depletion of some animals, birds, and fishes formerly associated with wilderness led to the erroneous conclusion that these forms would not tolerate man. We now know that the tolerance is greater than first believed and I hope that history will show that some forms can continue to tolerate even what we predict today they cannot. Witness the Canada goose in Ohio ponds, Illinois's Crab Orchard Refuge, and the city of Rochester, Minnesota; the canvasback and coyote within the city limits of San Francisco; moose around the streets in Anchorage. Of course they do not like it, but they are there. Nonetheless we are fortunate that these species can exhibit a great degree of tolerance.

What about the Alaskans? A drug detail friend of mine was having difficulty securing an appointment with an Alaskan psychiatrist. After protracted delays he finally got into his office. Without the formality of introduction or sweet words, the psychiatrist said, "What are you running away from in coming to Alaska?" The truth is, many come to Alaska to escape, perhaps for both good and bad reasons. But in sequence they came—sea otter hunters, whalers, gold seekers, commercial fishermen, depression escapees, military personnel, oil men and most recently the escapees of freeways, junk, pollution, and civil strife. These with the Eskimo, Indian, and Aleut make up a select people all associated directly or indirectly with the natural resources. Most love the wilderness, and its edge. The legislature, for example, contrary to a few comments that I have heard at this conference, includes many with a very reverent dedicated concern for the environment of both people and wildlife, and they would compare favorably on all counts with the legislatures of the other 49 states. This I say, in spite of our sad insistence in Alaska on following many of the mistakes of the older states in such matters as bounties, predator control, fish hatcheries, and politically oriented and appointed natural resource officials.

Regrettably, the conservationists failed to guarantee resource management program stability in its state constitution. The document is hailed as a model, strong governor, metro-concept of a constitution. Attempts to include a provision to assure some freedom from politics in conservation and education through a nonpartisan commission failed with a compromise "section 26" which permits creation of a commission or board by the legislature that can be dissolved by the next legislature. Members serve at the governor's pleasure, which provides for members little stability. Conservationists must insist on a constitutional amendment providing for a stable nonpolitical form of commission with staggered terms, removable for only specific cause and with wide powers in policy-making decisions. The day-to-day operations should be left to the department. Under the present government wounds created by the current administration will most certainly be vindicated by more wounds in the next administration. I cite an amended constitution, patterned after Missouri's amendment, as Alaska's greatest conservation need.

Now for a few remarks on our wilderness wildlife. Generally the larger and the longer lived the animals, the less erratic their population levels. The brown, grizzly, and polar bear, the mountain goat and wolverine have shown no dramatic natural changes in population levels. Recently most of these have declined under the hand of man. On some wilderness areas not reached by man there exists stable population of fish and game. I have in mind certain mountain goat, sheep, grayling, and cutthroat populations where apparently the environmental resistance parallels the reproductive capability. Here the biologist must carefully appraise the effect of any hunting, fishing, or other activities of man before endangering the species. I place goat and grayling in this delicate category, also those animals on the edge of their range such as sheep in part of the Brooks, Alaska, and Wrangell mountain ranges. It should be an axiom that any species on the edge of its range must be "delicate," else there would be no edge.

The polar bear has all but vacated the Alaska mainland and the recent oil exploration will further discourage its land ventures. I apparently have more concern over the plight of the polar bear, because of increased hunting pressure, than some biologists. It is hoped that the ambitious telemetry studies by the state and the Bureau of Sport Fisheries and Wildlife will give us more accurate information on numbers, movements, and the relation of Alaskan bear along our coast to the circumpolar populations of polar bear. The existing hunting restrictions and the so-called "landing law" are still not adequate to control the kill of polar bear. Sooner or later, a combination of vessel and aircraft will ply the arctic waters, much as along the coast of Norway, and then Alaska will require the support of federal regulation. I want to emphasize that state regulation alone is not adequate. This might apply also to some of the marine mammals. The late Senator E. L. Bartlett was instrumental in promoting the first polar bear conference and securing funds for the current studies. We must rely on the new Senators Ted Stevens and Mike Gravel and Congressman Howard Pollock from Alaska to seek support from Congress for continued interest in the polar bear. And here again I suspect that the interest of the national Sierra Club will be more important than the interest of the people of Alaska. Many disdain the use of aircraft in taking of any wildlife, including polar bear. Eventually this must cease.

The interior grizzly bear and the peninsula brown bear are in jeopardy because of their vulnerability to aircraft spotting, illegal hunting, and wanton killing. I exclude the Kenai Peninsula and Kodiak Island because I believe the staff of the national moose and bear ranges and the bureau will not permit an excessive kill on these locations. There always exists the threat of wiping out national refuges in the same manner they were created—by Executive order. Comments have already been made at this conference that we should take action toward Congressional support that will sustain the original Executive orders on which all the refuges in Alaska were created. The Alaska Sportsmen's Council has long supported this action to give the refuges a more secure status. To date the Alaska Congressional delegation has failed to support such a move because of the large portion of Alaska in a withdrawn status. More recently the interest in oil on the Kenai Peninsula and in the Arctic, and the native land claims have made the problem even more difficult.

The coastal brown bear is less vulnerable because of the generally unfavorable weather and heavy forest cover, but fewer bear elsewhere, diverts hunting pressure from the interior to the coast. Also the increased logging activity results either directly or indirectly in some additional legal or illegal hunting and the killing of nuisance animals.

If we could measure the illegal bear kill we would probably find it more serious than the legal kill. Part of the illegal kill is by uninformed pothunters, some by fishermen who think the bear a threat to salmon, and some by those who simply fear bear. Incidentally, I can assure you from personal experience that the breath of a brown bear makes one a pretty good tree climber. Education and preventative enforcement are needed and both will require more time and more money. Perhaps the only solution to legal hunting is by a strict quota and a regulated harvest, perhaps with permits issued by lottery. Such action is made difficult because guided hunts for nonresidents are planned one or two years in advance. But until the Alaska Department of Fish and Game can provide the regulation and the enforcement, the big brown bear will continue in jeopardy.

Many suggest that the destruction of the environment by logging will destroy the coastal brownie. I think not, simply because the logging is spread over a large area, over many years, and because only a small part of the watershed, in most cases less than 30 percent, will ever be cut. The climax forest is not necessary for brown bear, as is shown in the Alaskan Peninsula and western Kodiak Island where bear have no large tree cover. The early forest succession following logging may in some respects be superior to the climax forest because of the succulent grasses, forbs, and berries. Within 10 years of cutting, the seedling conifers begin to form dense growth of spruce, hemlock, and cedar, which is actually better bear cover than the old climax forest. So I do not hold the concern of some that logging will eventually doom the brown bear.

Turning now to the ungulates, moose, caribou, and deer populations have had their ups and downs. In the past 40 years the moose have extended their range to coastal areas, down the peninsula, and the western and Arctic coasts. The writings of explorers such as Vilhjalmur Stephansson say there was little evidence of moose on the Arctic coast until late in the last century. This is due in part to the changing environment in the face of glacier recession, partly due to better law enforcement, and partly due to the presence of fewer miners and trappers in the hinterland during winter when moose in open country and heavy snow were vulnerable to the dog team and hunter. Incidentally, I learned that the last dog-team mail trip had left Whitehorse just the other day. The snowmobile now becomes a true hazard since it will replace the dog team. Caribou have increased following the violent reindeer-caribou decline of the 30's. The recent hunting of cow moose and use of aircraft have provoked much public controversy. Locally, the removal of cows has reflected reduced populations but has resulted, in some instances, in better use of both the moose and the range.

Dall sheep are protected from legal hunting by the ¾-curl horn limit, meaning that a ram is legal only if it has a horn that is 270 degrees or more in circumference. Since it requires six years or more for a ram to grow a ¾-curl horn, it has the effect of protecting the younger rams. The regulation was promoted by biologist Robert F. Scott in the early 50's and adopted by the former Alaska Game Commission and the present Board of Fish and Game. Since then the sheep have held their own, and in fact have had some increase. The illegal kill associated with legal hunting may require more restrictions and better enforcement, particularly in accessible areas where small bands occur.

The hunter's conduct and hunting ethics in Alaska, as elsewhere, are degrading, and sometimes downright disgusting. Alaska cannot long afford wildlife merely as a replacement for a call to the butcher for a steak. The thrill of the chase and the challenge of a hunt should not be the minimum time between.leaving the bar, taking a short airplane ride, spotting a moose, landing, shooting, and dragging a hot bloody carcass through the plane and then back to the bar. This kind of hunting has now continued long enough to be considered standard. This scares me. Hunting should be a true wilderness experience. Ethics must intervene, the use of aircraft be severely restricted. Alaskans now do not tolerate the use of helicopters for hunting and there is growing animosity against the winged aircraft and the snowmobile. Unfortunately, modern day game biologists are overtrained and overimbued with the concept of controlling huntable game populations, regardless of the conduct of the hunter. Last fall I hunted for a week, apparently on a route followed by a pop maniac, for whenever I approached a beautiful muskeg vista, there was an aluminum pop can stuck on a stub. Pity the poor museum curator for the artifacts of this decade. How long before we ban the nonreturnable nondegradable container?

Depressed fur prices have removed the pressure from fur bearers except where beaver, muskrat, mink, and marten are the only source of income to some villages. The upland game bird and shorebird numbers are little affected by man, as yet, in Alaska. We hope the Rampart Dam proposal is embalmed and laid away together with the never-to-be-used brass dedication plate, the wilderness of the Yukon flats thus to be saved for its grayling, muskrat, ducks, geese, and moose. Here will some day be a wilderness boating area for those who can endure the mosquito. Boats leave no worn tether spots or eroded trails common to the horse-access wilderness areas.

Alaskan friends of the wolf will ensure a place for this truly wilderness predator. In 1968, both the legislature and the Board of Fish and Game acted to control the limit-bounties on wolves, and eliminated both the coyote and wolverine bounties. The wolf bounty will eventually go and actual protection be given the wolf. Progress is slow but we need to give patient consideration to the strong feelings of those who witness predation and see it only as a threat to prey species on which they depend for food.

Some of Alaska's most beautiful wilderness is accessible only by boat. Here marine animals are an interesting part of the fauna. Whales, though common in some locations, have never recovered from the early whaling days. Some are still being harvested by the Canadians, Japanese, and Russians. A few are taken and well used by the Eskimo of the Arctic coast. The limited and difficult walrus studies, though inadequate, reveal no cause for serious alarm. Regrettably, crippling losses from hunting and the taking of walrus for ivory alone represent a loss not yet resolved. Sea lions are everywhere persecuted, but still common. The returns of the fur seal and sea otter are successful conservation sagas of which the United States and treaty nations can be proud. Since World War II the Fish and Wildlife Service has looked to establishing sea otter on its entire former Pacific coast range but has been stymied by problems of transplants and funds. The state, under the able leadership of biologist John Vania, has made successful transplants.

The Atomic Energy Commission (AEC), which is working on Amchitka, rebuilt the airport and made, for the first time since World War II, an opportunity for fast air service. While the AEC does not acknowledge a blast threat to the otter or environment, it provided assistance and funds for removal of surplus sea otter from Amchitka for transplants the summer of 1968. The Department of Fish and Game's plans included commitments for stock to British Columbia and the State of Washington. Transplants are costly and success will depend not only on techniques but on the degree of protection from target shooters.

In summary then, industrial development now faces much of Alaska. Pioneering concepts and wilderness concepts are incompatible but Alaskans are awakening and the people maturing to the values of the wild country, uncontaminated. Wilderness wildlife to endure will require the support of an enlightened public. A constitutional amendment must be the basis for a more stable fish and game administration in Alaska. Conservationists must look to our progress and successes and not be daunted by our everyday failures. Alaskans have organized two units affiliated with the Sierra Club and this is a good sign of the growing interest of our people. Alaskans, too, contribute to the rise in human numbers with a young population and high birth rate.

# WILDERNESS STUDIES ON ALASKA WILDLIFE REFUGES

*Willard A. Troyer*
Wilderness Biologist
Bureau of Sport Fisheries and Wildlife, Anchorage, Alaska

The Alaska national wildlife refuges contain some of the unique and extensive potential wilderness areas remaining in the United States today. In these lands one finds a scenic array of lakes, rivers, beaches, glaciers, forests, and tundra inhabited by a diversity of wildlife. Caribou, brown bear, moose, black bear, mountain goats, Dall sheep, wolf, wolverine, and other wilderness animals are still abundant. The habitat also harbors hundreds of bald eagles; innumerable potholes support extensive waterfowl nesting grounds; and on the islands along the precipitous shorelines are some of the greatest marine bird colonies remaining in North America.

In addition to the scenic and wildlife resources, some of the areas contain significantly valuable archaeological sites. These sites along the Bering Sea and the Arctic Ocean may yet provide a key to many of the unknown facts of primitive man's migration into North America.

The 18 national wildlife refuges in Alaska vary in size from the 42-acre Hazy Islands to the 8,900,000-acre Arctic Range and collectively constitute slightly less than 20 million acres.

The Wilderness Act of 1964 directed the secretary of the interior, during the following 10-year period, to review all the roadless areas in the national wildlife refuges in excess of 5,000 acres and all roadless islands to determine their suitability for inclusion in the National Wilderness System.

During the first three-year period of wilderness review in Alaska, field studies were completed and public hearings held on six of the small island refuges. These included the Bering Sea, Bogoslof, Forrester, Hazy, St. Lazaria, and Tuxedni islands. All are occupied by large seabird colonies and have been recommended for wilderness status except for a small portion of Tuxedni Island.

Three more of the Alaska refuges were reviewed during the past summer. Chamisso Island, a small refuge in Kotzebue Sound, harbors the only pelagic seabird colonies in that portion of Alaska. The 25,000-acre Simeonof Island Refuge* lies in the Shumagin Island group off the southeastern coast of the Alaska Peninsula. It includes all the tidal waters within one mile of the island and is the only refuge in Alaska which includes jurisdiction over offshore lands. These waters are rich in marine resources and provide habitat for hundreds of sea otter and hair seal.

The 415,000-acre Izembek National Wildlife Range on the southwestern extremity of the Alaska Peninsula surrounds the largest known eelgrass beds in the world and is one of the more vital waterfowl refuges in Alaska. Nearly the entire Pacific black brant goose population feeds on the eelgrass during fall and spring migrations, and millions of other waterfowl and shorebirds utilize its vast resources. Under the Submerged Lands and Alaska Statehood acts, the saltwater lagoons do not come under the jurisdiction of the Bureau of Sport Fisheries and Wildlife. Oil companies are currently interested in prospecting for oil, but to date the State of Alaska has refused them exploratory privileges because of the possible danger to the valuable lagoon waters. We are very happy at these efforts so far and the Alaska Fish and Game Department is currently negotiating to gain management jurisdiction of these tidal lands so that they may dedicate them to waterfowl and other wildlife use.

A portion of the central part of the Izembek uplands was occupied by military forces during World War II and is still disfigured by deteriorating Quonset huts and a maze of roads. The access road to Izembek Lagoon from the nearby town of Cold Bay is also in this vicinity. The remainder of the uplands is a true wilderness with glaciated peaks exceeding 6,000 feet in elevation, broad valleys, and rolling tundra bisected by numerous streams. Brown bear, caribou, wolves, and wolverine thrive in this habitat. Approximately 300,000 acres will qualify for consideration as wilderness. Public hearings will be held May 16, 1970.

* Public hearings were held on Chamisso and Simeonof on November 13, 1969, in Anchorage, Alaska. No opposition to wilderness classification was raised.

Field studies for the Kenai National Moose Range will be completed during 1969. The 1,730,000-acre range is located on the Kenai Peninsula near the population center of Alaska. It is divided into two major geographic features consisting of the Kenai Mountains rising to 6,000 feet and their rolling foothills. The great Harding Icefield, with numerous glacial tributaries interspersed among these mountains, is of unmatched scenic splendor. The western two-thirds constitutes the Kenai lowlands, composed of rolling hills, muskegs, forests, streams, and is dotted with over 1,000 lakes.

The lakes and streams support a tremendous freshwater fishery and supply the spawning habitat for millions of salmon that ascend these waters each year. Wildlife abounds on the range consisting of moose, Dall sheep, mountain goat, black bear, brown bear, wolverine, and numerous small animals. Loons, grebes, and other water birds occupy the lakes, as do a substantial number of nesting trumpeter swans. Thus, the diversity of scenery and wildlife is unmatched, and it was these sources that caused George Shiras III to write of his 1911 travels in the *National Geographic Magazine*: "Were all of Alaska erased from the map except the Kenai Peninsula and its immediately adjacent waters, there would yet remain in duplicate that which constitutes the more unique and that which typifies the whole of this wonderful country."

Since his writings, the area has been subjected to increased pressures of civilization. A major highway now bisects the range, and recreational visitor use exceeds 300,000 annually. In 1958 most of the lowland portion was opened to oil exploration. Now approximately 2,000 miles of seismic lines crisscross the forests. Numerous access roads have been constructed to exploratory wells and one major oil field. Yet even with this commercial exploitation, portions of the forested lowland lake country still maintain much of their pristine character.

One of the primary objectives of the moose range is to maintain a fairly large population of moose. Since moose are dependent on a young forest in a seral stage of development, much of this lowland wintering area will be manipulated to meet this requirement. These activities then would conflict with the wilderness concept. However, it is imperative that selected portions of the lowland remain in a natural state. Currently, a canoe system linking nearly 100 lakes is being managed in as primitive a state as possible and it provides wilderness-type recreation. However, this entire area is covered by oil leases and whether any of it can be retained as wilderness remains in doubt.

All of the mountain area is still in a natural state and has not been subjected to commercial development. This region, called the Andy Simon Natural Area and comprising 830,000 acres, is a candidate wilderness area and will be reviewed for this purpose. We are hoping to get most of it in the wilderness system.

The 1,815,000-acre Kodiak National Wildlife Refuge covers about two-thirds of Kodiak Island. It was established in 1941 primarily to preserve the natural habitat of the Kodiak bear (called brown bear in other parts of coastal Alaska). It is a rugged land of mountains, valleys, and deep fiord-like bays. The greater portion of the valleys and mountainsides is covered with dense thickets of alder, willow, and elderberry interspersed with grassy meadows. Alpine meadows cover the higher mountains and on the southern extremity is rolling tundra. Flowers grow in profusion in this maritime climate, including fireweed and lupine, which splash the mountainsides in scenic splendor.

The rocky coastline, some 800 miles in length, harbors many seals, sea lions, and seabird rookeries, and whales and porpoises are found in the offshore waters. Salmon migrate up the numerous streams, and this is the home of approximately 2,000 Kodiak bear. Our national bird, the bald eagle, is an abundant nester along the streams and shorelines.

Although numerous commercial fishing sites ring portions of the seashore, the interior of the island is a roadless expanse of true wilderness. Alaska's big brown bear, and I cannot emphasize this too much, is dependent on a wilderness environment for its very existence. Pristine conditions are also essential to the survival of the bald eagle.

This, then, is a refuge with unusual wilderness qualities. These characteristics must be maintained if the objectives of the refuge are to be met. Yet I am very concerned because there has not been a great deal of national interest expressed in maintaining a wilderness environment on Kodiak and certainly, there has been little such interest from the local people.

Few people know the Aleutian Islands, and they are considered by many as remote, fogbound, bleak, and lifeless. Yet here are islands rich in wildlife resources, scenic beyond comprehension, relatively available with modern means of transportation facilities, where climatic conditions are not as bleak as many believe.

The Aleutian Islands, like a series of stepping stones, extend into the north Pacific from the Alaska Peninsula for over 1,000 miles. The nearly 70 named islands and the other smaller islets in aggregate constitute some 2,700,000 acres, a total of nearly 200 different islands. Although the Aleutians are treeless, supporting a dwarfed flora of willow and alder, alpine heather and meadows, they are of picturesque beauty. Active volcanoes tower in the sky; flowers grow profusely in season; and the irregular, rocky shorelines, reefs, and sand beaches create a special wild mood.

The islands provide sanctuary for unbelievable numbers of seabird colonies. The offshore waters with their extensive kelp beds are rich in marine life. It is here that the rare sea otter is making its comeback.

The largest of the islands, Unimak, is also inhabited by brown bear, caribou, and wolves. It alone constitutes nearly one million acres and is an area of high wilderness quality. On this island, Mount Shishaldin raises its lofty volcanic head to more than 9,000 feet. Salmon streams radiate from the mountains and flow through the grassy plains to seashore.

Many of the Aleutian Islands are completely unmodified by man; others are covered with decaying military remains of World War II, which mar the terrain extensively. Modern military and Atomic Energy Commission activities on some of the islands have also changed the natural environment, and several islands or portions of them will no longer qualify for wilderness status.

The Executive order that established the Aleutian Islands Refuge in 1913 stated that the reservation shall not interfere with the use of the islands for lighthouse, military, or naval purposes. Whether this exception will preclude any of these islands from being placed into the National Wilderness System still awaits a legal opinion.

Certainly the islands vary in physical characteristics and each has to stand on its own merits as to its wilderness qualities. Therefore, we in the Bureau of Sport Fisheries and Wildlife do not believe that the Aleutians can be covered in one wilderness review. We also do not think that this would be fair to conservation groups who also want to do some field studies in the area. We are now considering completing the wilderness studies by island groups. The task will be tremendous and time consuming, as each of some 200 islands and islets will have to be visited and its existing natural resources recorded. We have recently recruited a man who will be assigned to such a study on a full-time basis. Wilderness field studies will be completed this year on Unimak, Amak and Caton islands.*

The Nunivak National Wildlife Refuge is located in the Bering Sea about 20 miles from the mainland. This island has a tundra vegetation. Margins of the island are of low relief, but a number of old volcanoes occupy the interior regions. The million-acre-plus refuge was established as a sanctuary for musk-ox. The 31 animals transplanted

* Field studies have been completed on the million-acre Unimak Island and public hearings will be held in early 1971.

to the island in 1935 and 1936 have now increased to over 700 and are in danger of overgrazing their habitat. The island also harbors a sea-bird rookery of murres, puffins, gulls, and kittiwakes extending some 20 miles in length. Thousands of waterfowl and shorebirds use its lagoons, and a thriving reindeer industry provides income to resident Eskimos. The conflicts that might occur with a reindeer industry on lands under the wilderness system have not been determined but will need to be reviewed.

The Clarence Rhode National Wildlife Refuge formerly consisted of 1,870,016 acres but with a recent addition is now in excess of 2,800,000 acres. It lies in the Yukon-Kuskokwim Delta and is of low-lying tundra containing countless lakes, ponds, and brackish wetlands.

This extensive roadless area is one of the finest waterfowl production areas in North America. It is the major nesting area for black brant and for cackling, emperor, and Pacific white-fronted geese. Pintail, mallard, green-winged teal, and eider ducks are also well represented. However, for all their abundance, waterfowl are not as conspicuous as the innumerable smaller birds that fill the tundra air with a variety of sounds. Songbirds, gulls, terns, jaegers, godwits, plovers, sandpipers, dunlins, turnstones, phalaropes, and many others are present in impressive numbers.

The wetlands also support a tremendous population of fur-bearing animals. Fur, consisting of mink, fox, and land otter, is one of the major cash crops to the natives living in the area. Formerly, all the trapping was accomplished by dog sled but in recent years, the abominable snow machine has become more popular. This method of native use of the area may provide some complications in establishing wilderness in this region.

In the northeastern corner of Alaska lies the 8,900,000-acre Arctic National Wildlife Range, one of the greatest wilderness areas remaining on the North American continent. When it was established less than 10 years ago, opponents to the plan were often quoted as saying: "There was no need for setting aside such an area, for no one will ever set foot in that region of Alaska anyhow." Today oil exploration activities are near its border, and pressures are mounting to open up a portion of this great wildlife range to exploration.

This may be our last opportunity to preserve an arctic environment in pristine condition large enough to be biologically self-sufficient. Here is a wilderness where great herds of caribou roam unaffected by man; where the wolf howls under the northern sky; and the predator-prey relationship between wolf and caribou takes its natural course. The moving herds of buffalo so vividly described by western pioneers have vanished from the West. Are we going to let this same thing happen to the vast moving bands of caribou? Yes, there are other herds of caribou in Alaska, but are we sure that land use practices will not destroy many migration routes of these last great populations? A large tract of land dedicated to this cause may be our last chance to assure perpetuation of such an unusual spectacle.

The Brooks Range of Alaska bisects the Arctic Wildlife Range. To the north lies the vast arctic tundra, the summer range of over 100,000 caribou. The mountains are spectacular, and the wall of peaks is dominated by Mt. Chamberlain (9,131 feet) and Mt. Michelson (9,239 feet). To the south lie valleys warmed by winds from the Yukon River Basin. Rivers wind serpentine courses through a valley floor of lakes, oxbow sloughs, groves of spruce and cottonwood trees.

Not only do caribou and wolf thrive in this wildlife range but also moose, Dall sheep, grizzlies, black bear, wolverine, and a variety of smaller animals and birds.

Wilderness studies will get under way this summer on the Arctic National Wildlife Range but because of the vast size of the area and our limited knowledge of its resources, it is not anticipated that studies will be completed before the end of 1971. Some of you may be interested in knowing that we did get an appropriation this year for the first time. After July 1, 1969, there will be two refuge managers, who will manage this vast area by aircraft patrol.

The newly created Cape Newenham National Wildlife Refuge juts into the Bering Sea in southwestern Alaska. Covering 265,000 acres, it lies in one of the remote regions of Alaska. Storm-tossed seas, winds and rugged terrain have kept man from exploiting the area. The cape, surrounded by waters rich in marine resources, is the site of a great "bird city." A million or more murres, kittiwakes, and puffins make up the major bird population and cormorants, guillemots, gulls, and other seabirds are plentiful.

The rocky shorelines provide protection for the vast bird rookeries, and seals and sea lions by the hundreds abound in the water. In season, walrus haul out on the rocks. At the root of the cape are large, shallow tidal lagoons containing extensive eelgrass beds. These beds are used by several hundred thousand waterfowl, which pause to feed and rest during their spring and fall migrations. Several large streams drain the area and are filled with salmon during season—to the delight of the brown bear. In short, Cape Newenham is the site of one of America's most spectacular wildlife displays. Like so many of the refuges in Alaska, its value lies in retaining its physical and biological characteristics in a natural state.

Cape Newenham does have wilderness qualities, but no timetable has yet been set for conducting wilderness reviews.

Another small refuge, which will be reviewed for wilderness status during the year, is the Semidi Islands. These islands lie in the Gulf of Alaska between Kodiak Island and the Alaska Peninsula. The eight islands which make up the refuge encompass 8,400 acres of land. Their rocky cliffs support huge seabird rookeries of puffins, auklets, petrels, murres, and kittiwakes, and a fulmar colony which is thought to be the largest in Alaska. Currently the islands are remote, unmodified, and rarely visited by man.

This, then, is a brief report of the natural resources and wilderness values of the Alaskan refuges. In total, the lands within these refuges comprise one of the greatest opportunities for increasing the acreage of the National Wilderness System. They are quality lands established primarily for wildlife populations. They have, however, unique scenic qualities and are diverse in physical and biological characteristics.

The acreage that eventually is included in the wilderness system will depend greatly on you—the interested public. There are many things that cloud the issue and many problems will arise. The Alaska Native Land Claim issue has not been settled. How many acres will go to this cause and what rights will the natives be given which may interfere with wilderness status are questions that cannot be answered at this time. What additional areas in the Aleutians will be disqualified for consideration as wilderness by man's activities? Currently, there is little interest from a majority of the population in Alaska. They are endowed with a great wilderness area, and many fail to see the need for setting aside wilderness for the future. This is our biggest problem—getting the people behind us.

Fortunately, however, some residents of this great state are becoming concerned and demanding that our natural resources be conserved. The Alaska Chapter of the Sierra Club, formed in 1968, is growing rapidly. The Alaska Conservation Society is increasing its membership. The Izaak Walton League, Alaska Sportsmen's Council, and other conservation groups are demanding a greater voice in state affairs and making citizens aware of their rich heritage. Commercial fishermen and other groups directly dependent on natural resources are suddenly becoming aware of the need for long-term conservation practices. Pitted against these groups are many interests who are more concerned with exploitation than conservation of Alaska's resources.

Wilderness in Alaska must be a concern of the people of the nation. These are your federal lands; management policy of the future will greatly depend on your efforts.

# DISCUSSION

*Harry B. Crandell, planning officer, Bureau of Sport Fisheries and Wildlife:* I bring you greetings from the Land of the Great White Father. I also bring the greetings to our feathered friends in San Francisco from their feathered friends in Washington, where the birds do not stop coughing till noon.

I am not going to comment on the wilderness program in Alaska. I was sitting here listening to Will Troyer and I thought it was obvious that the wilderness program is in real good hands up there and anything that I could add would probably be superfluous. Instead, perhaps you might be interested in a very brief summary of some of the conflicts that we have run into in our wilderness program within the refuge system. Just a few places in the Wilderness Act apply to us, and lawyers are always interpreting them for us.

It is very difficult to come up with a wilderness program without previous guidelines. A wilderness philosophy has been developing since 1966. I think that we now have an emerging philosophy—an emerging program that is going to make a tremendous contribution to the American people. One of the first things that we discovered when we got into the wilderness review process was that the act was not specific regarding national parks and wildlife refuges, whereas it was more specific regarding national forests. As you know, the Forest Service was charged with studying, reviewing, and recommending to the Congress on suitability or nonsuitability as wilderness of already established primitive areas. But here was the park system of some

183

25 million acres and the refuge system of some now 30 million acres with no such charge. So, we developed a philosophy that through field studies we would determine whether a refuge qualified as wilderness or not, and went through an initial selection process of those refuges that remained in a natural or seminatural condition, or contained wilderness resources as set forth in the Wilderness Act. Just last month (February, 1969) we published in the *Federal Register* a list of 90 refuges, containing around 25 million acres, that qualified for study. We have finished reviews, including public hearings, on about one million acres within 30 of these. Twenty-seven of them are on Capitol Hill right now awaiting Congressional action. Further, we decided that refuges qualify for review—not wilderness areas. This was because of the problems we were confronted with in meeting the one-third requirement of the Wilderness Act. For example, we discovered that on a larger refuge we might have a half-dozen wilderness areas, or one wilderness area or, in some cases, two in the same refuge. This caused numbers to vacillate all over the blackboard. We had a difficult time telling somebody how far along we were in the program. However, we are on schedule. We expect to finish the job in 1974 within the time frame established by the Wilderness Act.

Another little conflict which had to be resolved was interpretation of the term "roadless island." It is in the act. Section 3(c) charges the secretary of the interior to review all roadless areas of 5,000 acres or more within the national park system and all such areas of, and all roadless islands within, the national wildlife refuge system. So the lawyers had a lot of fun defining the word "island." Does an ecological island qualify for review or does it have to be surrounded by water? However, we have more or less limited the definition to islands surrounded by water—the common definition. During our first Congressional hearings in the summer of 1968, we very deliberately brought this point up to the Congressional committee. We asked the question: "Is this little island that we have before you today what you meant when you passed the Wilderness Act?" And the Committee told us that that is exactly what they meant. Now, the reason that we brought this up was that 45 of the 90 study areas are islands. And they vary in size all the way from a few acres to over one million acres in Alaska. If the Congress did not mean these islands, field studies and reviews would be much less extensive than at present.

We feel that the Wilderness Act is one of the best things that has ever happened to the national wildlife refuge system. Very few refuges have legal protection afforded by an act of Congress. Almost all refuges are established by Executive order, secretarial order, public lands withdrawal, and purchased lands which are only approved by the

Migratory Bird Conservation Commission. So, just by a stroke of a pen the refuge can be dissolved, transferred, or abolished. But should a piece of the refuge be put into the wilderness system (or all of it), it would be protected by the Wilderness Act. In other words, once given Congressional protection it would take an act of Congress to abolish the refuge rather than just the signing of a bureaucrat's name to a typewritten document.

Being a native Coloradan I have a very definite opinion of what I think wilderness is. And it is, surprisingly enough, very similar to what most Westerners have in mind. I have learned since living in Washington, however, that not all people have the same thought. When one says "wilderness," being from the West, I have the high mountain peak, Forest Service-type wilderness in mind. But to people in the East, Great Plains, and South, "wilderness" is something different. We discovered this phenomenon in the Oregon Islands wilderness proposal where originally we recommended that these little bird rocks off the coast not be considered as wilderness for these reasons: (1) very small, (2) people couldn't get on them because of the heavy seas, (3) we did not want people on them because of the bird populations, (4) if you could get on the islands, you could look back to the shore and see highways, houses, and other evidences of man. Then Assistant Secretary Stanley Cain said: "Let's go to the public hearing and I'll make the decision after we get the citizen's views." At the hearing those people who lived around Highway 101 said: "Put it in wilderness—put it in the system. We want to make certain that from our homes we can always look out and see those rocks and know they are going to stay the same as they are today." So, the islands were recommended and are before the Congress right now. All of these kinds of inputs help to develop philosophy. Our philosophy now is that wilderness is relative. It is in the eyes of the beholder. What one person views as wilderness, another might not. Our wilderness reviews are based on this concept—what the local people feel to be appropriate will guide our determination, not what our individual concept of wilderness might be.

Wilderness is a social resource, since it benefits people. Possibly more people benefit from wilderness than will ever visit an area. This is because of knowledge that it is there. We, I think, learned this from the whooping crane. Very few people have ever seen a whooping crane, but they get a lot of satisfaction reading that the whooping crane arrived back at the Aransas Refuge each fall. So, with all the pressures that are going to be placed upon our resources in the future, we feel wilderness should be established throughout the country depending on the views of local people. Therefore, our attitude at public hearings is to present the proposal to the public and ascertain their views.

I would like to close with this: We can make the future happen. Even if we do nothing the future still is going to happen. But, by doing something, such as preserving wilderness, we make the kind of future we would like to have. As Charles Kettering said: "I am very interested in the future because I intend to live in it."

*Celia M. Hunter, chairman, Alaska Wilderness Council:* A few minutes ago I was asked: "What are you Alaskans going to do about all this?" And that was what I had in mind talking about this afternoon. In the first place, Alaskans are doing something about "all this" finally. It took us a while to get started because, as various panel members said, many residents started out with the idea that Alaska was the last frontier and their slogan was "get in, get it, and get out."

But as time went on more people came, liked what they found and settled down. Then they began to be aware of wildlife values which had not really mattered to them before, but which began to be the reason they wanted to stay. Then they became aware of increasing threats to those values. This was during the big military construction boom days of the 1950's when the DEW Line was being built. Suddenly Alaskans realized that their wilderness was finite because it was being ringed around on the north by the DEW Line, while it was being attacked on the south by all the other developments.

We have, for instance in the Cook Inlet area, urban problems that are as severe as any you have in the lower 48. An area there has about 100,000 people and the bumper-to-bumper traffic caused by people trying to return to town on a Sunday afternoon is just about as bad as trying to cross the San Francisco Bay Bridge in the rush hour.

The conservation movement in Alaska, however, is coming of age. Before 1960, few people there would have called themselves conservationists. As a matter of fact, when there were hearings on the formation of the Arctic Wildlife Range in the late 50's, Charles Callison, who then was with the National Wildlife Federation, testified before the Alaska Legislature in favor of the creation of the wildlife range. He was very poorly received by the legislators because they felt he was an outsider who was trying to interfere in Alaska's business—telling Alaska what to do with her own land.

It was this episode that actually created the Alaska Conservation Society. A number of us in the College area got together with John Buckley, who was then at the university, and decided to make our testimony jointly before Senator E. L. Bartlett when he brought the hearings to Fairbanks. We planned for each of us to present one certain area of argument for the range. Out of that perhaps one dozen people in 1960, the Alaska Conservation Society has grown until today there are over 480 members who are Alaskans, regular voting members, and well over 450 members outside of Alaska. This represents a tremendous increase in interest, in concern, and money spent and available for conservation in Alaska. It is still a long way from being enough, but it does give us hope.

Another asset that has developed recently is an explosion in conservation interest. Since 1966 the Alaska Conservation Society has added three local chapters to the parent society which still functions in the Fairbanks area. It may seem odd that we have local interests there which are getting in the way of our state interests, but we hope that our new chapter will take care of them.

Alaskans concerned with preserving some of the state's present de facto wilderness through inclusion within the National Wilderness Preservation System or other status, including creation of a state park system with provisions for zoning of wilderness areas, met in Juneau in February, 1969. The meeting was a tribute to the growth of conservation concern among Alaskans, for it included representatives of at least eight active conservation organizations, as well as drawing representatives of most of the government agencies having anything to do with land use classification and administration. As a result of this conference, the conservation groups formed the Alaska Wilderness Council. The council consists of representatives from each group, and will attempt to coordinate the efforts of conservationists to pinpoint outstanding wilderness areas and work for their preservation. Funding for the council efforts will be entirely from voluntary contributions, and funds are needed to get the work under way.

We receive support and assistance from other groups. The Alaska Chapter of the Sierra Club has two active groups functioning in Juneau and Anchorage. There is a new conservation interest on the part of the Southeast Alaska Mountaineering Association in Ketchikan. The Alaska Sportsmen's Council has been swinging more and more into the conservation concept rather than simply representing the hunting and fishing fraternity.

Another asset is the fact that the Alaska public opinion climate is changing rapidly. A few years ago, if you had written a letter to the editor in favor of saving the wolf, you would have been jumped on literally from every angle. Today, it is not the people who commend the wolf but those who denounce him who are jumped on in many knowledgeable and effective letters to the editor.

On the liability side, I think you have heard enough from professional resource managers at this conference who have outlined the situation in all its complexity. It is not a simple problem because it affects every level of activity and every geographic area. Just to mention snow machines will illustrate just one problem. The snow machine is one of the major threats to de facto wilderness in Alaska today because of its extreme mobility. In the Fairbanks area alone there are over 3,000 of them. In the Anchorage area there are over 6,000. Almost all of the native villages are using snow machines to replace the dog team. As a matter of fact there was a report in one of the papers telling about how the last holdout for a dog team in a certain village had taken to the "iron dog" finally. This means a lot in terms of the threat of intrusion on such wilderness areas as the upper part of the Koyukuk River in the Brooks Range, which we would like to see included in the proposed Gates to the Arctic national park.

Although Urban (Pete) Nelson has indicated that we do have more support at the present time for the conservation viewpoint in the legislature of Alaska, it still comes from a very small proportion of our elected representatives. One brief illustration will show something of the attitude of our Congressional delegation. One of our Juneau members was talking to one of our United States senators about the threat to Glacier Bay National Monument because of the mining and so on there. The senator said: "What's Glacier Bay?"

This sort of thing indicates that we have a tremendous educational job ahead of us as far as educating our legislature and Congressional delegation on the natural resource field. Since our Congressional delegation must introduce the legislation that will put areas in Alaska into the National Wilderness Preservation System, we are going to have to do an effective job of educating them quickly.

Now I would like to tell you of some of the things we need in Alaska. First of all we need some top people to work part time or full time on conservation problems. We need to lobby during the legislative sessions and pull together the separate efforts of all the different organizations, both government and private, that are concerned with land use. Then we need active and informed support from people outside Alaska. Many of you are members of the Alaska Conservation Society and receive our *Conservation Review*. We receive some financial support from outside groups for this publication to appear in printed form. We are very appreciative of this aid because we feel it is now far superior to the mimeographed one we had before.

We need your help in testimony when Alaska wilderness areas come up for Congressional review. This is a place where your numbers can count. Alaska has a population of under 300,000 people, even today, and not all Alaskans are fully behind all these conservation efforts.

I think that is the major message that I would like to leave with you and I would like to express appreciation to the Sierra Club for the opportunity that Alaska has had here to present the case for our wilderness and for our wildlife.

[Time did not permit questions following discussion. After the conference, Urban Nelson prepared these answers to the questions he had received during the session:

*Question:* Would you comment on the value and feasibility of a conservation amendment to the United States Constitution?

*Urban C. Nelson:* A citizen's right to clean air and water, his right to have all values weighed in publicly financed developments, and his right to have public renewable resources managed on sustained yield basis ought to be defined in the Constitution. Some might argue that one should not have the right to destroy one's own personal real property and thus deny future Americans the use thereof. Destruction of land through soil erosion because of poor farming practices, or destruction of land through strip mining without restoration, or destruction of unique American history, fauna, or flora is a loss that the entire nation endures, not just the current owner.

*Question:* Are there any species of shorebirds that might be affected by oil exploration on the North Slope?

*Mr. Nelson:* Both the long-distance-flying golden and black-bellied plover nest along the Arctic coast, as well as godwits, turnstones, and sandpipers. Pectoral, red-backed, and Baird's sandpipers are very abundant. Some damage is certain, but the extent will be dependent on better definition of both the extent of breeding ranges and the extent of oil development.

*Question:* How many reindeer now live in Alaska?

*Mr. Nelson:* Reindeer are the private property of individual or groups of native people, and as such they have the same protection as other domestic stock. The United States government also has reindeer. Current inventories show about 20,000 on the Seward Peninsula, 10,000 on Nunivak Island, and a total of about 2,000 on Kodiak, Hagemeister, and St. Lawrence islands.

*Question:* What laws exist curbing the use of airplanes in killing polar bear? What additional laws are needed to insure their preservation?

*Mr. Nelson:* State law prohibits taking polar bear *from* any aircraft, but does not prohibit spotting or locating animals. The state landing law prohibits possession of or transport in or out of Alaska of polar bear or parts unless taken in accordance with state regulations. Polar bear taken in violation of state law and transported to another state are in violation of federal law. State law is not effective beyond territorial waters. Polar bear taken on the high seas off the Alaska coast could be landed in another state having no laws pertaining to polar bear. What is needed are (a) state regulations effecting a conservative rigid annual quota of numbers of bear which can be taken, (b) enforcement of existing state regulations, (c) federal regulations based on federal law which could control the take of polar bear on the high seas by nationals, (d) treaty with circumpolar nations having polar bear.

  The remaining populations of polar bear live off the coast north of the 66th parallel. Some effort is being made to restrict hunting of polar bear; for example, guides are limited on the number of hunts, and aircraft are being used to monitor the taking and importation of polar bear in Alaska. The legal Alaska polar bear kill was 296 in 1965, 399 in 1966, 191 in 1967, and 351 in 1968.—Editor.]

## Part Five

# LUNCHEON

# REMARKS

*Jeffery Cohelan*
United States Congressman from California

We are faced with subdivided and spliced up hillsides, stripped of vegetation, loosened by heavy rains. Any freshman geology student can tell you this results in landslides, mud slides, and massive erosion. Careless exploitation of natural resources—even those lying thousands of feet below the ocean floor—can result in fouling our waters, our shores, our wildlife. After the *Torrey Canyon* broke up and loosed its cargo on March 18, 1969, and after that goo had seeped ashore, and after that oil had despoiled the beaches and the birds, man with his modern technology simply would not quit. Thousands of pounds of detergent were unleashed to clean up the sand. The result: a more deadly and ecologically disrupting compound than oil, one which killed life and vegetation with an alarming certainty. And so it is almost everywhere we look—man's inhumanity to man—an indirect but no less inhumane debilitation of our life. Matter is polluting the air, defiling the water, destroying the soil, disrupting nature's beauty and inviting nature's violence. Man's hope, if we can avoid nuclear annihilation, is that we will in time awake to what we are doing to the place where we live. We must awake to the fouling of our nest in time to reverse the destruction.

Men, for the moment at least, are led by governments. Change on the massive scale necessary to protect us in our environment must come through governmental action. Conferences like these, which educate the public including the legislature, are a fine way to move the government of men to the changes necessary to preserve the life

193

of man. One of those men, a man of government, who is and has been most vitally concerned with these issues of environmental life and death is happily our speaker today, Senator Henry M. Jackson of Washington. He is the chairman of the United States Senate committee that passes on almost all conservation legislation. Conservationist that he is, he is also a realist. He is a successful practitioner in one of the most sophisticated of all scientific disciplines—that of political ecology. Those of us who are constantly working within the framework of biological ecology know the physical limits. We understand the defined tolerances of natural elements. We know, for example, that inside the boundaries of the Redwood National Park there are certain irrefutable laws of nature regarding the survival of the unique redwood species. The political ecologist, working in the field of public affairs, does not enjoy the certainty of these limits. Particularly in Congress, representative of this giant nation's diversity, there are conflicting interests and forces which must be approached with reason, judgment, tolerance, and persuasion as well as parliamentary skills to successfully secure governmental decisions based on the best available information and the highest national interest.

Senator Jackson likes to tell his fellow Washingtonians of the frailty of public officials. He reminds us that when someone asked the Reverend Edward Everett Hale, chaplain of the Senate, "Do you pray for senators, Dr. Hale?" the good reverend doctor replied, "No, I look at the senators and I pray for the country."

# THE LEGISLATIVE PATH TO WILDERNESS

*Henry M. Jackson*
United States Senator from Washington

The past eight years have been very good years for those of us who, like Henry David Thoreau, believe that we need the tonic of wildness and that we can never have enough of nature.

Within this span of time our nation has witnessed a revolution of new policies, new legislation, and new programs designed to improve quality of life and the environment available to the American public.

A new attitude of concern for values that can neither be translated into the language of the marketplace nor computed in cost-benefit ratios or as a part of the gross national product is evident in citizen efforts to save parks, open spaces, and natural beauty from freeways, unplanned industrial expansion, and urban sprawl.

Congressman Joe Cannon, a former Speaker of the House of Representatives, once issued the ultimatum: "Not one cent for scenery!" Today, the conservation, natural beauty, and recreation budget is larger than the total federal budget of 50 years ago.

Speaker Cannon's ultimatum is no longer the law or fortunately the policy of this land. Politicians now speak of the importance of wilderness, natural beauty, and the quality of the environment without embarrassment and with a new sense of national urgency.

Those of you who have sponsored this Eleventh Biennial Wilderness Conference and the organizations you represent deserve a large measure of credit for the changes that have taken place.

You have played an important role in the enactment of the landmark measures of recent years: the Bureau of Outdoor Recreation; the open space and green span programs; air and water pollution control legislation; the Public Land Law Review Commission; and measures to authorize studies of pesticide use, our estuaries, and other public resources.

Another significant measure is the Land and Water Conservation Fund, increased in 1968 to provide one billion dollars partly earmarked from the sale of oil and gas leases from the outer continental shelf. Obviously we have a conflict of interest with oil. I do not think that we ought to stop all oil drilling on the outer continental shelf; instead, we must see that there are better regulations to avoid repetition of the Santa Barbara Channel oil blowout of January, 1969. This must be done because this very important source of revenue is not necessarily incompatible with a protected environment. The Land and Water Conservation Fund includes a lien on these oil revenues to as much as the maximum of $200 million a year for five years, these revenues making up the difference between appropriations and other sources and the total authorized. I want to increase the funds that are available because it can solve one of the hardest problems we face in conservation—getting money. Congress can authorize land acquisitions and it can appropriate funds, but still sometimes when the bills come in we don't have enough to pay them. The problem of getting the funds to complete acquisition of Point Reyes National Seashore is a good example. The Land and Water Conservation Fund can help to solve these vexing problems by keeping funds readily available for federal and state park and recreation purposes.*

Partly as a result of the fine work of the Sierra Club, Congress has acted to set aside and preserve for present and future generations a portion of the land, the mountains, the beaches, and the lakes which comprise our nation's natural heritage.

In 1961, Cape Hatteras in North Carolina was our only national seashore. Today there are six more—in the East, on the Gulf, and in the West.

In 1964, there were no national recreation areas. Today there are eight. All together these areas provide 2.4 million acres of prime recreational land.

In 1965, there were no national lakeshores. Today there are two and others are under study.

* Both presidents Lyndon Johnson and Richard Nixon cut back the budget for the Land and Water Conservation Fund. Mr. Johnson's last budget message requested only $154 million for fiscal year 1969; Mr. Nixon requested $124 million for fiscal year 1970. However, latest reports indicate that President Nixon will request appropriation of all money available in the fund—approximately $364 million —for fiscal year 1971, largely for already-authorized projects.—*Editor.*

Since 1960 we have established: four new national parks, six new national monuments, five new national memorials, four new national historic parks, 20 new national historical sites—one of the most recent of which commemorates the birthplace of our late President John Fitzgerald Kennedy.

During the last Congress alone we established: the Redwood and North Cascades national parks; the National Trails System; the National and Scenic Rivers System; and amended the Land and Water Conservation Fund Act to provide one billion dollars over the next five years.

In terms of national significance, one of the most important conservation measures of the 1960's was the Wilderness Act of 1964. From a legislative standpoint its attainment was also the most difficult that I have observed in my legislative lifetime. The legislative path to a statutory wilderness system for present and future generations has been long and tortuous. Wilderness advocates can vividly recall the early hope and promise of the wilderness concept; the frustration of 13 years of delay and compromise; and finally the joy of victory when President Johnson signed the act on September 3, 1964.

Unfortunately, some who contributed to the long and important effort that was required are not with us today. Particularly missed is Howard Zahnizer who described the concept of the first wilderness legislation in a speech before this conference in 1951.

To some the passage of the act "accomplished" the National Wilderness Preservation System. In reality, though, it was only the birth of a system. It was not the end of the path, but a beginning.

It was, however, an auspicious beginning. The initial 54 units brought nine million acres of unchanging beauty and wonder into the system for the American people's future use and enjoyment.

Since the passage of the act, public attention has been focused on the job of studying, recommending, and authorizing the addition of new areas to the system.

It was highly appropriate that the first addition to the wilderness system since its establishment was the San Rafael Wilderness, and the second the San Gabriel Wilderness, because both are here in California, the ancestral home of the Sierra Club.

Last year we also added the Mount Jefferson Wilderness, parts of three national forests in Oregon, and on the opposite side of the continent, the Great Swamp Wilderness of New Jersey.

With designation of the Great Swamp, we have taken a major conservation step in that we have established a wilderness area in what has been described as an island of beauty in the midst of a sea of increasing urban ugliness. This is not only a heart-warming story, but an example of our growing realization that we can beat back the tide of asphalt and cement when it threatens to engulf the last pure corner of the good earth.

Three other preservation measures, which the Senate Interior Committee and the Senate approved, died last year in the House. These were: Pelican Island in Florida; several island refuges in Wisconsin, Michigan, and Maine; and the Monomoy National Wildlife Refuge in Massachusetts. It is my hope that both bodies will act favorably on these measures during the present 91st Congress.

As this Congress gets underway, there are a dozen bills providing for new wilderness areas pending before the Senate Interior Committee. Two of the Forest Service proposals—the Desolation Valley Primitive Area and the Ventana Primitive Area, both in California—were the subject of Senate Interior subcommittee hearings and action in recent weeks.*

The Department of the Interior and the Department of Agriculture are now moving steadily forward with their review of additional areas as prescribed by the Wilderness Act. The Congress is proceeding with the required legislative action. In short, the act is working.

The major question now seems to be how are we going to meet the problems of management and protection of the wilderness environment? An important lesson may be traced in the evolution of the national park concept.

Public acceptance and public interest provided the support that permitted us to enlarge our national park system. But, the pressures of public demand for the use of the parks have in many cases made the preservation of wilderness values—both the wilderness experience and preservation of natural ecological systems—difficult, if not impossible.

The Wilderness Preservation System faces the same dilemma. We cannot expect to dedicate public resources and the services of public agencies to expanding the wilderness system unless the values embodied in the system are widely held. Wilderness must take its place, on its own merits, among all of the other urgent requirements for national attention and scarce funds.

Strong public interest is a valuable ally in legislative and appropriation struggles. But it will almost certainly be accompanied by increased pressures for use of wilderness areas. If new solutions are not found, the history of the park system will surely be repeated in the wilderness system.

* Wilderness designation was authorized by Congress for both these Forest Service primitive areas. President Nixon signed the bill for the Ventana Wilderness on August 18, 1969, and the Desolation Wilderness on October 10, 1969.—*Editor.*

I believe that new solutions can be found. The wilderness system must be considered as one aspect of a whole—a broad, diversified public program for outdoor experiences. It must be treated as a special and unique phase of a recreational and educational effort which encompasses the whole range of programs from city parks through national recreation areas and national parks to true wilderness.

Within this spectrum, there is an opportunity to provide meaningful benefits for every citizen, from disadvantaged, inner-city youth to the trained ecologist.

Today, our local governments have a total of about one and one-half million acres of land available for parks and recreation uses. These areas offer a tremendous opportunity to provide some of the benefits of outdoor recreation and diversity of experience to city dwellers. Unfortunately, much of this area is poorly planned and almost completely unmanaged. Imaginative and innovative programs are needed to make this wasting resource become productive.

At a different level, most national recreation areas do not provide a wilderness experience, but they do provide outdoor recreation to a wide and growing sector of the public. The Lake Mead National Recreation Area alone, for example, has served nearly five million visitors.

Participation in any one of our outdoor programs can show the Congress and the average citizen that the entire system is a relevant concern of public policy and a worthwhile expenditure of resources. Our recreational programs provide an opportunity to develop awareness, and appreciation of, and aspiration for the values of wilderness among many people who probably will not have direct contact with true wilderness areas.

Those of us who believe in the importance and the utility of the wilderness concept have the opportunity to enlist public support for the wilderness system and also for the management policies and restrictions concerning its use that are inevitable if its unique values are to be retained. But to do this we must provide effective support for other outdoor programs: programs that provide a week, or a day, or only a few hours of enjoyment for an individual or a family; programs that benefit the underprivileged, the city dweller, the middle-class suburbanite; programs which appeal to those with limited funds, time, or sophistication. Support for these programs can build a common bond among the proponents of outdoor activities. It can create a common cause in advancing wilderness objectives.

An example of an auxiliary double-purpose program is one I have introduced, a Youth Conservation Corps Bill, that will take many youngsters from 14 to 18 years of age off the streets and give them an outdoor experience. They are not eligible for employment during the summer because of federal laws prohibiting employment under 18. One of the major problems for youngsters these days is the lack of employment opportunity. Because of this and other problems the Child Labor Act requires complete review.

We found in Seattle, in the central area where most of the minority groups live, that hardly any of the youngsters have ever been in our city park—Woodland Park—only a few blocks away. The Snoqualmie National Forest is only 45 minutes east and Olympic National Forest is a similar distance west of Seattle; the North Cascades National Park is a little over an hour northeast while Olympic National Park is a little further west. If this legislation passes we will have an opportunity to provide more money for operation and maintenance of our parks and our outdoor systems. And by giving 14- to 18-year-olds the opportunity to render this service, we are also preparing them to become the future conservationists of this country. They can learn about the greatness of the outdoors and wilderness and what it means, and at the same time it will help go a long way toward improving human behavior in troubled areas of our cities.

On occasion, it is possible to enlist wide public support for a specific issue of great visibility. Emotional support based upon intense publicity, however, cannot be sustained over the long hard effort to implement programs which are necessary year in and year out. This kind of effort requires the continuing support of broad and diverse interest groups and the cooperation of decision-makers with varying constituencies. Support and interest of this nature will be forthcoming only when the participants share a common cause.

The advocates of wilderness, particularly those in our conservation organizations, have in many instances been the shock troops of the conservation movement. They have carried critically important issues to the forum of public decision when others have found it expedient to be busy at other tasks. This has been a notable public service and future historians will, in my judgment, find it to be such. I fear, however, that while the great battles of conservation are being won, the way may be lost.

While we have compiled an enviable, even an unprecedented record of legislative awareness of the value of wilderness, conservation, recreation, and man's total environment over the past eight years, we have not constructed a philosophy for future guidance.

Quite the contrary in fact. What we have done is to proceed piecemeal. We have repaired some of the faults, some of the mistakes of the past. We have set about to reclaim some of our streams and the air we breathe from the ravages of filth and waste.

We have responded to growing public pressures and demands for open space, for parks and recreation by setting aside some of the public domain for future use.

Through these years we have attempted to attain a pragmatic balance between the forces of exploitation and preservation; between development and restoration; and between quantity and quality. Often —as in the Santa Barbara Channel, the San Francisco Bay, and in our transportation program—the scales of this erratic balance have tipped away from the goals and the values that ought to be reached.

In large measure this is because we have not established the philosophical and institutional foundations that will support harmony, ecological stability, and the life-giving balance between man and his environment.

One of the popular catch phrases of today is "man's total environment." What does this mean? How can conservation's interests be served along with the other inescapable demands upon the environment?

As some of you may be aware, there are efforts underway to answer these questions, to formulate a philosophy commensurate with the needs of our time. For example, in July, 1968, Congressman George Miller and I convened a unique joint House-Senate colloquium to discuss "A National Policy for the Environment." The participants at the colloquium included five Cabinet secretaries, the president's science advisor, Laurance S. Rockefeller, Dean Don K. Price of Harvard, and many concerned members of Congress. The proceedings of the colloquium have stimulated a great deal of discussion in government, the universities, and abroad. In future proceedings of this nature we must involve all interested parties and give all viewpoints an opportunity for expression.

I have also introduced legislation that has as its purpose the establishment of a national strategy for the management of the human environment.

This legislation would lay the framework for a continuing program of ecological and environmental research and study.

It would establish in the office of the president a Council on Environmental Quality* to study and analyze environmental trends; the

* On January 1, 1970, President Nixon signed into law a bill establishing a national policy for the environment and a Council on Environmental Quality in the White House. Later that month President Nixon named Undersecretary of the Interior Russell Train as chairman, Dr. Gordon J. F. MacDonald, geophysicist at the University of California at Santa Barbara, and Robert Cahn, journalist for the Christian Science Monitor, as members of the council.—Editor.

factors that affect those trends; and how they relate to the conservation, social, economic, and health goals of the nation. The council would also advise and assist the president on the formulation of national policies to foster and promote the improvement of environmental quality, and in the preparation of an annual report on the quality of the environment.

This report would serve an important function by providing an annual comprehensive survey on the status of our environment and "Our Gross Natural Progress." The report would provide baselines against which we could chart our progress from year to year.

The need for an advisory body such as the proposed council is clear. We must do more to anticipate environmental problems and develop strategies for their resolution before they assume crisis proportions. It is far cheaper—in human, social, and economic terms—to anticipate the consequences of our actions at an early date and to find alternatives before massive expenditures are necessary to remedy mistakes.

Today we have the option of channeling some of our wealth toward the protection and improvement of our future. If we fail to do so in an adequate and timely manner, we may find ourselves confronted, even in this generation, with a wasteland—with a spent environment of asphalt and concrete.

In the recent Senate confirmation hearings on his appointment, Secretary Hickel said: "I believe we should devote a period of time to the consolidation of the gains that have been made and to a reassessment of our long-range objectives."

In my view, the period immediately ahead should not be devoted only to consolidation and reassessment.

But, if those in positions of major responsibility intend the future to be a period of consolidation, of reassessment, and of redefinition of national objectives, we must be certain that the time is well spent. Out of the reassessment should come laws, policies and stated goals that will insure the future well-being of those values the conservation movement has sought to attain. Those of us who have fought for the progress of past years must guide the reassessment so that it will indeed be a consolidation and basis for future action and not a loss of past gains.

Conservation's success in the future courses of public policy does not depend solely upon the fate of the Grand Canyon or the redwoods. It depends upon the development of a sound methodology to incorporate conservation values into public policies and actions which are evolving daily in response to the pressures of our times. That methodology does not exist today.

Formulating a national policy and developing new goals that are responsive to our needs and the needs of future generations cannot be done in an atmosphere of emotional conflict. It will be achieved, if it is achieved, by reasonable and thoughtful men who advocate their special concerns, but who recognize the legitimate concerns of others and the realities of life. It will not provide results that entirely suit any one point of view, but it can and, I hope, it will advance the aims of all.

# PRESENTATION OF THE JOHN MUIR AWARD

*Edgar Wayburn*

The John Muir Award was established by the Sierra Club in 1961 as its highest award for outstanding individual accomplishment over a period of years in fostering appreciation, interpretation, and preservation of scenic and wilderness values. In presenting the 1969 award to Senator Henry M. Jackson, the Sierra Club recognizes the achievements for wilderness and the environment of the Senate Interior and Insular Affairs Committee under his chairmanship. These achievements include more new units in the National Park System than ever before; the Land and Water Conservation Fund to finance them; the National Wilderness Preservation System; the National Wild and Scenic Rivers System; the National Trails System; and the Classification and Multiple Use Act for the public domain. Senator Jackson's strength and leadership made the difference in establishment of the North Cascades National Park and the Redwood National Park, and in preservation of a dam-free Grand Canyon.

Senator Jackson joins a distinguished list of previous recipients of the John Muir Award: William E. Colby, 1961; Olaus J. Murie, 1962; Ansel A. Adams, 1963; Walter A. Starr, 1964; Francis P. Farquhar, 1965; Harold C. Bradley, 1966; and Sigurd F. Olson, 1967.

[Editor's note: Upon receiving the Muir Award, Senator Jackson spoke briefly and eloquently: "May I accept this award in the name of all those who made it possible for us in the legislative end to do a few things in behalf of all the people of the country. I am most grateful for the loyal devoted support. It is a story about how a few people—

dedicated, determined, and with a righteous cause—can really accomplish a lot in a busy and sometimes unconcerned democracy. Never get discouraged by the fact that occasionally your numbers are not large, for I have learned through experience that the dedicated few can do much for the many who are not concerned. All of you in this room today belong to that qualitative and privileged few. I want to thank you for what you have done for your country."]

## Part Six

# WILDERNESS PLANNING AND PEOPLE

"The power of scenery to affect men is,
in a large way, proportionate to their degree
of civilization . . . as civilization advances,
the interest of men in natural scenes of sublimity
and beauty increases . . .

"Thus, (unless) government withhold them from the
grasp of individuals, all places favorable in
scenery to the recreation of the mind and body will
be closed against the great body of the people . . .
portions of natural scenery may therefore be guarded
and cared for by government . . . for the free enjoyment of the people . . ."

Frederick Law Olmsted, 1865

# INTRODUCTION

*Raymond J. Sherwin*
Judge, Superior Court, Solano County, California

For as long as I can remember, the general chairman of this conference, Dr. Daniel Luten, has been hammering away at the theme that without population control, other conservation measures were futile. At the time he first stated this theme publicly, his listeners tended to draw back as if the subject were likely to be so offensive that discussion of it would prejudice our other efforts.

Times have changed. Population control has become a recurrent subject of discussion at wilderness conferences. Some of those whom we once feared to offend by mentioning artificial means of inhibiting the proliferation of mankind are now contributing cogent arguments for reducing the rate of population growth to zero. These are some of those who have seen their efforts to relieve the degrading effects of poverty frustrated by unrestrained reproduction.

The nature of the discussion, in fact, seldom now concerns whether it is desirable to control population; rather, it concerns practical means of accomplishing what almost everyone now concedes to be necessary if the human race is to survive with sanity and inhabit a tolerable environment. This was the bent of Lincoln Day's wilderness conference speech four years ago. One of the practical suggestions that he then had to make concerned the necessity of careful planning of efforts in a number of directions. It is not a coincidence that one of the titles this afternoon concerns planning.

The modification of religious and ethical attitudes toward the entire subject is no more spectacular than the scope of investigation and

209

thought given to the uncomfortable details that obtrude between the acceptance of the desirability of population control and its effectuation. For example, I recommend to everyone an article by Bernard Berelson in the February 7, 1969, issue of *Science* entitled "Beyond Family Planning." He refers to the inadequacy of the results from today's national family planning program, inasmuch as it is based on voluntary contraception. Then he goes on to list and discuss some 29 additional proposals beyond family planning and the problems involved with each of them. In this regard, he subjects each such plan to the following critiques: scientific readiness, political viability, administrative feasibility, economic capacity, ethical acceptability, and presumed effectiveness.

The point is, we have a great deal to learn before we can reach the goal of a stable population, or a reduced one. What do we do in the meantime?

Of course, we must plan our conservation efforts to save what we can pending the millennium. I infer from the title of the presentation of one of our speakers that in his view only a worldwide approach will have the possibility of success. This title is "Conserving the Assets of Spaceship Earth." The allusion, of course, is to Barbara Ward's delightful eye-opener entitled "Spaceship Earth," in which she demonstrates so lucidly the effects of the constriction of the earth as the result of our communications breakthroughs, and the resulting exacerbation of the consequences of imbalances of wealth, power, and ideologies.

The danger in this approach, as I see it, is in the inherent slowness. The population is likely to get bigger before we can curb it. Worldwide cooperation on practical conservation is likely to be achieved with the deliberate speed of, say, a practical accommodation on arms control. Meanwhile, local bits of precious wild places and things may be eaten up by "developments," or highways, or drowned by reservoirs, or suffocated by our refuse. The special places where there is still space for wildness on a larger scale may yield secrets of mundane as well as aesthetic riches. We must not be diverted from guarding these places, whatever the energy cost, while working out the larger scheme. How can we plan for this, and is the planning enough?

This thought of planning leads to some vexing problems. Just to mention one of them: is the idea of planning consistent with the idea of wilderness—that is, do we manage wilderness? Our final speaker will touch on this.

# EARTH: THE END OF INFINITY*

*John P. Milton*

Deputy Director, International Programs Division
The Conservation Foundation, Washington, D.C.

Over the next several months the United States will be preparing for its first attempt to land men on the moon. Only a few months ago, we sent Apollo 8 hurtling on its half-a-million-mile journey through space, around the moon, and back to earth. Not since Copernicus has man known such a shift in universal perspective. Suddenly he has been confronted personally with the reality and awesomeness of the solar system and beyond. Challenged by the vast mystery of outer space, we are beginning to see the earth as it is: a small, delicate, incredibly beautiful planet whirling around a minor star. Will man be able to recognize the fragility of this life-sustaining beauty before destroying it? The Apollo astronauts voiced this same concern for our little globe when last December they radioed back from outer space:

> The vast loneliness up here of the moon is awe-inspiring
> . . . it makes you realize just what you have back there on
> earth.

Earth is precious in that it is a living planet. Its thin film of life intermingling with water, land, and air has evolved man and many other species. Man was nurtured and is sustained by this planet. Yet, incredibly, this child of the earth now threatens to extinguish both himself and the planetary biosphere that supports him. The end could come quickly, in a flash of thermonuclear fire, or slowly, through

---

* Views expressed herein are the author's and do not necessarily reflect the position of The Conservation Foundation.

the quiet squeeze of a million small pollutions, and lurking behind each of these possibilities is the growing specter of crowding, disease, malnutrition, and starvation for an increasing majority of mankind. Mankind has blundered before in his history as a species, but never before has he been confronted with such a formidable array of potentially irreversible disasters of his own contrivance. Not only are the power and magnitude of the technological threat to the planetary biosphere growing, but the speed with which new, untested technologies are being applied is accelerating. And the most important facet of all, the cumulative environmental impact of man's changes, is totally unknown. There may still be time to choose a better vision, but with each new dawn our options narrow.

These were some of my first thoughts when asked to consider planning for the protection of the earth's last wild places. Few of us question the value of preserving natural diversity. Thoreau wrote "in wildness is the preservation of the world" over a century ago. His words are even truer today than they were then. But how are we to arrest today's trend towards uniformity of cultures and natural environments? I think we all dream of a time when man will step softly in the few islands of wilderness left and when man's invention will be turned toward creating a world that encourages maximum natural and human variety. Nevertheless, we live in a time that illustrates another prophetic phrase from Thoreau: "The mass of men live lives of quiet desperation." What better description is there of the bureaucratic urban mechanism that increasingly absorbs most of our lives?

The wilderness that existed in Thoreau's day, the untamed parts of the planet resistant to man's civilizing efforts, is now much reduced. People have become the ecological dominants of earth. And yet, if world culture is to pass beyond the materialistic, infinite economic growth assumptions that now infect the world, it will need wildness and a wide diversity of human and natural environments to give man new resources and inspiration. The great tragedy of our time is that the explosive growth of our own populations and individual material desires is causing the extinction of global diversity. The few regions that remain as unprotected wilderness will continue so for only a moment more in the history of mankind. Today the oilmen and miners are in the process of raping North America's last great wilderness: the Arctic. The biologically diverse tropical forests of Latin America, Asia, and Africa are falling before the land hunger of millions of malnourished people. The rich wildlife of Africa is now only a shadow of what roamed that continent several generations ago. We are adding to the list of extinct species approximately one more mammal every year, and 300 additional mammals are close to extinction. The earth's greatest free-flowing rivers such as the Congo, the Zambezi, the Nile, the Amazon, the Mekong, the Peace, the Colorado, the Yukon, and the Mackenzie are already dammed and controlled or are beset with plans for flood control, hydropower, and irrigation. Most of the last remaining wild oceanic islands and island groups such as Aldabra, Galapagos, New Guinea, Dominica, Dahlak, and many of those in the Pacific Trust Territory are threatened by a variety of developments, particularly colonization, invasion of exotic species, mining, agriculture, and mass tourism. The oceans and seas are the focus of accelerating demands for offshore oil, whaling, fishing, and even sea-bottom mining. Even the remotest icecaps, forests, and oceans already have been contaminated by pesticides such as DDT, radioactive wastes, and a rapidly growing number of other pollutants.

Clearly, this is our last chance to adopt a less arrogant attitude toward the biosphere and to decide to save the few wild places of the earth we have left. What wilderness we save in the next generation or two will be all that will remain. Little, if any, of today's unprotected wilderness will survive future change unless we plan and act to preserve it over the next few years. Of necessity, we require a massive effort to protect only a representative sample of the most typical as well as the most unique habitats. Yet, the forces now affecting the pace of technological change, industrialization, and urban growth throughout much of the world are growing rapidly. If we are to plan for the retention of environmental diversity, then we also must understand and act in recognition of these forces. If we fail to give attention to the broader environmental system within which our wilderness protection efforts take place, then planning for protection will fail. A number of important factors contribute to our current rapid loss of wilderness: technological revolution, competition for raw materials, and dedication to economic growth.

First, the creation rate of new technology and its application is growing exponentially. This means that the number and complexity of impacts affecting wilderness are building up at an ever increasing rate. One of the most dangerous aspects of this burgeoning technological revolution is that we have consistently failed to foresee the risks and impacts involved in each new application of technology. As the growth of our technology accelerates, the probabilities of unforeseen new environmental hazards also are accelerating. This dangerous problem is compounded by our tendency to commit ourselves to massive development schemes, such as huge dam-building projects and colonization programs. The large long-term investment of time, capital, and talent required by such grandiose programs means a great restriction in our ability to shift into alternative choices as our requirements change and as our understanding of the environmental risks and benefits grows.

The worldwide exportation of medical technology that triggered the population explosion was an early mistake now grown to a full-blown life of horror for many millions of people. Currently, various other technological introductions abroad are fostering the spread of diseases such as schistosomiasis, sleeping sickness, malaria and a whole range of pollution and urban stress-related diseases with which the United States is all too familiar. Similarly, new dam-building and irrigation activities are causing the salting and waterlogging of agricultural areas, shoreline erosion, destruction of fisheries, and the loss of rich sediments that sustain agricultural fertility. Not content to restrict our mistakes with pesticides to the highly developed nations, we are marketing vast quantities of destructive, persistent chemical poisons in new environments and among new people who lack the knowledge to evaluate the health hazards and environmental degradation that they are risking. Massive colonization of tropical soils that rapidly leach or erode and cannot sustain development still continues to create vast rural slums; this colonization is supported directly through governmental resettlement programs and indirectly through spontaneous colonization following new roads. Many such little-known rural disaster areas export large numbers of impoverished people now contributing to the staggering growth of urban slums in underdeveloped countries. Assistance agencies continue to foster overgrazing, wind erosion, and eventual destruction of nomadic cultures through provision of new water supplies in arid lands. Destruction of earth's rich ocean fisheries through overfishing continues at a headlong pace; often, as in the case of the Peruvian anchovies, this valuable fish protein goes to fatten chickens and livestock in the rich nations while locally protein-starved people in Latin America go hungry. We talk of exporting abroad dramatic new technologies, such as atomic power plants, despite the mounting evidence of grave bio-medical hazards and ecological deterioration due to radioactive wastes and thermal pollution.

A particularly ominous consequence of these multiplying technological impacts is the danger that we could trigger some unanticipated and truly irreversible change of disastrous proportions. The bewildering growth of chemical pollutants, fertilizers and pesticides has already led to a vast array of unanticipated and often irreversible degradations. Now our approach to radioactive waste problems is beginning to repeat the old pattern: a single purpose, reductionist approach to problem definition, followed by single factor innovation, application, trial-by-error, and then gradual understanding of the broader ecological implications. Our first mistake, now obvious, resulting from this new atomic technology was bomb testing and its radioactive atmospheric fallout which dangerously contaminated the biosphere. Now we are concentrating on the construction of giant nuclear power plants and seem hell-bent on ignoring the serious biological dangers posed by this new widespread application of atomic technology. Both government and private industry respond weakly to the warnings of concerned experts who are worried about the dangers of reactor explosion, accidental leakage, and radioactive pollution problems from disposal of air, water, and solid wastes. Radioactive cesium 137, strontium 90, iodine 131, krypton 85, tritium, radium, and thorium are some of the new elements man has already released into the biosphere, there to pursue a complicated course through living things. Once these elements escape into the biosphere, there is no conceivable way of recapturing them. We must not allow our former history of environmental laissez-faire to apply to the utilization of atomic energy. We are in grave danger that radiation damage may become extensive before we are even aware of it; and in a system as complex as the biosphere, the causes may be far removed in location and time from the effects. The risks are too great and the potential damage is irreversible. Even the most remote wilderness would not escape severe contamination from widespread radioactive pollution.

Another important factor that will affect the quality and distribution of tomorrow's wilderness is the rising demand of both highly developed and developing nations for the planet's available raw materials. According to Durward Allen, those of us now living in North America (about seven percent of mankind) are using approximately half the total world output of natural resources to sustain our affluent industrial society. The per capita consumption of environmental resources in North America, Europe, the Union of Soviet Socialist Republics, Japan, and Australia/New Zealand continues to climb steeply. The per capita pollution of the earth caused by this growth in material wealth also continues to climb. By contrast, the per capita demand for and pollution of environmental resources in the less developed regions is markedly lower.

Philip Hauser, the sociologist, estimates that the entire current resource output of the world would provide for only half a billion people at North America's current level of living. As the "revolution of rising expectations" sweeps into every earthly nook, wilderness faces the prospect of literally being swallowed by the appetites of individual desires for more material goods, and by a rising tide of individuals. With a rapidly growing human population of already three and one-half billion, prospects for our species' future welfare, indeed the very survival of all species and some modest protection of the existing diversity of wilderness on a global scale, appear grim. As competition, particularly from the developing countries, increases for earth's fixed amount of land, water, and air resources, many potential and existing wilderness parks and reserve areas at home and abroad will face more severe development pressures.

Population growth and distribution, of course, will exert the primary pressure forcing both new technological applications and rising consumption of raw materials and space. Without a stable human population on earth, better controls on technology and the utilization of space will be futile. There is considerable evidence that mankind has already passed beyond the point of optimum population. By the end of this century the world population could easily reach seven billion. Unfortunately, the most rapid growth is occurring in those less developed regions already suffering terribly from stress and overcrowding, disease, starvation, and malnutrition. This impoverished part of the world, which now numbers two-thirds of the total human population, is doubling every 20 to 35 years. Among the highly developed minority of nations, the doubling time ranges from 50 to 200 years.

The misguided application of relatively sophisticated Western medical technology without provision for birth control assistance helped fuel this catastrophic increase; clearly, those of us living in the rich nations, who are now fat from the resources drawn from abroad, bear great responsibility for the less-developed world's problems. In addition, it has allowed us to pollute far more of the global environment than the bulk of mankind. One of the saddest aspects of overpopulation and its consequences is that once a society is severely afflicted with too many people, it becomes increasingly difficult for the culture to solve the problem. For example, malnutrition, particularly if suffered at an early age, can cause permanent damage to the human nervous system and result in lowered intelligence. This means lowered capability to improve one's own condition and that of succeeding generations. If large numbers of people are affected, whole societies may be caught up in a vortex of increasing cultural and ecological decay. In planning for wilderness protection on a global scale, massive population control efforts must form the solid base for any realistic protection of natural diversity and improvement of the human environment.

I would like to mention one other factor that is absolutely essential to realistic wilderness protection. Our culture has been dominated by an assumption that our economy must always continue to expand. With more economic growth there would be more jobs, more industry, more goods, and more wealth. The obvious result would be a continuously improving life for everyone. Even today, in our national concern for more equitable distribution of wealth, this obsessive infinite growth assumption is still accepted. Only recently have we come to realize that the growth of our Gross National Product may also be the same as the growth of our Gross National Pollution. Because we have never placed a price tag on good health (medicine benefits only when we are sick), sound food, clean air, clean water, a quiet environment, beautiful and varied natural surroundings, or a national life style that minimizes environmental consumption and degradation, we have made the catastrophic mistake of equating the expansion of material, industrially produced wealth with an increase in the quality of our lives. Our gross national product is surpassed only by our gross national greed. No species has ever been able to expand its influence indefinitely, and man is no exception. The next economic era on our planet might be termed "The End of Infinity." We still have time, however, to determine how we will come to terms with our faulty assumption of infinite growth.

Somehow, we must make the transition to a society where growth of technology, growth of resource demand, growth of population and growth of materialistic economic greed are supplanted by a focus on developing and sustaining a new dynamic equilibrium between human society and the biosphere that supports it. The assumption that we must continue increasing production in order to accommodate more and more people at higher and higher economic levels must be replaced by a concern for the long-term quality of living for man both as an individual and as a species inextricably bound up in the health of the biosphere. Unless we can succeed in this, all of life—including man—is threatened with extinction or severe degradation.

I feel that to plan for protecting a global system of wilderness reserves in isolation from the irresistible forces of environmental change is a tragic delusion. To safeguard wilderness we also must bring about a change in man's perception of himself in relation to the planet Earth. We require an assessment of man's ecological, cultural, and psychological needs as a functioning partner in the biosphere.

What are the potentials for the emergence of ecologically sensitive man—and the limitations? We require a redefinition of man's cultural values to better harmonize with biospheric processes. We require clear identification of serious social and ecological conflicts in man's current utilization of the earth. We require the cultural means to identify and work toward new concepts of ecologically harmonious change.

We require a creative new series of possible life styles as valid alternatives to the environmentally disruptive patterns our culture is now intertwined with. We require methods to reform environmental decision making through legal, educational, political, and economic means. We require that this country revoke the assumption that a small, rich establishment controlling industry, science and education has the right to devastate the earth for the profit of a few. At present, most of us in the United States (particularly the young who will have to live longest with the consequences of industry's greed) feel an overwhelming sense of futility for effective reform and reversal. Unless the wheels of change are prepared, unless government exhibits true leadership to meet the deep-running crises of our time, violent revolution—rather than constructive evolution—will provide the outlets for the frustrations of the coming age.

Stated more simply, wilderness preservation must be integrated with the positive development of an ecology of man and the biosphere. In our development of a world technology capable of such astonishing feats as sending a man to the moon, we have come to realize that development of comparable biological and ecological understanding has fallen far behind. In this situation lie the seeds of our growing dilemma. We find ourselves with sophisticated, often dangerous tools in our hands—ones of our own fashioning—and with no concept of where, how, why, or when to use them. The creation of positive, operational ecology for man is long overdue in a world where his time for choice is running out.

Several specific lines of immediate action are necessary if we are to successfully redirect Western society's economic growth bias into fostering the harmonious growth of cultural variety and maximum preservation of natural diversity.

First, we need to develop a strong national policy to stabilize our own population growth. Such a policy must be implemented through a spectrum of simultaneous actions. Governmental incentives to encourage small families and discourage large ones, massive research into the development and application of birth control techniques, legalized abortion and sterilization clinics, and widespread birth control education are only a few of the actions that could be taken now.

Following adoption of such enlightened policies at home, the United States will better be able to act as a leader to help solve the much greater global problem of population increase. Until we can demonstrate an ability to control our own population size, our arguments concerning deficiencies in other nations' population policies will have limited validity. Assuming that we can get our domestic house in order, other avenues for immediate efforts are clear. Through our support of multilateral institutions such as the United Nations, the World Bank, the Asian and Inter-American Development Banks, and the Organization of American States we should seek the establishment of large-scale population control programs as an issue of first priority. In our own bilateral programs such as the Agency for International Development, the Alliance for Progress, and the Peace Corps, birth control assistance should become the central focus. In all of these programs, not only is an emphasis on new techniques required, but even more importantly the means for gaining cultural acceptance must receive high priority. The problems of adequate birth control extension alone, even if the necessary technologies and social understandings exist, will be overwhelming.

Second, we must develop adequate institutions for establishing and implementing national, regional, and local policies for the environment. Our country can no longer afford to allow the right of special interests to degrade the environment and defer the costs to society as a whole. We must prepare now for the protection, restoration, replacement, or rehabilitation of environmental resources before or while they are being used. Similarly, we must support the adoption of effective national environmental policies and institutions elsewhere. However, the most difficult environmental problems to solve will continue to be those requiring adequate international cooperation to protect the biosphere. A rapidly growing number of problems such as air pollution, atmospheric particulate matter and carbon dioxide increase, pesticide and radioactive contamination, marine pollution, and the destruction of ocean fisheries and mammals respects no national boundaries. It is becoming increasingly apparent that the biosphere is an incredibly complex, globally functioning ecosystem, which bears no relation to civilization's current political and economic compartmentalization of the planet Earth. Somehow we must achieve strong international control over all these adverse biospheric changes, despite national jealousies and ambitions. This will be the hardest task of all.

Third, we must look much more carefully at existing programs of international assistance to assess their full environmental impact. The social and ecological costs of such programs have often been much higher than the benefits received, despite the fact that many adverse environmental impacts could have been avoided if industries or international agencies responsible had taken the trouble to study and anticipate ecological consequences. We must insist on the redirection of such international programs. Despite the mounting evidence of grave ecological crisis at home due to misapplication of technologies, little attention currently is given to the adverse environmental consequences of introducing alien Western technologies into the natural systems and traditional cultures of less developed countries. We are exporting many familiar mistakes and creating a large number of new catastrophes through massive private investment abroad and through programs of international assistance and lending agencies.

We must require that both bilateral and multilateral agencies involved in foreign aid build ecological criteria into the process of project selection at an early stage. In the past, attention to economic and engineering feasibility factors have dominated the international development process. This is no longer good enough. Environmental science should also play a major role in all pre-investment survey and action phases of development if we are to avoid creating more future horror stories. Careful post-audits of the success and failure of past development projects should also be initiated (perhaps most objectively by an independent agency). If we are to achieve harmonious introduction of new technologies abroad, this will demand much more research (particularly applied research) into the precise ecology of these regions to make ecology more predictive. The worldwide monitoring of ecosystem changes, including those caused by man-induced stresses and pollutions, should be a central part of increasing our understanding of biospheric processes. Further, where our funds are assisting industrial development abroad, we must begin to require that adequate pollution controls be included as part of the exportation of all industrial technology. Another helpful approach would be to search out and study those successful examples of man in cultural and ecological harmony in which new technologies have played a positive role. We still know very little about how to solve one set of socio-ecological problems without introducing a series of disequilibriums. Much could be learned from those cases in which man has achieved a measure of environmental harmony.

Fourth, mankind must start to direct its tremendous scientific and technical talent into a search for new substitute technologies that cause a minimum of disturbance to the natural environment while still accomplishing important human objectives. For example, hydropower, fossil fuels, and atomic energy all often bring about serious environmental side effects whose long-term cumulative risks and measurable costs are higher than the energy's demonstrable benefits. If we shift from one source to another, we only shift our environmental problems. Shouldn't we now be engaged in an intensive, heavily subsidized search for new energy sources that are "clean," economically feasible, and relatively free from adverse consequences? Hydrogen fusion, solar power, and the fuel cell are all promising areas for major investigation. Such innovations could be profoundly beneficial, but our society must state its goals clearly to move in such a direction.

A great deal of time, talent, and cash will be needed.

Fifth, we must seek the involvement of a far broader spectrum of mankind in the conservation of the biosphere. The size, rate, and speed with which we are presently destroying earth's mantle of life requires this. Environmental concerns are still limited to a very small percentage of people, and key industrial and political decision makers still initiate most actions with little thought for their total impact on society. The development of an effective strategy for greater world-wide involvement in conservation will depend on such things as increased utilization of all public media, accelerated action in working directly to influence all levels of decision making, greatly expanded legal action in environmental affairs and the involvement of many other formerly uninvolved interest groups in solving environmental problems.

One particularly effective avenue would be the creation of a power-ful and large national environmental lobby, backed up and given strength by a sizable and active membership. Most traditional con-servation organizations, although all are involved in very effective work, have not been able to exert direct lobbyist pressure due to their nonprofit, tax deductible status.* The creation of a specific lobby group for the protection of environmental resources could do much to counteract the existing overwhelming dominance of Congress by special interest lobbies promoting a vast array of environmentally destructive industries. Similar environmental lobby organizations could be set up in other countries where the political systems follow a similar decision making pattern. On a personal level, each individual also has the option to boycott, and encourage others to boycott, industries whose products and production are causing environmental pollution.

Sixth, I suggest that we must begin thinking of wilderness reserves and natural areas in relation to the cultural and natural systems sur-rounding them. The threats now facing water-lacking Everglades National Park and the pesticide-ridden bodies of both eagles and ospreys in their coastal sanctuaries are due to external influences that act to destroy wildness. Future planning for protecting the earth's wild places will be concerned increasingly with a wide variety of relevant factors outside the strict park or reserve boundary. Effective wilderness protection will increasingly depend on the creation of reserves that include relatively whole self-sustaining environmental systems rather than fragmented bits of wild nature.

* This is no longer true of the Sierra Club. Since it lost its tax deductibility in 1966, the club has been extremely active on Capitol Hill. A number of recent votes shows the effectiveness of this activity.—Editor.

Seventh, there is a need to initiate a series of demonstration projects, both domestic and international, to show how ecological principles can be effectively built into development change. Such work, along with the collection of positive case histories that analyze historical examples of ecologically sound development, could provide valuable guidance and insight into how the whole development process must be reformed and restructured. Its particularly great value would come from the fact that it would provide specific positive guidelines for redirecting future change.

Lastly, a major restructuring of the educational system will be needed to allow people to effectively attack the multiple aspects of any specific environmental problem. We must include ecology as a basic unifying element in educational reform. Traditional education has emphasized the development of narrowly defined, exclusive disciplines with little communication between them. The organization of separate departments in our universities has deepened the lack of communication between disciplines and the estrangement from reality. This emphasis has fomented the reductionist philosophy that has led to today's environmental crisis. What is now needed is a creative, flexible, unified, problem- and process-oriented approach to education. Environmental problems always exist in the context of multiple factors and processes simultaneously interwoven and operating. Education and training must deal with this fundamental reality. Humpty Dumpty has been broken apart and analyzed; now we must put him back together again.

I have spoken very little about traditional planning for the location, selection, and creation of park and reserve systems. Obviously, this is of primary importance in effective safeguarding of earth's wilderness. Excellent park planning work continues to be done by many private groups such as International Union for Conservation of Nature and Natural Resources, International Biological Program, World Wildlife Fund, the Sierra Club, and The Conservation Foundation; their efforts deserve substantially increased support. However, we also should be acting directly to obtain increased park planning assistance throughout the world from international agencies such as the Agency for International Development, the Peace Corps, the Organization of American States, the Food and Agriculture Organization, and the United Nations Educational, Scientific and Cultural Organization. These same groups are fostering the proliferation of technological forces now obliterating planetary organic diversity—certainly they should also be acting to retain a broad spectrum of this diversity in parks and reserves. At a minimum, we should try to preserve several examples representative of each identifiable natural ecosystem on our planet.

Nevertheless, we must recognize that the best planning, implementation, and protection to create such a global system of safeguarded wilderness will fail unless mankind can overcome its fundamental disharmony with the biosphere. Must man always require catastrophe to convince him of the necessity for change? I hope not. However, the very destructive capability of this brave new civilization means he *must* be able to anticipate and forestall future degradation. Short of establishing a new dynamic equilibrium with the world's environment, first wilderness and its many forms of life will vanish into oblivion as man's demands upon the biosphere increase. Then man himself will become an endangered species. In short, we face the end of infinity.

# CONSERVING THE ASSETS
# OF SPACESHIP EARTH

*R. Buckminster Fuller*
Professor of Comprehensive Design, Southern Illinois University

Mr. Milton has given a most extraordinarily confident inventory of the conditions confronting us. As my subject I have given the conservation of resources of Spaceship Earth for all generations to come. I would like to introduce, if I can, some thoughts that I hope will be useful. Certainly there is a world society coming and today's literate society is becoming increasingly aware of the problems we are all talking about here. Humanity has an extraordinary number of conditioned reflexes; reflexes developed because man has come through great vicissitudes and out of utter ignorance, mankind has made many amazing mistakes.

All of this does not add up to say that man is stupidly ignorant and does not deserve to prosper. It adds up to the realization that in the design of universal evolution, man was given an enormous safety factor as an economic cushion. Within this cushion man learns by trial and error to dare to use his most sensitively intuited intellectual conceptioning and greatest vision. He joins forces with all of humanity to advance into the future in full accreditation of the individual human intellect's conception of the potential functioning of man in universe.

Our little Spaceship Earth is only 8,000 miles in diameter, which is almost a negligible dimension in the great vastness of space. The nearest star to us is our energy-supplying mother ship—the sun—and the sun is 92,000,000 miles away. The next nearest star to us is 100,000 times further away. It takes two and one-half years for light to get to us from the next star. This is the kind of space distance pattern that we are flying. Our little Spaceship Earth is right now traveling at 60,000 miles an hour around the sun and, at the same time, is also spinning axially which, at a latitude central to the United States, adds approximately 1,000 miles per hour to our motion. Each minute we both spin at 100 miles and zip in orbit at 1,000 miles per hour. That is very swift spin and zip. When we launch our rocketed space capsules at 15,000 miles an hour, that additional acceleration speed which we give the rocket to attain its own orbit around our speeding Spaceship Earth is only one-fourth greater than the actual speed of our big planetary spaceship.

Spaceship Earth is so extraordinarily well invented and designed that, to our knowledge, humans have been on board it for over two million years without even knowing that they were on board a ship. And our spaceship is so superbly designed as to be able to keep life regenerating on board despite the phenomenon of entropy by which all local physical systems lose energy. So we have to obtain our biological life regenerating energy from another spaceship, the sun.

Our sun is flying in company with us, within the vast reaches of the galactic system, at just the right distance to give us enough radiation to keep us alive, yet not close enough to burn us up. And the whole scheme of Spaceship Earth and its live passengers is so superbly designed that the Van Allen Belts—which until very recently, we didn't even know we had—filter the sun and other star radiation which, as it impinges upon our spherical ramparts, is so concentrated that, if we went nakedly outside the Van Allen Belts, it would kill us.

Inasmuch as we are learning more intimately now about our Spaceship Earth and its radiation supply ship sun on the one hand, and on the other its moon, acting as the earth's gravitationally pulsing "alternator," which together constitute the prime generator and regenerator of our life-supporting system, I must observe here that we are not going to be able to sustain life at all, except by our successful impoundment of more of the sun's radiant energy aboard our spaceship. We could burn up the Spaceship Earth itself to provide energy—which is what we are really doing when we burn fossil fuels or utilize atomic energy—but this really gives us very little future.

It is obvious that any real wealth that we have on earth is a forwardly operative metabolic regenerating system. Quite clearly we have vast amounts of energy-income wealth such as sun radiation and moon gravity to implement our forward success. Therefore living only on our energy savings by burning up the fossil fuels which took billions of years to impound from the sun, or living on our capital by burning up our earth's atoms is lethally ignorant and also utterly irresponsible to our coming generations and their forward days. And our children and their children are our forward days.

Spaceship Earth's designed infusion of the radiant energy of the stars is processed in just such a way that man can carry on safely. A man can go out and take a sunbath but is unable to take in enough energy through the skin to keep himself alive. So part of the invention of Spaceship Earth's biological life-sustaining is that the vegetation on the land and the algae in the sea employ photosynthesis to impound adequate life-regenerating amounts of radiation energies. Of course, man cannot eat all the vegetation—as a matter of fact, he can eat very little of it. Man cannot eat the bark or the wood of the trees, or the grasses, but there are many other animals and creatures that can. And the animals that can eat the vegetation, plus a few of the fruits and tender vegetation petals, can be eaten by us.

That we are endowed with such intuitive and intellectual capabilities as that of discovering the genetic code, the structure of basic particles and other fundamental principles governing the basic design controls of life systems is part of the extraordinary design of our Spaceship Earth, its equipment, passengers and internal support systems. It is therefore paradoxical but strategically explicable, that up to now we have been misusing, abusing and polluting this extraordinary chemical-energy energy-interchanging system for successfully regenerating all life aboard our planetary spaceship.

One of the interesting things to me about our spaceship is that it is a mechanical vehicle, just as is, for example, an automobile. If you own an automobile, you realize that you must put oil and gas into it, and you must put water in the radiator and take care of the car as a whole. A man with a car begins to develop quite a little thermodynamic sense; he knows that he either has to keep his machine in good order or it's going to be in trouble and fail to function. We have not been seeing our Spaceship Earth as an integrally designed machine which to be persistently successful must be comprehended and serviced in total.

Now, no instruction book came with our Spaceship Earth and I find this fact very significant. In view of the infinite attention to all other details displayed by our ship, it can be taken as deliberate and purposeful that an instruction book was omitted. Lack of instruction has forced us to find that there are two kinds of red berries—red berries that will kill us and red berries that will nourish us. And we had to find our ways of telling which-was-which red berry before we ate it or otherwise we would die. So we were forced, because of the lack of an instruction book, to use our intellect which is our highest faculty, to devise scientific experimental procedures and to effectively interpret the significance of the experimental findings. Thus, because the instruction manual was missing, man is learning how he can safely anticipate the consequences of an increasing number of alternative ways of extending our satisfactory survival and growth—both physical and metaphysical.

Quite clearly all of life as designed and born is utterly helpless at the moment of birth. The human child stays helpless longer than does the young of any other species. Apparently, it is part of the invention "man" that he is meant to be utterly helpless through certain anthropological phases until he begins to get on a little better because he begins to discover some of the physical leverage-multiplying principles inherent in universe, as well as the many non-obvious resources around him which will further compoundingly multiply his knowledge-regenerating and life-fostering advantages.

I would say that designed into this Spaceship Earth's total resources was a big safety factor which allowed man to be ignorant for a long time until he had amassed enough experiences from which to extract progressively the system of generalized principles governing the increases of energy-managing advantages over environment. The designed omission of the instruction book on how to operate and maintain Spaceship Earth and its complex life-supporting and regenerating systems has forced man to discover retrospectively just what his most important forward capabilities are. Man's most important resource is his intellect. His intellect had to discover itself.

After discovery, man's intellect had in turn to compound the facts of his experience. Comprehensive reviews of the compounded facts of experience by intellect brought forth awareness of those generalized principles underlying all special and only superficially sensed experiences. Objective employment of those generalized principles in rearranging the physical resources of environment can lead to humanity's eventual total success on this planet, and readiness to cope with far vaster problems of universe.

As we begin to fix our present position aboard our Spaceship Earth, we must first acknowledge that the abundance of immediately consumable, obviously desirable or utterly essential resources has been sufficient until now to allow us to carry on despite our ignorance. Being eventually exhaustible and spoilable, they have been adequate only up to this critical moment. This cushion-for-error of humanity's survival and growth up to now apparently has been provided just as the embryo bird inside the egg is provided with liquid nutriment to develop it to a certain point. But then by design, the nutriment is exhausted at just the time when the chick is large enough to locomote on its own legs. And so, as the chick pecks at the shell seeking still more nutriment, it inadvertently breaks open the shell. Stepping forth from its initial sanctuary, the young bird must now forage on its own legs and wings to discover the next phase of its regenerative sustenance.

My own picture of humanity today finds us just about to step out from amongst the pieces of our just one-second-ago broken eggshell. Our innocent, trial-and-error-sustaining nutriment is exhausted. We are faced with an entirely new relationship to universe. We are going to have to spread our wings of intellect and fly or perish—that is, we must dare immediately to fly by the generalized principles governing universe and not by the ground rules of yesterday's superstitious and erroneously conditioned reflexes.

I am reminded so often just how we are cerebrally booby-trapped by yesterday's misinformation-polluted environment. Possibly the most lethal pollution we have is information pollution, the effect of which can blind us from seeing the costly eventualities of the more familiarly recognized water and atmosphere pollutions. Even today at lunch, I heard one of our prominent speakers speak about "the four corners of the earth" as a seemingly logical way to speak about the earth. A cosmological model of a wide, four-cornered planar earth surrounded by infinitely extensive waters discloses how the earliest historical humans explained the sum of their experiences to themselves. Because the sun and stars quite obviously passed over and returned under it, the world was implied to be a thick but penetrable watery slab extending horizontally to infinity in all planar directions.

All the perpendiculars to that slab's base plane were mathematically demonstrated as parallel to one another. Those perpendiculars then were extended in only two directions in relation to man's erroneously conceived flat earth. Those two exactly opposite, positive and negative, exclusively perpendicular directions in respect to the horizontal earth plane were the seemingly obvious concepts "up" and "down." Anyone who still uses the words "up" and "down" is subconsciously reflexing to the ancient concept of a flat earth. And that means approximately everybody today. I always ask the audiences as I address them, for a show of hands by any who do not use the words "up" and "down." No hands are ever raised. Science, of course, has found no single direction of universe that can be logically designated as "up" and another opposite celestial direction which is "down."

But we now know that we do not live on a flat slab and that we do live on board a spherical spaceship speeding around the sun at 60,000 miles per hour and spinning axially as it orbits. None of the perpendiculars to a sphere is parallel to one another. The first aviators flying completely around the earth within its atmospheric mantle and co-hered to the planet by gravity, having completed half their circuit, did not feel "upside down." They had to employ other words to explain their experiences.

So aviators evolved the terms "coming in" for a landing and "going out" when taking off. So when people say "up," they really mean "out," and when they say "down," they mean "in"—toward the center, the center of some specific, focal, unitary mass in the universe. Each individual's "in"-wardness is unique and specifically directional. The "out"-wardness is common to all the individual "in's" and is omni-directional. You come in toward various bodies in the universe and you go out from them. Those are the proper words. And if you should ever wish to challenge your own conditioned reflexes, try saying that you are going "outstairs" and "instairs." Just begin to try to discipline yourself, first, into speaking correctly, and you gradually will find after perhaps only a week that you are really thinking about being on board a spaceship.

Anyone spontaneously seeking to prove his "practical" sense who says, "Never mind that theoretical stuff—let's get down to earth!" probably banging the table with his fist as he says it, discloses himself as insane. We must reply to him, "Where and what is that 'down to earth' phenomenon?" Only yesterday, society spoke of an insane man as a "lunatic." Now history's first real luna-tics are history's most widely celebrated heroes for they are the earthian astronauts who first landed on luna—the moon—and are moon-touchers, ergo luna-tics. The moon viewpoint of earth first glimpsed realistically by humans through the television receivers at Christmastime, 1968, will soon become the natural way in which earthians will think of earth's celes-tial functioning. But on that Christmas, 1968, occasion the president of the United States while congratulating the moon-circumnavigating astronauts after their return to mother Spaceship Earth spoke of the astronauts' going up to the moon and back down to earth.

And our senior TV commentator, who is continually faced with the challenge of ameliorating his language to coincide with new informa-tion, said as the astronauts' TV camera was aimed at the earth, "There is our earth floating there!" Floating in what? There is nothing in which the earth floats; there is no gravitational displacement of one body by another. Our earth planet was at that moment; and continues to be, flying a fancy spin-around formation in company with the moon as the two together orbit the sun at a speed four-fold that which we impart additionally to our greatest space rockets. The earth's posi-tion in space is kinetically maintained by a combination of its precessionally maintained, mass-velocity momentum, and its orbital radius restraints—provided most prominently by the sun's gravity and secondarily by the other planets.

All the misconceptions expressed in our outmoded conditioned reflexes are found to be deep rooted in our twentieth-century self-misinformed "common sense." Common sense was assumed by society to be the antithesis of lunacy. It still is. But now we know that the lunacy conforms strictly to the cosmological reality and that the "down to earth" common sense of yesterday is fundamentally misinformed. This is perhaps a basis for the intuitive discrediting of the older generation by world youth who are directly informed by watching the astronauts as to the nature of celestial beauty.

This is just one of many indications of what I mentioned earlier—that man is on the verge of conscious and responsible participation in his own evolutionary transformation—and I include evolution of the environment as a major part of the evolution of humanity. Man's unconscious participation in the past has carelessly ruptured his earth, polluted his air and water, corrupted his children in order to sell any kind of toy guns, dope, smut and anything that would make money, and has made all moneymaking sacrosanct. But if we discover that man is necessary to the invention of universe, we can understand somewhat better what he is inadvertently doing. Some years ago, I asked myself whether man had a function in universe and if so, what it might be. My experience-informed answer went as follows:

The astronomers have given us their observation of the "red shift" which indicates that vast and remote star groups are probably receding from us in all directions because the light coming from them is redder than that from nearer groups. This indicates an expanding universe. An expanding universe is also predicted by the law of entropy or increase of the random element filling ever more space. We have also learned experimentally that unique behaviors are always countered by somewhat opposite behaviors although these behaviors need not be mirror images, one of the other. Therefore: an expanding universe would infer a concurrently contracting universe. So I began to look for those experiences which demonstrate the existence of such a contracting universe—even though none has been observed or mentioned by the astronomers.

I saw that around our own planet, we have high and low atmospheric "pressures," which might better be called expanding and contracting atmospheric patterns. I discovered clues to the operation of a contracting universe from the example of our own planet. Spaceship Earth is not radiant. It is not sending off energy in any important degree: As compared with a star, it is dead. Earth is receiving energy from the sun, but is not losing it at the same rate. We are receiving about 100,000 tons of star dust every day—even our physical imports from universe are, as yet, much greater than exports. Therefore, we are a collecting or concentrating center, possibly one amongst myriads in universe. All planets in universe may be collecting points as foci of the contracting phase in universe.

At the surface of the earth, in the topsoil, and the waters, the ecological balance becomes operative. The vegetation's chlorophyll inhibits the sun's radiation instead of allowing it to be reflectively rebroadcast back into space. The sun-inhibited energy impounded by the vegetation is further inhibited by insects, fish and mammals. Both botanicals and zoologicals are gradually pressured into the growing earth crust and finally are concentrated into coal and oil rather than being broadcast off to universe in all directions. By dissipating these energy concentrations, man may well be upsetting the expansion-contraction balance of universe.

The ecological balance is fascinating when viewed chemically. We find all biological systems continually sorting and rearranging atoms in methodical molecular structures. To ensure performance, each species is genetically and environmentally programmed. Each sorts and reassociates atoms as its genes cope with and alter environment, which in turn alters species behavior.

Thus we see that all the star dust, cosmic rays and other radiation randomly dispersed into universe by all stars are being methodically converted by the biological activity around our spaceship's whole surface—in the sea and on the land—into progressively more orderly "organic" chemical structures. Thus biological life on earth is anti-entropic. Earth is acting as an anti-entropic center as may well be all planets in universe.

Of all the anti-entropic sorters and rearrangers on earth, none compares with brain driven man. We find man continually differentiating and sorting out his experiences in his thoughts. As a consequence, we find him continually rearranging his environment so that he may eat, be clean, move about and communicate in more orderly and swifter ways.

Dr. Wilder Penfield is the head of the Neurological Institute of McGill University in Montreal. He is one of the world's leading electrode probers of the brain. The brain probers have now identified, for instance, the location of various memory banks. Dr. Penfield says, "It is much easier to explain all the data we have regarding the brain, if we assume an additional phenomenon 'mind,' than it is to explain all the data if we assume only the existence of the brain." Why? Because they have found, so to speak, the telephone sets of the brain, they have found the wires connecting the telephone sets, they have found the automatic message-answering service and the storage systems; but a great deal goes on in the conversations over the wires that is not explicable by the physical brain's feedback. I have submitted what I am saying to you to leading neurologists, and they have not found fault with it—so far, there have been no objections and there seems to be some affirmation of what I am about to say to you.

We have a phenomenon that we speak about as a generalization. In science, a generalization is very different from a literary generalization. Generalization in the literary sense usually means that you are trying to cover too much territory with some statement. The scientific meaning is precise: it means "the discovery and statement of a principle that holds true without exceptions." I will give you an example. I am going to talk about a piece of rope. I would have in my hands a foot length of three-quarter-inch Manila rope. But I can also say to you, "I am going to take an imaginary piece of rope," and I, not specifying nylon or Manila, immediately generalize a rope concept from our mutual experiences. I am going to pull on that piece of rope and as I pull on it very hard, it contracts in its girth. As it gets tauter, it gets tighter. This means that it goes into compression in its girth in planes at 90 degrees to the axis of the pull. I have found a great many human beings who think that tension is something independent of compression. I have found experimentally, however, that tension can only be operative when compression is also present. A cigar-shaped vertical compression member that is loaded on its neutral axis tries to "squash." This means that its girth tries to get bigger. Which means that its girth expands and is tensed. So I find that compression is never innocent of tension, but that they are cooperative in axes arranged at 90 degrees to one another. Sometimes I find tension at what we might call "high tide" or in highly visible aspect, and compression at "low tide" or almost invisible aspect, and vice versa. We have here a generalization. We have found by experiment, "Tension and compression only coexist." That is quite an advance over the first generalization just saying, "I take a piece of rope and pull on it," which was already a second-degree generalization (first, we had a generalized rope concept). It is a third-degree generalization when I say, "Tension and compression only coexist."

A system subdivides universe into all of the universe that is outside the system and all of the universe inside the system. Every system, as viewed from inside, is concave, and as viewed from outside, convex.

Concave and convex only coexist. Concave and convex are very different from one another. Convex diffuses energies by increasing wave lengths and widening angles. Concave concentrates energies by decreasing wave lengths and reducing angles. Although not the same and not exactly opposite, concave and convex only coexist.

In addition to tension and compression and concave and convex, I can give you a number of other such coexistences. This brings us then to another and further degree of generalization wherein we say that there is a plurality of coexistent behaviors in nature which are the complementary behaviors. That caused the mathematicians to generalize further. They developed the word "functions." Functions cannot exist by themselves. Functions only coexist with other functions. They are sometimes covariables. When I say "functions only coexist," I have gone a little further than the special cases of concave and convex or of tension and compression which were themselves highly generalized. Then I'll go further still and say, "Unity is a plural and at minimum two." This last is the generalization that greatly advanced quantum physics. We may go a little further in generalization, as did Einstein when he gave us his "relativity." You can't have relativity without a plurality of cofunctions.

Now, I shall give you another progression of events. You have seen a dog tugging at one end of a belt. He tenses it as he grips it compressionally—with the concave and convex surfaces of his teeth. I am sure that you will agree that the little dog will never say, "Tension and compression only coexist," even though his brain coordinated them. The dog will not say, "Concave and convex, tension and compression are similar cases of coexistence of functions." I think the neurologists go along with me in saying that what we mean by mind—in contradistinction to the brain of the animal or of man—is man's ability to generalize.

We have seen how an enormous amount of special case experiences finally led to a progression of generalizations. There were about six degrees of progressive generalization, and as we went from one case to another and to higher and higher degrees, it was accomplished with fewer and fewer words, until finally we used only one word, "relativity." Now this orderly simplification happens to be exactly the opposite of the mathematician's law of the increase of the random element. It is, instead, the decrease of the random element. Generalization is the law of progressive orderliness.

The mind of man seems to be the most advanced phase of anti-entropy witnessable in universe. And if there is an expanding universe there logically is a contracting universe. Possibly man's mind and his generalizations, which weigh nothing, operate at the most exquisite stage of universe contraction. Metaphysics balances physics. The physical portion of universe expands entropically. The metaphysical contracts anti-entropically.

So now we have found a function for man in universe, which was our objective. Man seems essential to the complementary functioning of universe. Therefore the probability of humanity annihilating itself and thus eliminating the anti-entropic function from universe is approximately zero. This does not, however, mean that man on earth may not eliminate himself. It suggests that there are—as the Cambridge University astronomer, Dr. Fred Hoyle, suggests—hundreds of millions of other planets in universe with men living on them.

This brings us to the observation also that to keep nature's ecological balance intact, when she finds the conditions are becoming unfavorable for any of her "cogwheel" species necessary for the system, she introduces many more starts of that species. She makes enormous numbers of seeds for this and that tree when she sees that such trees are not going to prosper. The seeds multiply in number, float off in the wind, randomly distribute in order to increase the probability of an adequate survival number to keep the system in balance.

Nature makes enormous numbers of babies whenever the species "man" has low chances for survival: witness the extraordinary rise in birth rates in time of war. Also, the rate of conversion from an agricultural-craft economy to an industrial economy is directly related to both birth rates and life span increase in the converted economy. The original European colonists in North America had an average family of 12 children—but many of these children died soon after birth. The average life expectancy for those who survived was 27 years. As industrial tools such as community water distribution and sewage systems, electric power, telegraph and telephone came into use, the birth rate went down and expectancy of life span increased. Today the birth rate in the United States is about two children per family and the average life expectancy is more than 70 years. Although there are larger numbers of humans now alive in the United States of America, the total number of babies born each year is decreasing. Population increase in all industrialized countries of the world, including Russia, is now holding consistently to this same pattern of birth rate decline and life expectancy increase—Japan has achieved approximate population equilibrium.

Because the additional, annually arrived human beings are decreasing in the industrialized countries, their population increase is due exclusively to people living longer. Because the highest death rate used to occur predominantly in the first four years of life, the decline of death in these years means that, momentarily, the big bulge in population increase through not dying is in the under-25-year-old people. That bulge will grow progressively older so that by 1985 the average population age in the industrialized nations will be 30 years, and the birth rate will be so lowered so as to begin to show a total population decrease. The population expansion through birth control is unique to the as yet nonindustrialized India, African, South and Central American countries. China, well on her way toward industrialization, has already instituted rigorous birth controls.

We can say quite clearly that the craftsman's hold on life was poor and that his numbers multiplied slowly if at all. We can say that industrialized man's chances of living out his "four score and ten" are high. We can say that the so-called population explosion is misleading terminology because the increase in numbers alive is due primarily to cessation of death at an ever increasing age. If man is to live only to 90, then the population increase will cease when the average age of people alive is 45 years. If man could learn how to keep human life going on indefinitely at a level of good health, vigor, and agility, then man might also stop producing new babies entirely.

Because of the tie-up of population characteristics with industrialization and because of the acceleration of industrialization rates in countries now and forwardly becoming industrialized, we can foresee a maximum world population reached in the year 1990, and a twenty-first century in which world population begins to decline. As world industrialization advances, the number of babies born will decrease to rates matching the accidental deaths. Stabilization of Spaceship Earth's population will probably occur at around five billion people and then there would be as yet five acres of dry land and 17 acres of water averaging one-half mile deep for every human on the planet. Life will still be sparse enough around the surface of Spaceship Earth and natural resources for life support will as yet be abundant if adequately conserved.

Man is beginning to transform from being utterly helpless and only subconsciously coordinated with important evolutionary events. We have gotten ourselves in a lot of trouble, but now at the critical transformation stage, we are getting to a point where we are beginning to know a little something. Man is probably coming to the first consciously assumed responsibility of man in universe. And with his responsibility, man will be preoccupied with the safeguarding of the innate faculties of the newborn. Man's mind, refined to understanding, tolerance and love, will compound for all humanity the ever increasingly augmentable advantages inherent when each child is born in the presence of less misinformation and is endowed with as yet undamaged, unfrustrated love drives to apprehend, comprehend, understand, and be understood. Each child will employ regeneratively the ever more reliable information, and thereby potentially discover and designingly employ on behalf of humanity an ever greater inventory of the generalized principles inter-accommodatively governing universal-metaphysical and physical evolution.

# CONSTRUCTING THE MAN-MADE WILDERNESS

*George Macinko*
Professor of Geography
Central Washington State College

My invitation to this conference came from Chairman Dan Luten, who suggested that I might look at a landscape architect's review of *Wilderness in a Changing World*, the book that resulted from the Ninth Biennial Wilderness Conference. The review in question lamented the fact that the environmental design skills of the landscape architect and the regional planner found no place in the wilderness conference. Dan further suggested that I might address myself to the question of whether one truly can design a wilderness.

Brushing aside the contradiction implicit in the architect's criticism—the Wilderness Act specifies that a wilderness is to be contrasted with those areas where man and his works dominate the landscape—I began my assignment. From the outset, it seemed readily apparent that nothing more could be put into any wilderness design than existed in the mind of the would-be designer. For this reason it seemed equally apparent that the environmental designer would have to consult the environmental specialist—the ecologist—to flesh out his design. Because I already had consulted ecologists and was familiar with the writings of an even larger group, I was convinced that the complexities, interrelations, and unknowns in ecosystem functioning were such that any contrived wilderness could be at best but a greatly simplified version of the original. The score might be fairly good with respect to birds, the larger mammals, and the more prominent plants, but would fall far short in terms of the invertebrates and other less conspicuous biota. For example, F. Fraser Darling at the Sixth Wilder-

237

ness Conference (1959) referred to a Danish study indicating that the biomass of animals above ground is equaled by that below ground. To further emphasize the complexity of wilderness and our relative ignorance of it, Darling asks if you can list the things present, their associations, and their proportional incidences. If you can, he counts you lucky, for few geographical areas are so well known.

I was familiar with many such examples and I was sympathetic to S. Dillon Ripley's idea that the complexly woven and integrated systems we call ecosystems are not only more complicated than we think they are, but are more complicated than we *can* think. This, then, was the background from which I would have developed the point that our lack of knowledge guaranteed that the man-made wilderness would be at best a much simplified and a less than satisfactory imitation of its prototype. In true sporting fashion I had decided I would not chide the design professionals for taking on the wilderness (admittedly an unknown and unfamiliar area) before they had demonstrated fully acceptable work in the city (a familiar and presumably better known area).

This simple plan went awry when I read Stephen Spurr's contention that wilderness is a sociological concept peculiar to each man and each generation. Spurr first made this contention at the Eighth Biennial Wilderness Conference (1963) and later elaborated on it in the Sixth Horace M. Albright Conservation Lectureship presented at the University of California, Berkeley (1966), under the title "Wilderness Management." Here was a respected ecologist who in the latter work not only said that wilderness could and should be managed, but also argued for an expanded definition of wilderness.

The apparent clash between the words "wilderness" and "management" can be resolved, according to Spurr, by simply taking the second definition of wilderness in the *Oxford Universal Dictionary*, "a piece of ground in a large garden or park, planted with trees, and laid out in an ornamental or fantastic style, often in the form of a maze or labyrinth." Spurr then went on to contend that if the essence of wilderness is a place where one is isolated from the sights, sounds, and smells of human activity, then the perception of a place as wilderness will differ among observers depending on their various experiences. As a result, he concludes that to a seventeenth-century Londoner, wilderness might conform to the definition cited above. To Longfellow, it was the forest primeval. To Thoreau, a rather domesticated pond at Walden. To the Sierra Club member, a mountain meadow. But Spurr pleaded for a much greater expansion of the definition of wilderness. On the grounds that each man has his own version of wilderness, Spurr argued that to some urbanites wilderness may even be a thicket in a city park, or a backyard in a suburban home. How the latter provides isolation from the sights, sound, and smells of human activity is never made clear.

Elastic definitions aside, Spurr's argument that an ecosystem has reality only at a given point of space and at a given point of time is compelling. Spatially, he argued, the ecosystem changes gradually along a continuum as changes occur in climate, soil, and land, while temporally it is subject to change diurnally, seasonally, and over a period of years. For this reason he said there never was a constant wilderness and never will be. He emphasized the point that nature cannot be locked up and preserved indefinitely at some particular stage, for change inevitably will take place because of death, migration, and genetic evolution. Since succession is bound to occur, Spurr said you cannot preserve an area intact, but you can approximate a previously existing ecosystem by careful ecological manipulation. He argued that such manipulation is management; we should admit this explicitly and then consciously manage wild lands to achieve our objectives. It should be noted that creating a wilderness for Spurr is largely a process of a limited and unobtrusive use of technical skills to supplement the natural process of regeneration. The aim is to avoid the introduction of obvious man-created incongruities into the landscape. No doubt the wilderness purist will recoil from the suggestion that wilderness should be managed, but I find no quarrel with some degree of wilderness management—a practice already engaged in— though I would brook far less than Spurr.

Examination of the total American environment discloses landscapes which range from those wherein visible signs of man's presence are absent or minimal to those in the heart of large urban areas where man's impact is all-pervasive. To the former we assigned the name "wilderness." How far toward the latter one can slide and still meaningfully apply the same wilderness designation is subject to some arbitration, but I find the mind boggles at the notion of the suburban backyard wilderness. Nor can this stretching in terminology be excused by recourse to a secondary definition in the dictionary. The High Sierra, Balboa Park, and a suburban backyard conjure up different images. To apply the term wilderness indiscriminately to all three, and presumably to all variations between, is to strip the term of its meaning. Meaningful use would require that such an all-embracing term be subdivided into wilderness type 1, wilderness type 2, etc., thereby specifying the context in which the term is used. Now, it seems unarguable that the context of the Sierra Club wilderness conferences and the 1964 Wilderness Act validates the meaning of wilderness as an area of earth minimally influenced by man and containing significant numbers of wildlife. This meaning and this context preclude the suburban backyard wilderness.

An analogy may prove useful here, for context is all-important. The analogy suggested itself to me last evening when I sat down at the banquet table and noticed that the first item on the menu was hearts of lettuce. Now imagine for a moment that you are at home some evening. The doorbell rings and a solicitor announces that he is collecting for the Heart Fund. You make a contribution only to find out later that it was used to support activities at the local pool hall. Would you be content with an explanation of this seeming diversion of funds which had as its justification the fact that the word "heart" can be defined as "the game of cards" or "the suit of cards so marked," or alternatively, if you discovered that your contribution had been used to support research into lettuce blight on the grounds that one of the meanings of heart is "the central or most vital part of anything"? Instead, would you not feel that the context as cited demands the definition of heart as "a hollow muscular organ of vertebrate animals that by its rhythmic content acts as a force pump maintaining the circulation of the blood"? And finally, would you be placated by an argument that suggests no concern need be generated over the deterioration of hearts of the latter type (circulatory pumps) because hearts of the former type (card games and vegetables) were thriving? All this suggests that Spurr's use of secondary and tertiary definitions of wilderness was inappropriate as it served more to obscure than to enlighten.

Perhaps I dwell overlong on semantics, but I believe we have here the entering wedge whereby the process of definition can be used to permit the alteration and destruction of wilderness while at the same time insisting that wilderness is being maintained—although in a different form. I would be less chary about this were I not aware of a similar though more advanced trend in my own field of geography where during the past decade geographers, with the help of others, have used the pages of that otherwise admirable magazine, *Landscape*, to blunt the distinction between man and nature and thence between man-made and natural. Starting with the unarguable premise that man is part of nature, the argument by means of circumlocutions concludes that redwood forests and the Golden Gate Bridge are equally natural objects, and if natural objects of the former type (those representing the living world) increasingly give way to natural objects of the latter type (those representing the nonliving world), it is only the sophistically naive who feel pangs of remorse over this trend.

The attempt to clarify thinking on the relationship between man and nature is needed because wilderness does have many values worthy of recognition. Prominent among these are the value of wilderness as an ecological landmark—as a standard for judging man's management systems—and the value of natural biota for medicinal purposes and as a gene pool. Perhaps more important than these scientific values is the potential value of wilderness as a civilizing influence on man in that the qualities of foresight and forbearance, the capacity for wonder and compassion (human attributes necessary to save wilderness) are also fundamental to the salvation of man.

Starker Leopold, for one, sees a vast difference between the creation of a botanical garden and the maintenance of an undisturbed natural area. The difference largely is that in maintaining wilderness man shows respect for nature as it exists, whereas in the garden, he arranges, rearranges, and manages for his own interests. At a time when international aggression and strife are increasing, the exercise of respect for nature and the humility that must accompany such respect might well prove salutary to the passions of man.

Six years ago the late Aldous Huxley prophesied that only by shifting his collective attention from the merely political to the basically ecological aspects of the human situation could man hope to mitigate and shorten the time of troubles into which it seemed he was moving. Huxley's prophecy, vindicated by the events of the past six years, was based on his belief that power politics in the context of nationalism raises problems that, except by war, are practically insoluble. The problems of ecology, on the other hand, he held to "admit of a rational solution" and these, he believed, could be "tackled without the arousal of those violent passions always associated with dogmatic ideology and nationalistic idolatry." In further elaboration of these sentiments, he noted that while there might be arguments about the best way to raise wheat in a cold climate, or reforest a denuded mountain, such arguments never led to organized slaughter. Organized slaughter, he said, resulted from questions such as: Which is the best nation? the best religion? the best political theory?

Huxley believed politics were unlikely to improve until it was understood that the basic problem confronting twentieth-century man was ecological. Only with this understanding could man make a break with the irrelevant and anachronistic politics of nationalism and military power to consider more fundamental issues, such as: "How does the human race propose to survive and, if possible, improve the lot and the intrinsic quality of its individual members? Do we propose to live on this planet in symbiotic harmony with our environment? Or, preferring to be wantonly stupid, shall we choose to live like murderous and suicidal parasites that kill their hosts and so destroy themselves?"

Huxley's position was as ecologically conservative as it was politically liberal. On both counts he proved to be prescient. Ten years ago Wallace Stegner at the wilderness conference said: "A nervous man might even fear for the carbon cycle: we may need our wilderness for making oxygen." One need not be a nervous man today to harbor such fears, as Paul Ehrlich so amply demonstrated in his keynote address yesterday morning. This was even more fully developed in the December 1968 issue of the *Population Bulletin* wherein LaMont Cole, a Cornell ecologist, raised just the same specter. In introducing Cole's analysis, Robert Cook, past president of the Population Reference Bureau, reminded us that the thin slice of the earth we know as the biosphere is a "fabulously implausible" occurrence. Cook asked that we consider the odds wherein earth organisms that survive within a temperature range of about 120 degrees find those conditions here on earth when, in the universe, temperatures range over perhaps 26 million degrees. And, he reminded us, life as we know it depends on a mixture of gases which is almost incredibly exotic by galactic standards. For example, oxygen must be mixed with other gases in proper proportions just to keep from exploding.

Given the unique and fragile nature of our biosphere we have been fortunate that until recently no creature could significantly affect it. However, man's newly acquired technological prowess in conjunction with the precipitous increase in his numbers now poses serious problems to the biosphere. Let me return to Cole for but one example. His calculations of the oxygen supply for the 48 conterminous United States indicate that the amount of oxygen produced by photosynthesis within our borders is not quite 60 percent of the amount consumed by our combustion of fossil fuels. Assuming Cole's calculations to be even approximately correct means that we are absolutely dependent on oxygen imported from outside—chiefly that from the Pacific Ocean brought in by atmospheric circulation. In a world apparently committed to increasing industrialization and thereby to an accelerating use of fossil fuels, it would be prudent to maintain satisfactory oxygen levels by establishing safeguards on photosynthetic processes. This elementary precaution seems to have been neglected. Although nearly 70 percent of the earth's annual supply of oxygen is produced by marine diatoms and though we add 400 to 500 new chemicals each year to the store of nearly one-half-million man-made substances inflicted on ourselves and our environment, only a minute fraction of these has been tested for toxicity to marine diatoms.

Because the end of the production of new chemicals is nowhere in sight and because environmental problems, real and potential, have become so serious, man can no longer trust to luck and hope that environmental modifications will turn out to be harmless; he must insure this outcome. To do so he must adopt a conservative attitude toward the biosphere and himself. Man must collectively, and soon, decide what quality of biosphere and what quality of life he wants and then institute the pollution controls and population incentives needed to get and sustain them.

Had I read Cole's statement more than a month ago I would have reacted in my usual fashion. That is, I would have discussed it with my colleagues, brought it to the attention of my classes, and perhaps incorporated it within my own writing efforts. However, after reading a story about the Environmental Defense Fund (EDF) and its attorney, Victor Yannacone, in the February 3, 1969, issue of *Sports Illustrated*, I am more or less convinced that my previous procedure is an inadequate prescription for present and future environmental disorders. Yannacone argues persuasively that the traditional conservation position is essentially negative in that it assumes a defensive position at the outset. "Rather than asserting rights and demanding justice, organized conservation has been educating each generation to the position that the natural environment is absolutely subject to ruthless, unscientific, ecologically suicidal degradation in the quest for private gain." Yannacone notes that the penalty for adopting this defensive position, rather than having the public assert its primacy in all aspects of environmental use, is the belief that in order to protect their national heritage conservationists must buy it at the price set by the exploiters. Yannacone concludes that conservationists must instead work toward a reversal of these positions, essentially placing the would-be exploiter in the position wherein he must justify socially and economically his environmental manipulation schemes before he can act. And he would use litigation as the primary means to bring about this fundamental reversal of positions and attitudes.

I affirm that EDF is correct in its belief that the people of the United States are constitutionally entitled to the full benefit, use, and enjoyment of the American environment and that the right to a sound environment must replace the right to pollute. Further, I believe that Yannacone may also be correct when he says that at this time in our history litigation may be the only way—or at least the most effective way—to focus the attention of legislators on environmental problems. Therefore, I believe that conservationists, myself included, must be prepared to go to court in the interest of the environment rather than simply write letters to editors and congressmen. The following example of a type that can be duplicated almost daily in any major newspaper may help to make clear the necessity for new modes of action if environmental improvement is to be attained.

The February 6th Seattle *Post-Intelligencer* ran a news item headed "SST Pollutants May Turn Sky White or Earth Warmer Scientists Caution." The article went on to say that though the scientists were not sure of the exact effects of the vaporous by-products of the supersonic transport (SST), they were greatly concerned that the SST would leave a trail of water vapor, carbon dioxide, and soot in the stratosphere where it might remain aloft for years, thereby adversely affecting the atmosphere in a progressively accumulative way. Consequently, the scientists called for major experiments before the SST's were activated. However, the paper reported The Boeing Company apparently was not concerned with the problem and was conducting no major research in the area prior to flying the SST.

Now, as I near the end of my paper I think it proper to return to the wilderness role of the landscape architect and regional planner. Because in the final analysis it is man's total environment that is most important, and because this total environment should have included in it a full range of landscape, I would encourage the design specialists to proceed with the construction of an experimental wilderness in the same sense that Athelstan Spilhaus has promoted the experimental city. Both ideas are worthy of implementation.

An experimental wilderness should produce at least two benefits: first, disclose some of the limitations on technology, and by demonstrating that confidence in technology sometimes goes unrewarded, might help avert more dangerous future situations when man may well have survival at stake rather than simply wilderness preservation; second, help to ease pressures building on true wilderness areas. Since wilderness implies wildness, low density, and but a modest number of viewers, the quasi-wilderness should be welcomed as a means of siphoning off that part of the recreational crowd to whom true wilderness means little. Though the experimental man-made wilderness should be promoted, efforts to acquire and maintain natural wilderness must proceed unabated because the two concepts are not interchangeable.

In *Round River* Aldo Leopold stated, "The last word in ignorance is the man who says of an animal or plant: 'What good is it?' If the land mechanism as a whole is good, then every part is good, whether we understand it or not. If the biota, in the course of aeons, has built something we like but do not understand, then who but a fool would discard seemingly useless parts? To keep every cog and wheel is the first precaution of intelligent tinkering."

We would do well to pay heed to Leopold's admonishment that we are the recipients of an environment which was a long time making and which, in man's absence, generated a magnificent complex of living things. Though man now has the power, or may soon get the power, to engage in environmental manipulations on a truly prodigious scale, it is not at all certain that he can with impunity substitute his plan for nature's. In man's headlong flight to conquer nature, he tends to behave as though he were not subject to any ecological laws. This overdose of hubris is not the formula for a long and productive stay on earth—no matter what it does for the human ego.

The basic problem of man is ecological—how to establish a satisfactory and homeostatic ecosystem on planet Earth with man as a member. In this attempt he is likely to encounter many pitfalls. Among the most important may be his fantastic powers of adaptation.

René Dubos put it very well when he said, "Man can learn also to tolerate ugly surroundings, dirty skies, and polluted streams. . . . He can live without the fragrance of flowers, the songs of birds, the exhilaration of natural scenery, and other biological stimuli of the natural world." This tolerance enables him to overcome effects that are unpleasant or even traumatic when first experienced. The ultimate result, said Dubos, "can be and often is an impoverishment of life, a progressive loss of the qualities that we identify with humanness and weakening of mental and physical sanity." These words remind us that creating a desirable future requires a vision of what we think life ought to be. It may be that in the furtherance of such vision the wilderness conferences make their greatest contribution.

# DISCUSSION

*Robert R. Curry, assistant professor of environmental sciences, University of California at Santa Barbara*\*: I propose that the total combined area of ecological preserves and wilderness areas existing in the world by the year 2000, 31 years from now, will determine the distribution of and directly influence every living human being left on earth in the year 2050. This proposal is based upon a premise that world population growth for the next 80 years will create such stresses on the world food reserves that at least one, and possibly two, worldwide famines will occur. These great famines which will affect, in varying degrees, everyone on the earth will hereafter be referred to as "GF I" and "GF II."

My idea is that the world's intrinsically viable ecosystem preserves, in addition to giving pleasure and knowledge to the present population, will act as the biotic reserves for plants and animals able to repopulate the denuded, soil-free, scorched earth after human, plant, and animal population crashes that accompany famines. It is the opinion of many natural and social scientists that the world is on the brink of its first major decline in Homo sapiens populations. As an environmental scientist, I am no longer concerned about the population explosion—with our effective socio-political phase lag that has already occurred—but I now wish to consider the nature of the world between population crests and consider the number of "explosions"

* Dr. Curry is now assistant professor of geology, University of Montana, effective fall 1969.

246

to occur before we develop the moral philosophy to willfully maintain our human populations in balance with animal and plant food resource populations.

Stress is usually placed on the aesthetic and scientific values of the existence of the wilderness areas per se to the population. With these values I entirely agree. However, there are other rationales for preserving as many examples of our natural world as possible. Throughout the three-million-year-long evolution of mankind, icecaps have offset populations of plants and animals living over large areas of the earth's crust. During periods of waxing glaciers, examples of the biota survived in refugia from which they spread outward to repopulate the glaciated regions after the ice melted. Man himself may have been able to populate the Americas by periodically "wintering over" through 20,000 or more years of Ice Age, occupying ice-free refugia along the Arctic Ocean shores and interior Alaska at times when a low sea level permitted his crossing of the Bering Strait land bridge while icecaps extending from British Columbia to New York blocked his passage into southern North America and South America.

I can picture a population crisis at time of world famine that is much more destructive to plant and animal life than any of the geologic crises that may have occurred in the past. Man's ability to modify and extract his natural resources has never been surpassed by other organisms inhabiting the earth for the last billion years. Of all the people who have ever lived on earth, one out of 20 is alive today—and almost 50 percent of these have not yet borne children. We can perhaps support a population doubling by the year 2000 if we greatly increase our efficiency of resource use and distribution. But if present population growth rates continue, by A.D. 2050 the world will reach the most extreme and numerically optimistic upper theoretical limit of sustainable human population of 30 billion people. These 30 billion could just be sustained at mere minimum starvation levels without motivation, intellect, or cares for the future of mankind. They would exist for short life spans of less than 30 years at the lowest possible standard of living. Long before this could ever happen, man's aggressiveness and geopolitical immaturity will force famine on at least parts of the world's populations with resultant unrest and pressures that will be felt strongly throughout the world. A biologically realistic population limit for the world is six to eight billion people—a limit to be reached about the year 2000. Stanford biologist Paul Ehrlich predicts that major regional famines may begin as soon as 1975—only six years from now.

By "population crash" I imply that total world populations will rapidly drop from six billion to as low as one billion rather than merely level off at six billion or slowly decline. This prognosis is based upon a biologic population model in which world raw materials, grossly deficient for existing populations, are unequally distributed among a powerful few. When imbalance is critical, a sort of chain reaction occurs wherein, for instance, malnutrition decreases resistance to disease, death rates rise rapidly among the aged and very young, medical care becomes overtaxed, world epidemics decrease the reproductive capacity of surviving populations, and within perhaps as little as 20 years the world population crashes.

During and immediately before a population crash, food demands upon all productive lands and seas will be extreme. The sea can actually supply relatively little of the demands of a population of 20 to 30 billion, and the land wilderness areas will come under heavy attack. Today's protective legislation will be ignored or declared invalid in time of supernational emergency, and our ecological preserves may suffer the same fate as that of some of the woods and maintained game preserves of Europe during World Wars I and II. Ecologists will agree that it is imperative that examples of all species of plants and animals survive GF's I and II. One could argue that only those species upon which man is dependent for food should be preserved, i.e., domesticated animals and plants, but clearly this would create such a depauperate population with so imbalanced an ecosystem that subsequent human populations would not be able to develop to our present potential. Cattle and sheep would be the least able to survive in a world without human population to care for them. When cattle and sheep return to a wild state for lack of domestic care, they do not long survive in areas without winter range. Some populations might learn to migrate great distances to follow available feed, but even these would be susceptible to diseases that could wipe out domestic varieties lacking inherited natural resistance.

Even today we are just learning the value to mankind of some of our animal and plant colleagues. Our top predator, the duck hawk, has just given us the warning about our worldwide systemic contamination with DDT. The lowly molds have existed for more than two billion years but gave us penicillin, terramycin, and the other antibiotics in only this century. The bacteria living on the fungus in a rotting wilderness log may prove to be the key to permitting humans to directly consume cellulose at some date after A.D. 2050—yet the fungus might not survive soil removal and deforestation during the great famines.

The idea of multiple famines derives from my optimistic belief that mankind, as a species, will be able to survive world famines and accompanying disease in numbers of perhaps one billion individuals who are strong, disease and stress resistant, and live in remote areas. Since natural population crises accompanying crashes in most mammal groups generally result in increased fecundity and overall reproductive success after the crash, human populations may spring back to critical limits of five to six billion in 50 to 100 years—long before the earth would be naturally restored to an ecological balance after the soil destruction of the first great famine.

Only true complete wilderness entities, complete ecologically unto themselves, can act as adequate refugia upon which future populations can call for breeding stock for future food sources.

I believe ecologists, conservationists, and concerned parent-citizens should press for legislation to set aside and protect by international law and virtual geographic inaccessibility large enough areas of wilderness representing all the major types of world biota (including those of the sea) to permit our great-grandchildren and their great-grandchildren to at least understand the potential population diversity of stable ecosystems, and the dynamic range of species and population densities occurring within natural systems unmodified by monocultural extractive processes and philosophies. Clearly this action should be begun with utmost haste and urgency. An international body such as the United Nations should be best able to coordinate the actions of individual nations in setting aside preserves, but agencies such as the United Nations move much too slowly. The first United Nations Environmental Congress is scheduled for June, 1972, in Stockholm. With this sort of timing, I fear that the first congress may be the last. I suggest an environmental congress in 1971 to be supported by the scientific and conservation organizations of the world. Specific protective legislation as well as potentially salvageable ecosystems could be proposed so that a mandate may be presented to the United Nations in 1972.

With political and technological breakdown during prolonged famines, fuel reserves will be exhausted rapidly, and only those naturally selected individuals who are able to seek out on foot, and survive in, the ecological preserves will be able to draw upon them. Possibly the numbers of humans surviving will be small enough to avoid destruction of the refugia yet diverse enough to assure a large gene-pool for slow repopulation during the approximately 10- to 30,000-year periods necessary to naturally renew a small portion of the world's soil cover.

Ferren MacIntyre, assistant professor, Scripps Institution of Oceanography, University of California at San Diego: It is not easy to follow
a speaker like Robert Curry for my topic has relevance only if we get
past Great Famine I. But there are at least two ways we can do this:
by taking to heart Swift's Modest Proposal, or more likely by a technological debauch that will make our previous remodeling of the planet
look like an infant at his mud pies. In either case I foresee an ultimate
problem far more subtle than starvation of the belly: we have to learn
to survive technology's starvation of the soul. A partial—but essential—
answer is with unmanaged wilderness.

As a hard-nosed physical scientist, well accustomed to logical rigor,
it bothers me that I find the arguments of the wilderness managers
logical and compelling, but their conclusion unacceptable. Their
arguments state that man has so altered the earth that no true wilderness survives, and that the retention of even the semblance of wilderness for sentimental reasons in the face of increasing pressures will
require careful planning and priority setting. Their conclusion has
been most forcefully put by arch-manager Stephen Spurr, who says in
Tomorrow's Wilderness, the book based on the Eighth Biennial Wilderness Conference: "I submit that we should identify the values we
wish to create and then set ourselves deliberately to create a wilderness
with these values." I find myself asking: "What if the oxymoron
'planned wilderness' reflects a basic incompatibility? What if it turns
out once again that the ends are the product of the means? What if
the value we need (not wish) to create is unplanned, spontaneous,
messy, natural wilderness?"

The conclusion follows from the argument if, and only if, one ac-
cepts the underlying axioms that are never mentioned, that wilderness
managers share with all of technological man. One of these runs, "The
earth is man's, and the fullness thereof."

But this is medieval superstition writ large, embodying all the
wisdom of the old belief that the sun revolves around the earth because man lives here. We see ourselves as the finale of evolution: from
an unbiased point of view we may not even be the most interesting
species currently living on our planet. It is entirely possible that a
visitor from a truly advanced civilization would see us as we see
baboons: aggressive, successful, obnoxious, and poor neighbors—and
ignore us in favor of philosophical discourses with whales.

The good Lord gave man stewardship, not domination. If we have
any just claim to our role as keepers of the ecosystem, it lies in our
ability to empathize with the rest of nature, to recognize ourselves as
part of the system, and to care for our fellow mortals as we care for

ourselves. Humility to recognize that we may never know what we *need* to have on a given tract of land is part of the stewardship.

The idea that wilderness ought to be wild smacks of preservationism, and that is a dirty word. Preservationists are known to be emotional, and their arguments are correspondingly discounted in reasoned discussion. But the emotion that drives a preservationist is more basic than pensive nostalgia for the trees of his childhood. It is the species' gut urge to survive. Preservationists are not fundamentally worried about saving trees, marshes, mountain lions, and sea otters, but about preserving mankind itself. Nature, like the coal miner's canary, is a sensitive indicator of what lies ahead for man. If wilderness cannot survive, neither can we.

There is ample evidence to show that man as man can coexist with nature. One can look back some 20,000 years to the Cro-Magnon artists who painted the wonderful animals of Lascaux and identify completely with them, their art, culture, awareness of life and its mysteries. All these have been with man since he became man, with or without technology. But there is no evidence at all to suggest that man can survive without the natural environment. Such indications as we have suggest that the future of hyper-urban man will parallel the much faster evolution of that other urbanized species, the rat. The rat comes in two urban varieties. One is the brown ghetto version: unruly, belligerent, clever, adaptable, and savage. The other is the antiseptic, white, Anglo-Saxon, Protestant version found in the citadels of research and technology: chosen for uniformity, docile through stupidity, and incapable of surviving outside of its air-conditioned cage.

With examples like this before us, I am afraid that what the wilderness managers are doing is irrelevant to the needs of the occasion. I am reminded of a similar irrelevancy that occurred at the last New York world's fair where the Vatican exhibited the "Pietà." The problem was accommodating the vast number of people who wanted some acquaintance with one of the world's great works of art. The solution was typical, technological-manager: put the "Pietà" behind glass, light it dramatically, and run the people past on a three-tiered conveyor belt to the accompaniment of soft music. That was an elegant engineering solution—but what did it have to do with art? A plastic model shown on TV would have done as well. The viewer checked off "Pietà" and went on to the Walt Disney movie. What did he see of tragedy? Loss? Love? Relevance? Identification? He was denied all benefit of personal interaction with the sculpture because the manager solved the wrong problem. What frightens me is that the manager probably had a clear conscience about it all and was totally unaware that he was incapable of recognizing the real problem. I am similarly suspicious of wilderness managers, for like technologists everywhere, they can solve nearly every problem they can recognize, but no others. I am afraid that this is not enough.

Man's need to manage nature is more than a quirk of the wilderness planners' psyches, for it has been with us for a long time indeed. Its first expression seems to have been the Pleistocene overkill that wiped out the large mammals of the Ice Age. It appeared later as sorcery and despotism, then still later disguised as agriculture and technology. In the nineteenth century it surfaced in the Marxian concept that only those things produced by man have value, that everything in nature ought to be brought under man's rational control. For 40,000 years we struggled to mold the protean forces of nature into man's image, succeeding finally by inventing God the Creator and God the Father. Then with the help of psychology we debunked God the Father, and now seem bent upon replacing God the Creator with a thousand manic managers.

The need to manage nature remains a deep-seated psychological drive. It hits me every time I get my hands on a pair of pruning shears. Snip! (neaten). Snip! (organize). Snip! (manipulate)—but I recognize this as a vestigial urge that no longer serves its original purpose. I can control the impulse and keep my hedges bushy. But, since the managers seem unable to control the impulse by themselves, I suggest that we redirect their psychological drive into useful pursuits. In order to do this, I would like to submit a new classification of wilderness which will be a fitting job for these managerial talents. We have heard about many kinds of wilderness this weekend: etymological, de facto, statutory, mishandled, lost—but we have not talked about the most important kind of all. We have not faced up to the problem of adequate per capita wilderness.

As population grows our technological dogma asserts that we can expect more and better of the goodies of life. If the technological culture is viable, it must also deliver more and better of the things that make man human. This includes enough variety of so-called empty space and unplanned wild land so that each person can find his own level of wilderness, and enough area so that the wilderness is self-sustaining and not in need of constant rehabilitation. This is a need that increases directly as the population increases; meeting it is a challenge that will separate the real wilderness planners from the mere tinkerers.

Why is wilderness so vital? Because we are human. A person who was all cold superego without the wild promptings of the id might be a logically impeccable thinker. But he would be a pitiable failure as a human being, and one with no psychic reserves to fall back on in times of stress. Such, I believe, is the plight of an urban civilization without its wild back country: eventually it dies of a surfeit of rational management. This is only a hypothesis, of course, but it is one which we are actively testing. What if it is right? What if there is an absolute need for untouched, unplanned, unmanaged wilderness where man can escape from himself, where society's id can recuperate from technology's superego? What if the reason that man is lonely in space, and has not made contact with other more advanced civilizations on nearby planets, is that no other technological civilization thought to leave itself this sort of escape room?

Astronomers, searching the sky for signs of such extraterrestrial life, have made estimates of the probability of life arising on other planets. Shklovskii and Sagan, in their provocative book *Intelligent Life in the Universe*, suggest that there are probably 100 billion inhabitable planets in our galaxy, with 50,000 to one million extant civilizations scattered among them. Some of these civilizations will be technological—by which one means that they have achieved at least the ability to communicate over interstellar distances. (By this definition, mankind is just entering its technological period.) Freeman Dyson has shown that in a mere 3,000 years a technological civilization could—and probably would—so alter the appearance of its central sun that earth-based astronomers would be aware of the existence of the civilization even though it made no attempt to communicate. Why then have we seen no indication of such extraterrestrial technologies?

One thought-provoking answer that comes out of the probability estimates is that the average lifetime of a technological civilization is a critical parameter. If this lifetime is 10 million years, there should be an advanced neighbor within 100 light-years of us, and intercultural chatting should be commonplace. If, on the other hand, the lifetime is on the order of 100 years, we may be the galaxy's only living example of a technological civilization.

The reason that we have not detected signs of extraterrestrial life may simply be that technological civilizations just naturally kill themselves off within a century. Perhaps as soon as technology anywhere learns to do something, it tries it. It does not really matter what its final try might have been.

This is a sobering thought. It suggests that perhaps man is not unique in his failure to adapt to success. Perhaps nearly all species that become dominant over their planetary environment fail to recognize that they are unstable in their manufactured substitutes. Perhaps everywhere economics takes precedence over ecology. Perhaps everywhere practical managers ignore the literal truth of Thoreau's vision: "In wildness is the preservation of the world."

*Session Chairman Raymond J. Sherwin:* On examining the wording of the questions submitted to the panel, it looks to me as if the audience has answered some of the questions posed by the speakers today. It seems to me also that the subjects raised by these questions could serve for an entire wilderness conference.

The first set of questions is directed to George Macinko. What you gentlemen have been discussing is profoundly radical and subversive in the context of the present political, economic, and technological paradise. How do you propose to accomplish your solutions? Should conservation groups use civil rights tactics to try to obtain their objectives?

*George Macinko:* I think that we can do without the more radical type of civil rights tactics, the sort dependent on violence. I tried to make the point that if man is to have any future he must keep his aggressive and violent tendencies in hand. The compassion and the understanding that are necessary to provide for the continued life of the so-called lower organisms provide him with a test of his ability to use the same type of feeling and knowledge necessary to his own survival.

So, would I support civil rights tactics? Not of the more destructive sort. Conservationists should use the courts more than they have in the past. They should choose their issues wisely and work on those things that are both important and have the backing of the greater part of the scientific community. Their appeal to the general populace will be largely emotional, but when the issue gets into court it must be backed up with hard data. If there is to be continued recourse to the courts, it has to be in a fashion that tries to avoid building up a backlog in the court system because of a limited capacity there, and instead allows the courts to function as quickly and smoothly as possible.

Finally, is this a subversive doctrine? I wonder how subversive it is to suggest that man should begin now, in 1969, to do the types of things that might insure that he has a future as lengthy as his past. As far as I know, it is pretty generally agreed that man has been on planet Earth in sort of a recognizably human form for something more than one million years. If his tenure is to extend that far into the future, then it would seem obvious that he will have to live under conditions far different from those that now prevail. I believe it prudent, not subversive, to suggest he delineate the demographic, physical, and economic framework of a viable, long-term future and then move with all due haste toward a life style which fits such a framework.

*Chairman Sherwin:* The next series of questions is for John Milton. The first one asks what is the best solution to the problems of power generation of electricity? The questioner comments that if fossil fuel steam plants pollute the atmosphere, hydroelectric dams destroy the ecology of rivers and adjacent land areas, and nuclear power causes thermal pollution and is dangerous, what is the best source, or least damaging source, of power?

*John P. Milton:* My answer is muscle power. Wind and solar power are pretty good too.

Aside from utilizing our sinews, I don't know and I don't think anybody does. But my point is precisely that. Nobody has spent much time, our society has not spent nearly enough time, nor money, nor talent, to find out what the answers are. That is the main point. Until our society is willing to devote its tremendous technological capacity to discover viable alternative energy sources that do not pollute, that are clean, we are not going to solve this problem. It is still going to be with us if we shift from any one of the existing energy sources to another. If in Los Angeles we have a problem with fossil fuel smog, and then we shift to atomic energy, we may find we have to have our plants located near the coast where they can get water for cooling; but at the same time many plants probably will be located near areas of high earthquake fault probability. We also have the thermal pollution problem. On the other hand, we might go to the Grand Canyon, build some dams and create some hydropower. But what a horrible price to pay in loss of wilderness and spiritual values. Under the existing alternatives, you are going to have serious problems whatever you do, whatever energy technology you pick under the present system. The only answer is for us to insist that the world's top decision makers start placing very high priority on discovering new, clean, and economically feasible alternative energy sources. Because we didn't have this before we are all now in bad trouble. Despite industry and political lobby pressures, the people of this country must insist on an ecologically sound national energy policy.

*Chairman Sherwin:* What processes do you envision for the "how" of redirecting decision making? Also, what do problems of schistosomiasis have to do with technology?

*Mr. Milton:* I have recently finished a study of the impact of a varied series of international development projects, many of which were sponsored by development banks such as the World Bank, various United Nations agencies, the Agency for International Development, and other bilateral assistance programs. My purpose was to trace the flow of funds from our own pockets through the assistance agencies and then determine, with good documentation, the ecological effects on the less-developed world. After finding out what happened, my main concern was in seeing how the whole international decision making process might be made more environmentally sound. The case study was the basic technique used in this investigation and I would like to give one example of a particular case study.

In December, 1958, the gates of the first dam across Africa's Zambezi River were closed, beginning the creation of 1,700-square-mile Lake Kariba. World Bank financing provided much of the capital needed to construct the massive, multimillion-dollar hydroelectric and flood-control project. The hazards of initiating such huge river basin development schemes without adequate ecological and social investigations are well illustrated by this project; few attempts were made beforehand by the responsible agencies to look into the potential ecological impacts on the region and its people. One of the most immediate impacts, of course, was the flooding out of some prime alluvial agricultural land along the Zambezi River itself. As the waters rose, the people who inhabited these rich alluvial soils had to move up into the highlands to adopt a new way of life and land use. They had been agriculturalists. Now they were forced to become pastoralists or to adapt to a new system of upland agriculture. Many chose to adopt their old-style agricultural practices on the hillsides and dry uplands; but these regions were not sustained by the fertility of the Zambezi River. The Zambezi had formerly deposited many nutrients which regularly fertilized the alluvial soils. Resettlement in the uplands was difficult under the population densities they now had to support. Also the resettled people were now in competition with the existing pastoralists. Their society began to go down very rapidly. Severe problems of overgrazing, soil erosion, deterioration and resultant malnutrition and general lowering of cultural morale appeared. A real mess.

Another impact was the failure of fishing along with proliferation of weeds in Kariba Lake. Originally, the projected benefits of fish production were estimated at 20,000 tons per year. In 1963, only 4,000 tons were taken by 2,000 fishermen. By 1967, the yield had declined to 2,100 tons supporting only 500 fishermen. The spread of predacious fish species, chemical pollution, faulty clearance of lake bed trees and shrubs, and the spread of water weeds, all contributed to declining yields. Because the area could not be fished properly, there was less available fish protein. (More fish protein was to have been one of the benefits from the dam.) In addition, recent studies have found that water weeds caused an increase of evapotranspiration; more water than had been anticipated was passed by these water plants into the atmosphere. If this proliferation of plants continues, we may see some serious reduction of the amount of storage water available for hydropower.

Another important impact was the irregular release of water behind and below the dam. Before Kariba, there had been a regular seasonal pattern of flooding integrally related to agricultural patterns. The local Tonga peoples used to plant both just before the rainy season and after the floods receded along the river's edge. This gave them two crops each year. After dam construction, power production requirements became paramount; massive amounts of water were discharged unpredictably. It was impossible for the agricultural people downstream to plant their crops on a regular basis anymore. Likewise, erratic lake-edge areas were made unavailable. This meant that these people also were forced up into the hills, later to settle in relatively unproductive areas. The impact on their whole culture was severe. There is good evidence that some of these people are now migrating to urban areas where they add their numbers to the local slums.

I would like to mention one other unanticipated impact. The lakeshore edge became a new habitat: a low, shrubby forest, which spread along the considerable lakeshore. This new zone was ideal for proliferation of tsetse flies. Prior to the dam, tsetse was only found in a couple of small pockets. The tsetse flies spread out into the new habitat, and began to infect the cattle populations with trypanosomiasis. In one area studied, cattle populations were halved by serious outbreaks of the disease. The amount of animal protein available for food was drastically reduced. The impact on people themselves by tsetse-carried sleeping sickness is still unknown.

This little story illustrates the kind of complex disaster that our international "assistance" programs often have created. They are all disasters due to inattention to the natural biological systems being affected by development projects. The same sort of thing has happened in the case of the Russian-built Aswan Dam, where the dam and other Nile barrages caused rapid erosion of the Nile Delta, threatened loss of agricultural land, the destruction of the multimillion-dollar sardine fishery in the Mediterranean, waterlogging, and loss of soil nutrients.

A particularly important impact of damming tropical rivers relates to the other question that was asked on its relation to schistosomiasis and malaria. In the case of the Aswan Dam (and the earlier barrages built there) we now have some clear evidence. A number of expert ecologists have studied the introduced Nile system of perennial irrigation and found that the incidence of schistosomiasis, a blood fluke parasitic on man, rises spectacularly where old natural flooding systems have been replaced by extensive perennial irrigation projects. The parasite is carried at one stage in its life history by a snail which lives in irrigation ditches. The snail itself finds it difficult to live under the old normal system of occasional flooding; it requires permanent water to survive and reproduce well. When permanent irrigation ditches are constructed to give higher crop productivity, the snails and the schistosomes they carry are able to proliferate. At a later stage in its life cycle, this little parasite passes from the snail into the water; when people go down to the irrigation ditches to tend rice, bathe, or wash, it penetrates the body through the skin, passes into the bloodstream, and attacks various internal organs of the body. Huge numbers of people are now so infected in the Nile Delta, and control of the snails and parasites or cure for the disease is difficult, costly, and often impossible. With a greatly increased incidence of the disease in large river basin populations, you can imagine the individual and cultural impact. It is very, very serious. Yet in most tropical river areas without year-round irrigation, the problem is controlled by nature.

What does all this have to do with ecology and the process of decision making? It means that the people of this country must insist that all agencies, whether bilateral or multilateral development agencies, build ecological factors into the whole international development process. This means including ecology in the criteria used for the selection of aid projects. It means devising ecological pre-investment surveys to give some attention to these problems. It means including ecologists and social scientists in the carrying out of the projects. It means evaluating the ecological, social, and economic success of the projects afterwards.

At present no post-audits are initiated on these subjects. Nobody is going back to see if development projects succeeded or not. And yet we continue to spend billions of dollars all around the world. This is scandalous and incredible. Right now development agencies are planning to initiate the biggest river basin development ever: the Mekong Project. Yet these same ecological considerations have been and are being given short shrift.

*Chairman Sherwin:* Dr. Fuller said that industrialization brings down birth rates very rapidly, implying we need not be concerned about population growth. Mr. Milton, do you agree?

*Mr. Milton:* No. Obviously, the planet now has an incredible population problem. The one-third of the world that comprises the highly developed (overdeveloped?) nations does have a lowering birth rate. However, this one-third is on the way to becoming one-fourth of the total world population. The less-developed nations will soon contain three-quarters of the global population. We have no evidence that birth rates are going to drop over the foreseeable future in the less-developed parts of the world. And the populations of the rich regions also continue to grow, even though more slowly. However, this does mean that the split between the rich nations and the poor nations is going to become more and more severe. This is the single most important problem facing all men of all nations. I don't think that there is any question about being alarmed. We must be alarmed about it or we are doomed.

*Chairman Sherwin:* The final question asks whether you feel our present failure to control our own population is a result of political failure or scientific ignorance?

*Mr. Milton:* Both are involved, but the failure is largely social, psychological, and certainly political. Science is a tool, and political timidity has prevented our use of science to see, study, and help solve the problem. This is part of a vast political and scientific failure to press for a deep and comprehensive understanding of the whole biosphere upon which man depends.

Up to now scientific policy has been specialized and applied to single purpose problems; the world's political systems have just not been willing to deal with whole systems. Our failure to give attention to whole systems has led to such things as the planetary spread of medical technology without at the same time introducing adequate birth control mechanisms. The result has been a catastrophe of incalculable, almost unthinkable, proportions.

# WE MUST EARN AGAIN FOR OURSELVES WHAT WE HAVE INHERITED

## A Lesson in Wilderness Economics

*Garrett Hardin*

Professor of Biology
University of California, Santa Barbara

To some it may seem anathema to mention wilderness and economics in the same breath. Certainly, in the past, some of the most dangerous enemies of wilderness have been men who spoke the economic lingo. Despite this historic tar I think the brush of economics is a proper one for painting a picture of wilderness as a problem in human choice.

Economics may be defined as the study of choice necessitated by scarcity. There is something improper in speaking of the "economics of abundance" as Stuart Chase once did. With true abundance all economics ceases, except for the ultimately inescapable economics of time. Of the economics of time there is no general theory, and perhaps cannot be. But for the things of the world there is an economics, something that can be said.

Although there really is no such thing as an economics of abundance, the belief that there is, is one of the suppurating myths of our time. This belief had its origin partly in a genuine economic phenomenon, "the economy scale." For complex artifacts in general the unit cost goes down as the scale of manufacture increases. In general, the more complex the artifact, the more striking the economy of scale: the cost per unit to build a million automobiles per year is far, far less than the cost per unit when only one is manufactured. Because artifacts are so pervasive in modern life, most of us unconsciously assume the bigger the better, and the more the cheaper. It takes a positive effort of imagination to realize that there are things the supply of which cannot be multiplied indefinitely. Natural resources in general, and wilderness in particular, fall in this group.

This is obvious enough to Sierra Club members. It should be obvious to everyone, but it is not. Discussing some proposed improvements in a national park, the *Toronto Financial Post* said: "During 1968 and early 1969, campsites will be expanded and roads paved to enable the visitor to enjoy the wilderness atmosphere that was nearly inaccessible only a few years ago." This is an astonishing sentence, but I will bet that one would have to argue with the writer for quite a while before he could be made to see the paradox in proposing to build a road into the wilderness.

Wilderness cannot be multiplied, and it can be subdivided only a little. It is not increasing; we have to struggle to keep it from decreasing. But population increases steadily. The ratio of the wilderness available to each living person becomes steadily less—and bear in mind that this is only a statistical abstraction: were we to divide up the wilderness among even a small fraction of the total population, there would be no wilderness available to anyone. So what should we do?

The first thing to do is to see where we stand, to see what the possibilities are, to make a calendar of possibilities without (initially) making any judgment of their desirability. On the first level of analysis there are just three possibilities.

1. The wilderness can be opened to everyone. The end result of this is completely predictable: absolute destruction. Only a nation with a small population, perhaps no greater than one percent of our present population, a nation that does not have at its disposal our present means of transportation, could maintain a wilderness that was open to all.

2. We can close the wilderness to everyone. In a limited sense, this action would preserve the wilderness. But it would be a wilderness like Bishop Berkeley's "tree in the quad" when no one is there: does wilderness really exist if no one experiences it? Such an action would save wilderness for the future but it would do no one any good now.

3. We can allow only limited access to the wilderness. This is the only course of action that can be rationally defended. Only a small percent of a large population can ever enjoy the wilderness. With suitable standards and a detailed study of the variables, we can (in principle) work out a theory for maximizing the enjoyment of wilderness under a system of limited access.

Whatever theory we adopt, we shall have to wrestle with the problem of choice, the problem of determining what small number among a vast population of people shall have the opportunity to enjoy this scarce good—wilderness. It is this problem of choice that I wish to explore here.

What I have to say applies not only to wilderness in the sense in which that term is understood by all good outdoorsmen, but also to all other kinds of outdoor recreational areas—to national parks, to ski areas and the like. All of these can be destroyed by localized overpopulation. They differ in their carrying capacity, to use a term taken from game management. The carrying capacity of a Coney Island (for those who like it, and there are such people) is very high; the carrying capacity of wilderness, in the sense defined by Howard Zahniser, is very low. In the Wilderness Bill of 1964 Zahniser's felicitous definition stands for all to admire:

> A wilderness, in contrast with those areas where man and his own works dominate the landscape, is hereby recognized as an area where the earth and its community of life are untrammeled by man, where man himself is a visitor who does not remain.

The carrying capacity of Coney Island is, I suppose, something like 200 people per acre; the carrying capacity of a wilderness may be less than one person per square mile. Whatever the capacity, as population inexorably increases, each type of recreational area sooner or later comes up against the problem of allocation of a scarce resource among the more than sufficient number of claimants. The problem of limited access must be faced.

How shall we limit access? How shall we choose from among the too-abundant petitioners those few who shall be allowed in? Let us run over the various possibilities.

1. *By the marketplace.*—We can auction off the natural resource, letting the richest purchase it, or purchase tickets for admission. In our part of the world and in our time most of us unhesitatingly label this method unfair. Perhaps it is. But don't forget that many an area of natural beauty that we enjoy today was passed down to us unspoiled in an estate of the wealthy of past times. This method of allotment has at least the virtue that it preserves natural treasures until a better, or perhaps we should merely say a more acceptable, method of distribution can be devised. The privilege of wealth has in the past carried many of the beauties of nature through the first destructive eras of nascent democracy to the more mature stages when people are capable of appreciating beauty. A somewhat different privilege in China, the privilege of religion, preserved the dawn redwood in temple gardens while all the rest of the species was being cut for timber and fuel by impoverished people outside.

2. *By queues.*—Wilderness could be made available on a first come, first served basis, up to the extent of the carrying capacity. People would simply line up each day in a long queue and a few would be allowed in. It would be a fatiguing and wasteful system, but it would be fair. But it might not be stable.

3. *By lottery.*—This would be eminently fair, and it would not be terribly fatiguing or wasteful. In earlier days, the decision of a lottery was regarded as the choice of God. We cannot recapture this consoling belief (now that "God is dead") but we still are willing to abide by the results of a lottery. Hunting rights in several states where big game abounds are allocated by lottery.

4. *By merit.*—Whether one regards this as unfair or fair depends on the complexion of one's political beliefs. Whether it is fair or not, I will argue that it is the best system of allocation.

Anyone who argues for a merit system of determining rights immediately raises an *argumentum ad hominem.* He immediately raises the suspicion that he is about to define "merit" in such a way as to include himself in the meritorious group. The suspicion is justified, and because it is justified it must be met.

To carry conviction, he who proposes standards must show that his argument is not self-serving. What I hereby propose as a criterion for admission to the wilderness is great physical vigor. I explicitly call your attention to this significant fact: I myself cannot pass the test I propose. I had polio at the age of four, and got around moderately well for more than 40 years, but now I require crutches. Until today, I have not traded on my infirmity. But today I must, for it is an essential part of my argument.

I am not fit for the wilderness I praise. I cannot pass the test I propose. I cannot enter the area I would restrict. Therefore I claim that I speak with objectivity. The standard I propose is not an example of special pleading in my own interest. I can speak loudly where abler men would have to hesitate. I hope that what I have the right to say can be accepted by all.

To restrict the wilderness to physically vigorous people is inherently sensible. What is the experience of wilderness? Surely it has two major components. The first is the experience of being there, the experience (to use Thoreau's words) of being refreshed "by the sight of inexhaustible vigor," of being emotionally overwhelmed by the vast and titanic forces of nature.

The experience of being there is part of the experience of wilderness, but only a part. Dropped down from a line by helicopter into the middle of a wilderness we would miss an important part of the total experience; namely, the experience of getting there. The exquisite sight, sound, and smell of wilderness is many times more powerful if it is earned through physical achievement, if it comes at the end of a long and fatiguing journey for which vigorous good health is a necessity.

Practically speaking, this means that no one should be able to enter a wilderness by mechanical means. He should have to walk many miles on his own two feet, carrying all his provisions with him. In some cases, entrance might be on horse or mule back, or in a canoe, or by snow-shoes; but there should be no automobiles, no campers, no motor-cycles, no totegotes, no outboard motors, no airplanes. Just unmech-anized man and nature—this is a necessary part of the prescription of the wilderness experience.

That mechanical aids threaten wilderness is already recognized by managers of our wildernesses. Emergency roads, it is said, should be used sparingly. I submit that this cautious policy is not cautious enough. I submit that there should be no emergency roads, that the people who go into the wilderness should go in without radio trans-mitters, that they should know for certain that if an emergency arises they can get no help from the outside. If injured, they must either somehow struggle to the outside under their own power, or (if lucky) catch the attention of another rare wanderer in the wilderness and get him to help. For people who are physically prepared for it, the wilderness is not terribly dangerous—but such danger as there is, is a precious part of the total experience. The knowledge that one is really on one's own is a powerful tonic. It would be a sentimental cruelty to deprive the wilderness adventurer of the tonic knowledge that death is possible.

There is not even a public interest in making the wilderness safe. Making great and spectacular efforts to save the life of an individual makes sense only when there is a shortage of people. I have not lately heard that there is a shortage of people.

There is, however, a public interest in making the wilderness as difficult and dangerous as it legitimately can be. There is, I think, a well-founded suspicion that our life has become, if anything, too safe for the best psychological health, particularly among the young. The ever-greater extension of the boundaries of legal liability has produced a controlled and fenced-in environment in which it is almost impossible to hurt oneself—unless one tries. The behavior of the young clearly indicates that they really try. Drag races, road races, rumbles, student sit-ins, marches, and tauntings of the police—all these activi-

GARRETT HARDIN | 265

ties look like the behavior of people looking for danger. I do not wish to deny that some of the activities may arise from other motivations as well, e.g., idealistic political beliefs. I am only saying that it looks like a deliberate seeking of danger is part of the motivation of our obstreperous young. I think they are right to seek danger. I think we should tear down some of the fences that now deprive people of the possibility of danger. A wilderness without rescue services would in a small way contribute to the stability of society.

There is another respect in which the interest of society could be furthered by a rigorous wilderness. From time to time a president of the United States tries to improve the physical condition of the average citizen by pummeling him with rhetoric. The verbal assault consists pricipally of the words "responsibility," "duty," and "patriotism." These rhetorical duds no longer move the young. The negative motivation of shame is, in general, not as effective as the positive motivation of prestige. A wilderness that can be entered only by a few of the most physically fit of the population will act as an incentive to myriads more to improve their physical condition. The motivation will be more effective if we have (as I think we should) a graded series of wilderness and park areas. Areas in which the carrying capacity is reckoned at one person per 1,000 acres should be the most difficult to enter; those with a capacity of one per 100 acres should be easier; those with one per 10, still easier; and so on. Yosemite Valley should, I suggest, be assigned a carrying capacity of about one per acre, which might mean that it could be opened to anyone who could walk 10 miles. All automobile roads should come to a dead end 10 miles short of the valley. At first, of course, the 10-mile walkers would be a very small class, but once the prestige factor took effect more and more people would be willing to walk such a distance. Then the standard should be made more rigorous.

I am sure other details of such a system would eventually have to be faced and worked out. It might be necessary to combine it with a lottery. Or some independent, easily administered test of physical fitness might be instituted. These are details, and in principle can be solved, so I will not spend time on them. But whatever the details, it is clear that many of our present national parks, forests, and other recreation areas should be forever closed to people on crutches, to small children, to fat people, to people with heart conditions, and to old people in their usual state of physical disrepair. On the basis of their lack of merit, such people (and remember, I am a member of this deprived group) should give up all claim of right to the wilderness experience.

The poet Goethe once said, "We must earn again for ourselves what we have inherited," recognizing that only those things that are earned can be precious. To be precious the heritage of wilderness must be open only to those who can earn it again for themselves. The rest, since they cannot gain the genuine treasure by their own efforts, must relinquish the shadow of it.

We need not be so righteous as to deny the excluded ones all experience of the out-of-doors. There is no reason in the world why we cannot expand our present practice of setting up many small outdoor areas where we permit a high density of people to get a tiny whiff of the outdoors. Camping cheek by jowl with thousands of others in an outdoor slum does not appeal to me personally (I have not visited Yosemite Valley in 30 years) but there are people who simply love this slummy togetherness—a fact that Sierra Clubbers sometimes forget or find hard to believe. By all means, let us create some *al fresco* slums for the people—but not in the likes of Yosemite Valley, which is too good for this purpose. But there will be little lost if some of the less attractive forest areas are turned into outdoor slums to relieve the pressure on the really good areas. We must have lakes that fairly pullulate with water-skiers, in order that we may be able to set aside other lakes for quiet canoeing. At the terminus of six-lane highways we must have beaches that fairly writhe with oily bodies and vibrate to a steady cacaphony of transistor radios—in order to maintain other beaches, difficult of access, on which we forbid all noisemakers.

The qualities we seek in wilderness can be achieved only by adopting a policy of variety in management, and selling the concept of merit as the ticket for entrance to the most restricted areas.

The idea of wilderness is a difficult one, but it is precisely because it is difficult that clarifying it is valuable. In discovering how to justify a restricted good to a growing nation of 200 million people, we find a formula that extends beyond wilderness to a whole spectrum of recreational activities in the national commons. The solution of this difficult case erects a framework into which other cases can be easily fitted.

# APPENDICES

# Appendix A

## THE RETURN OF THE SEA OTTER
### Margaret W. Owings

Rafting in dark clusters around the Aleutian Islands or diving and feeding along the restless shores of the Pacific, the sea otter survives a monstrous past at the hands of man. Sea otter herds were scattered and slaughtered, their once unlimited freedom in the lap and slap of the sea nearly gone, until a turning point in 1911 when the International Fur Seal Treaty halted further exploitation. Today following a valiant return, *Enhydra lutris*, a species once decimated but now rebuilding a population out of fragile remnants, has become a symbol of American wildlife.

The Alaskan harvest of sea otters began in 1741 when Vitus Bering's vessel returned from remote islands with dark rich furs and inflamed the greed of a reckless, barbaric cast of men. For 75 years the hunters carried out unparalleled slaughter: 750,000 pelts were taken. By 1867 when Alaska was sold to the United States, the northern fur trade was finished. Today in the northern waters some 30,000 otters have regained their habitats in isolated island colonies. One of them, the island of Amchitka, was set aside for "sea otter restoration" but the Atomic Energy Commission has twice selected this area for experimental nuclear blasts.

Along the California coast remnants of the sea otter population represent a conservation challenge and achievement. In an ugly chapter of American history, the Pacific coast from Washington to Baja California was plundered for two centuries. Padres of Spanish missions and Russians with enslaved Aleuts stripped Pacific waters of otter herds. Aleuts were said to have killed 800 otters during one week in San Francisco Bay as firearms replaced arrows and clipper ships initiated trade with Boston. By the 1911 Fur Seal Treaty, the slaughter totaled an estimated one million skins. Only small gene pools of these animals remained unnoticed along the coast until 1938 when a herd was reported off the Monterey shore. In 1969 a census of California's central coast reported a comeback: 1,014 otters.

Population growth of the sea otter has been deliberate, due in part to the female's long and solicitous care of her pup which prevents her from bearing young oftener than every two years. Lying motionless on its mother's chest while she licks and grooms it, the pup is carried about or left to float while she dives for food.

Large beds of kelp (*Macrocystis* and *Nerocystis*) are common throughout the sea otter range in California and offer protected areas for resting, for the otter rarely leaves water for land. It swims belly-up with propulsion from its webbed hind feet. Diving among the shore reefs for mollusks, these playful and intelligent animals scatter and regroup in communities which appear to have an internal vitality. The California sea otter is unique in its use of a tool—a rock which it carries in the loose fold of skin under the armpit. Lying on its back, it places the rock on its chest and uses its nimble forepaws like hands to break the shells of mollusks. Observers have seen otters eat 21 kinds of food, most notably sea urchins, mussels, crabs, and abalones. Sea urchins feed on the root-like structures of kelp. Kelp beds nurture and protect vast fish populations as well as sift particles of nutrient for abalones. It is the food chain, and the balance of nature at work.

The State of California established a Sea Otter Refuge which stretches for 75 miles along the Monterey coast. One-third of the 1,014 otters grouped outside the refuge have caused bitter complaints from the abalone industry. Abalone fishermen, however, before moving south to Morro Bay, reduced the harvest around Monterey by 42 million pounds: mounds of abalone shells visible near processing plants illustrate another story. Twenty-six otters once were transplanted from the critical region by the state Department of Fish and Game, but the tagged animals returned 45 miles to their place of capture. The abalone industry then pressured legislators to allow the "taking" of sea otters outside their refuge by Fish and Game, or others by permit. Strong public opposition prevented the passage of the bill.

Today no one expects the otter ever to repopulate its former range because its unique evolutionary development, unspecialized for habitat between moving tides and shoreline, places it in a delicate survival category. Having no subcutaneous fat, the otter relies on a blanket of air trapped among the fibers of its fur for buoyancy and insulation. Oil spills can coat its fur, destroy warmth, and cause chill and death.

Through man's careless pollution, the otter could be lost. Through man's unwillingness to share another marine resource, the otter could be destroyed. Through resumption of the fur trade—"Six hundred selected fresh sea otter pelts auctioned in Seattle, 1970"—the old pattern could return. Is man to move forward, or retrogress to a shameful past? The future of the sea otter is unknown. But its value is infinite.

# Appendix B
## ENDANGERED SPECIES

The following list includes some of the species of wildlife in the Nearctic region (Canada, Mexico, United States) and oceans and oceanic islands adjacent to North America that are endangered by man and his activities—animals hunted for hides, feathers, trophies or sport; captured for live animal trade; combated as alleged pests; or whose habitat has been destroyed by man, introduced species, or diseases.

For more complete lists, see the International Union for Conservation of Nature and Natural Resources *Red Data Books* (Mammalia, Aves, and Pisces).

Late in 1969 the United States Congress passed, and the president signed, the Endangered Species Conservation Act of 1969, the complete text of which appears in this book as Appendix C. The act will protect not only species endangered within the boundaries of the United States and its possessions, but also those endangered anywhere in the world. Means for determining endangerment are specified in the bill and in the regulations later formulated by the Department of the Interior.

## NEARCTIC REGION
### Canada, Mexico and United States

*Mammals*

| | |
|---|---|
| Polar bear | *Thalarctos maritimus* |
| Barren Ground grizzly bear | *Ursus richardsoni* |
| Glacier bear | *Ursus americanus emmonsi* |
| Northern swift fox | *Vulpes velox hebes* |
| Black-footed ferret | *Mustela nigripes* |
| Eastern panther | *Felis concolor couguar* |
| Florida cougar | *Felis concolor coryi* |
| Texas ocelot | *Felis pardalis albescens* |
| Texas margay | *Felis wiedii cooperi* |
| Mexican grizzly bear | *Ursus nelsoni* |
| Red wolf | *Canis niger* |
| San Joaquin kit fox | *Vulpes macrotis mutica* |
| Lower California pronghorn | *Antilocapra americana peninsularis* |
| Sonoran pronghorn | *Antilocapra americana sonoriensis* |
| Peninsular bighorn | *Ovis canadensis cremnobates* |
| Tule elk | *Cervus nannodes* |
| Key deer | *Odocoileus virginianus clavium* |
| Columbia white-tailed deer | *Odocoileus virginianus leucurus* |
| Wood bison | *Bison bison athabascae* |
| Indiana bat | *Myotis sodalis* |
| Spotted bat | *Euderma maculatum* |
| Kaibab squirrel | *Sciurus kaibabensis* |
| Delmarva Peninsula fox squirrel | *Sciurus niger cinereus* |
| Utah prairie dog | *Cynomys parvidens* |
| Texas kangaroo rat | *Dipodomys elator* |

| | |
|---|---|
| Salt-marsh harvest mouse | *Reithrodontomys raviventris* |
| Beach Meadow vole | *Microtus breweri* |
| Block Island meadow vole | *Microtus pennsylvanicus provectus* |
| Atlantic walrus | *Odobenus rosmarus rosmarus* |
| Florida manatee | *Trichechus manatus latirostris* |
| Southern sea otter | *Enhydra lutris nereis* |
| Guadalupe fur seal | *Arctocephalus philippi* |
| Caribbean monk seal | *Monachus tropicalis* |

## Reptiles and Amphibians

| | |
|---|---|
| Gila monster | *Heloderma suspectum* |
| American alligator | *Alligator mississipiensis* |
| Blunt-nosed leopard lizard | *Crotaphytus wislizenii silus* |
| San Francisco garter snake | *Thamnophis sirtalis tetrataenia* |
| Santa Cruz long-toed salamander | *Ambystoma macrodactylum croceum* |
| Texas blind salamander | *Typhlomolge rathbuni* |
| Inyo County toad | *Bufo exsul* |
| Houston toad | *Bufo houstonensis* |
| Pine Barrens tree frog | *Hyla andersoni* |
| Bog turtle | *Clemmys muhlenbergi* |

## Fishes

| | |
|---|---|
| Piute cutthroat trout | *Salmo clarki seleniris* |
| Greenback cutthroat trout | *Salmo clarki stomias* |
| Gila trout | *Salmo gilae* |
| Apache trout | *Salmo sp.* |
| Devils Hole pupfish | *Cyprinodon diabolis* |
| Comanche Springs pupfish | *Cyprinodon elegans* |
| Owens Valley pupfish | *Cyprinodon radiosus* |
| Big Bend gambusia | *Gambusia gaigei* |
| Clear Creek gambusia | *Gambusia heterochir* |
| Pecos gambusia | *Gambusia nobilis* |
| Mohave chub | *Gila (Siphateles) mohavensis* |
| Humpback chub | *Gila cypha* |
| Moapa dace | *Moapa coriacea* |
| Cui-ui | *Chasmistes cujus* |
| Pahrump killifish | *Empetrichthys latos* |
| Gila topminnow | *Poeciliopsis occidentalis occidentalis* |
| Modoc sucker | *Catostomus microps* |
| Unarmored threespine stickleback | *Gasterosteus aculeatus williamsoni* |
| Fountain darter | *Etheostoma fonticola* |
| Shortnose sturgeon | *Acipenser brevirostrum* |
| Longjaw cisco | *Coregonus alpenae* |

## Birds

| | |
|---|---|
| Whooping crane | *Grus americana* |
| California condor | *Gymnogyps californianus* |
| Everglade kite | *Rostrhamus sociabilis plumbeus* |

| | |
|---|---|
| Southern bald eagle | *Haliaeetus leucocephalus leucocephalus* |
| American peregrine falcon | *Falco peregrinus anatum* |
| Ivory-billed woodpecker | *Campephilus principalis principalis* |
| Southern red-cockaded woodpecker | *Dendrocopos borealis hylonomus* |
| Imperial woodpecker | *Campephilus imperialis* |
| Slender-billed grackle | *Cassidix palustris* |
| Bachman's warbler | *Vermivora bachmanii* |
| Kirtland's warbler | *Dendroica kirtlandii* |
| Dusky seaside sparrow | *Ammospiza nigrescens* |
| Cape Sable sparrow | *Ammospiza mirabilis* |
| Masked bobwhite | *Colinus virginianus ridgwayi* |
| Puerto Rico plain pigeon | *Columba inornata wetmorei* |
| Eskimo curlew | *Numenius borealis* |
| Yuma clapper rail | *Rallus longirostris yumanensis* |
| Aleutian Canada goose | *Branta canadensis leucopareia* |
| Tule white-fronted goose | *Anser albifrons gambelli* |
| Mexican duck | *Anas diazi* |
| Puerto Rico parrot | *Amazona vittata* |
| Puerto Rico short-eared owl | *Asio flammeus portoricensis* |
| Attwater's prairie chicken | *Tympanuchus cupido attwateri* |

## OCEANS AND OCEANIC ISLANDS
### Adjacent to North America

*Oceanic Mammals*

| | |
|---|---|
| Fin whale | *Balaenoptera physalus* |
| Blue whale | *Balaenoptera musculus musculus* |
| Humpback whale | *Megaptera novaeangliae* |
| Greenland right whale | *Balaena mysticetus* |
| North Pacific right whale | *Eubalaena sieboldi* |
| North Atlantic right whale | *Eubalaena glacialis* |

*Birds*

| | |
|---|---|
| Hawaiian gallinule | *Gallinula chloropus sandvicensis* |
| Hawaiian crow | *Corvus tropicus* |
| Honey-creeper: eight species | *Drepaniidae* family |
| Hawaiian hawk | *Buteo solitarius* |
| Puaiohi | *Phaeornis palmeri* |
| Dark-rumped petrel | *Pterodroma phaeopygia sandwichensis* |

*Appendix C*

ENDANGERED SPECIES CONSERVATION ACT OF 1969

91ST CONGRESS
1ST SESSION

# H. R. 11363

————

## IN THE HOUSE OF REPRESENTATIVES
MAY 15, 1969

Mr. LENNON (for himself, Mr. GARMATZ, Mr. DINGELL, Mr. PELLY, Mr. DOWNING, Mr. KEITH, Mr. KARTH, Mr. DELLENBACK, Mr. ROGERS of Florida, Mr. POLLOCK, Mr. HANNA, Mr. GOODLING, Mr. LEGGETT, Mr. McCLOSKEY, Mr. ANNUNZIO, Mr. FREY, Mr. LONG of Louisiana, Mr. BIAGGI, and Mr. FEIGHAN) introduced the following bill; which was referred to the Committee on Merchant Marine and Fisheries

————

# A BILL

To prevent the importation of endangered species of fish or wildlife into the United States; to prevent the interstate shipment of reptiles, amphibians, and other wildlife taken contrary to State law; and for other purposes.

*Be it enacted by the Senate and House of Representatives of the United States of America in Congress assembled,* That, for the purposes of sections 2 through 5 of this Act, the term—

(1) "Secretary" means the Secretary of the Interior;

(2) "fish or wildlife" means any wild mammal, fish, wild bird, amphibian, reptile, mollusk, or crustacean, or any part or products or egg thereof;

(3) "United States" includes the several States, the District of Columbia, the Commonwealth of Puerto Rico, American Samoa, the Virgin Islands, and Guam; and

(4) "person" means any individual, firm, corporation, association, or partnership.

SEC. 2. Except as provided in section 3 of this Act, whoever imports, in violation of sections 2 through 5 of this Act, from any foreign country into the United States any species or subspecies of fish or wildlife which the Secretary has determined, in accordance with the provisions of such sections, to be threatened with worldwide extinction, shall be punished in accordance with the provisions of section 4 of this Act.

SEC. 3. (a) A species or subspecies of fish or wildlife shall be deemed to be threatened with worldwide extinction whenever the Secretary determines, based on the best scientific and commercial data available to him and after consultation, in cooperation with the Secretary of State, with the foreign country or countries in which such fish or wildlife are normally found and, to the extent practicable, with interested persons and organizations and other interested Federal agencies, that the continued existence of such species or subspecies of fish or wildlife is, in the judgment of the Secretary, endangered due to any of the following factors: (1) the destruction, drastic modification, or severe curtailment, or the threatened destruction, drastic modification, or severe curtailment, of its habitat, or (2) its overutilization for commercial purposes, or (3) the effect on it of disease or predation, or (4) other natural or man-made factors affecting its continued existence. After making such determination, the Secretary shall promulgate and from time to time he may revise, by regulation, a list in the Federal Register of such fish or wildlife by scientific, common, and commercial name or names, together with his determination. The Secretary shall at least once every five years conduct a thorough review of any such list to determine what, if any, changes have occurred relative to the continued existence of the species or subspecies of fish or wildlife then on the list and to determine whether such fish or wildlife continue to be threatened with worldwide extinction. Upon completion of such review, he shall take appropriate action consistent with the purposes of this Act. The Secretary shall, upon the request of any interested person, also conduct such review of any particular listed species or subspecies at any other time if he finds and publishes his finding that such person has presented substantial evidence to warrant such a review.

(b) In order to minimize undue economic hardship to any person importing any species or subspecies of fish or wildlife which are determined to be threatened with worldwide extinction under this section, under any contract entered into prior to the date of publication of such determination in the Federal Register of such species or subspecies, the Secretary, upon such person filing an application with him and upon filing such information as the Secretary may require showing, to his satisfaction, such hardship, shall permit such person to import such species or subspecies in such quantities and for such periods, not to exceed one year, as he determines to be appropriate.

(c) The Secretary may permit, under such terms and conditions as he may prescribe, the importation of any species or subspecies of fish or wildlife listed in the Federal Register under this section for zoological, educational, and scientific purposes, and for the propagation of such fish or wildlife in captivity for preservation purposes, unless such importation is prohibited by any other Federal law or regulation.

(d) The provisions of section 553 of title 5 of the United States Code shall apply to any regulation issued under this section.

SEC. 4. (a) Any person who violates the provisions of sections 2 and 3 of this Act or any regulation or permit issued thereunder shall be assessed a civil penalty by the Secretary of not more than $5,000 for each such violation. No penalty shall be assessed unless such person shall be given notice and opportunity for a hearing on such charge. Each violation shall be a separate offense. Any such civil penalty may be compromised by the Secretary. Upon any failure to pay the penalty assessed under this section, the Secretary may request the Attorney General to institute a civil action in a district court of the United States for any district in which such person is found or resides or transacts business to collect the penalty and such court shall have jurisdiction to hear and decide any such action.

(b) Any person who willfully violates the provisions of sections 2 and 3 of this Act or any regulation or permit issued thereunder shall, upon conviction, be fined not more than $10,000, or imprisoned for not more than one year, or both.

(c) For the purposes of facilitating enforcement of sections 2 and 3 of this Act and reducing the costs thereof, the Secretary, with the approval of the Secretary of the Treasury, shall, after notice and an opportunity for a public hearing, from time to time designate, by regulation, any port or ports in the United States for the importation of fish and wildlife, other than shellfish and fishery products imported for commercial purposes, into the United States. The importation of such fish or wildlife into any port in the United States, except those so designated, shall be prohibited after the effective date of such designations. Such regulations may provide exceptions to such prohibition if the Secretary deems it appropriate and consistent with the purposes of this subsection.

(d) The provisions of sections 2 through 5 of this Act and the regulations issued thereunder shall be enforced by either the Secretary or the Secretary of the Treasury, or both such Secretaries. Either Secretary may utilize by agreement the personnel, services, and facilities of any other Federal agency or any State agency. Any employee of the Department of the Interior or the Department of the Treasury authorized by the Secretary or the Secretary of the Treasury may, without a warrant, arrest any person who, within the employee's presence or view, violates the provisions of this Act or any regulation or permit issued thereunder, and may execute a warrant or other process issued by an officer or court of competent jurisdiction. An employee who has made an arrest under this Act may search the person arrested at the time of the arrest and seize any fish or wildlife or property or items taken, used, or possessed in violation of this Act or any regulation or permit issued thereunder. Any fish or wildlife or property or item seized shall be held by the employee or by a United States marshal pending disposition of the case by the court, commissioner, or magistrate, except that the Secretary may, in lieu thereof, permit such person to post a bond or other surety satisfactory to him. Upon conviction, any fish or wildlife seized shall be forfeited to the Secretary for disposal by him. Any other property or items seized may, in the discretion of the court, commissioner, or magistrate, be forfeited to the United States or otherwise disposed of.

(e) In carrying out the provisions of section 2 through 5 of this Act, the Secretary may issue such regulations as may be appropriate.

SEC. 5. In carrying out the provisions of sections 2 through 4 of this Act, the Secretary, through the Secretary of State, shall encourage foreign countries to provide protection to species and subspecies of fish or wildlife threatened with worldwide extinction, to take measures to prevent such fish or wildlife from becoming threatened with extinction, and shall cooperate with such countries in providing technical assistance in developing and carrying out programs to provide such protection, and shall, through the Secretary of State, encourage bilateral and multilateral agreements with such countries for the protection, conservation, and propagation of fish or wildlife. The Secretary shall also encourage persons, taking directly or indirectly fish or wildlife in foreign countries for importation into the United States for commercial or other purposes, to develop and carry out, with such assistance as he may provide under any authority available to him, conservation practices designed to enhance such fish or wildlife and their habitat. The Secretary of State, in consultation with the Secretary, shall take appropriate measures to encourage the development of adequate measures, including, if appropriate, international agreements, to prevent such fish or wildlife from becoming threatened with worldwide extinction.

SEC. 6. (a) The Secretary of Agriculture and the Secretary shall provide for appropriate coordination of the administration of this Act and amendments made by this Act, with the administration of the animal quarantine laws (21 U.S.C. 101 et seq., 21 U.S.C. 111, 21 U.S.C. 134 et seq.) and the Tariff Act of 1930, as amended (19 U.S.C. 1306).

(b) Nothing in this Act, or any amendment made by this Act, shall be construed as superseding or limiting in any manner the functions of the Secretary of Agriculture under any other law relating to prohibited or restricted importations of animals and other articles and no proceeding or determination under this Act shall preclude any proceeding or be considered determinative of any issue of fact or law in any proceeding under any Act administered by the Secretary of Agriculture.

SEC. 7. Section 43 of title 18, United States Code, is amended to read as follows:

"§ 43. Transportation of wildlife taken in violation of State, National, or foreign laws; receipt; making false records

"(a) Any person who—

"(1) delivers, carries, or transports or causes to be delivered, carried, transported, or shipped for commercial or noncommercial purposes or sells or causes to be sold any wildlife taken in any manner in violation of any Act of Congress or regulation issued thereunder, or

"(2) delivers, carries, or transports or causes to be delivered, carried, transported, or shipped for commercial or noncommercial purposes or sells or causes to be sold in interstate or foreign commerce any wildlife taken in any manner in violation of any law or regulation of any State or foreign country; and

"(b) Any person who—

"(1) sells or causes to be sold any products manufactured, made, or processed from any wildlife taken in any manner in violation of any Act of Congress or regulation issued thereunder, or

"(2) sells or causes to be sold in interstate or foreign commerce any products manufactured, made, or processed from any wildlife taken in any manner in violation of any law or regulation of a State or a foreign country, or

"(3) having purchased or received wildlife imported from any foreign country or shipped, transported, or carried in interstate commerce, makes or causes to be made any false record, account, label, or identification thereof, or

"(4) receives, acquires, or purchases for commercial or noncommercial purposes any wildlife—

"(A) taken in violation of any law or regulation of any State or foreign country and delivered, carried, transported, or shipped by any means or method in interstate or foreign commerce, or

"(B) taken in violation of any Act of Congress or regulation issued thereunder, or

"(5) imports from Mexico to any State, or exports from any State to Mexico, any game mammal, dead or alive, or part or product thereof, except under permit or other authorization of the Secretary or, in accordance with any regulations prescribed by him, having due regard to the requirements of the Migratory Bird Treaty with Mexico and the laws of the United States forbidding importation of certain live mammals injurious to agriculture and horticulture;

shall be subject to the penalties prescribed in subsections (c) and (d) of this section.

"(c) Any person who knowingly or has reason to know violates the provisions of subsection (a) or (b) of this section may be assessed a civil penalty by the Secretary of not more than $5,000 for each such violation. Each violation shall be a separate offense. No penalty shall be assessed unless such person shall be given notice and opportunity for a hearing on such charge. Any such civil penalty may be compromised by the Secretary. Upon any failure to pay the penalty assessed under this section, the Secretary may request the Attorney General to institute a civil action in a district court of the United States for any district in which such person is found or resides or transacts business to collect the penalty and such court shall have jurisdiction to hear and decide any such action.

"(d) Any person who knowingly and willfully violates the provisions of subsection (a) or (b) of this section shall, upon conviction, be fined not more than $10,000 or imprisoned for not more than one year, or both.

"(e) Any wildlife or products thereof seized in connection with any violation of this section shall be forfeited to the Secretary to be disposed of by him in such manner as he deems appropriate.

"(f) For the purpose of this section, the term—

"(1) 'Secretary' means the Secretary of the Interior;

"(2) 'person' means any individual, firm, corporation, association, or partnership;

"(3) 'wildlife' means any wild mammal, wild bird, amphibian, reptile, mollusk, or crustacean, or any part or egg thereof, but does not include migratory birds for which protection is afforded under the Migratory Bird Treaty Act, as amended;

"(4) 'State' means the several States, the District of Columbia, the Commonwealth of Puerto Rico, American Samoa, the Virgin Islands, and Guam; and

"(5) 'taken' means captured, killed, collected, or otherwise possessed."

SEC. 8. Section 3054 of title 18, United States Code, is amended by inserting "42," after "to enforce sections" and by inserting a comma after "43".

SEC. 9. Section 3112 of title 18, United States Code, is amended by inserting "42," after "to enforce sections" and by inserting a comma after "43".

SEC. 10. The first paragraph in section 44 of title 18, United States Code, is amended by deleting "wild animals or birds, or the dead bodies or parts thereof," and inserting "any wild mammal, wild bird, amphibian, or reptile, or any mollusk or crustacean, or the dead body or parts or eggs thereof."

(b) Section 44 of title 18, United States Code, is amended by adding at the end thereof a new paragraph to read as follows:

"In any case where the marking, labeling, or tagging of a package under this section indicating in any way the contents thereof would lead to the possibility of theft of the package or its contents, and affect the ability to insure the package and its contents, the Secretary of the Interior may, upon request of the owner thereof or his agent or by regulation, provide some other reasonable means of notifying appropriate authorities of the contents of such packages."

SEC. 11. (a) Section 2 of the Black Bass Act (44 Stat. 576), as amended (16 U.S.C. 852), is amended to read as follows:

"SEC. 2. It shall be unlawful for any person knowingly to deliver or receive for transportation, or to transport, by any means whatsoever, in interstate or foreign commerce, any black bass or other fish, if (1) such delivery or transportation is contrary to the law of the State, territory, or the District of Columbia or any foreign country from which such black bass or other fish is found or transported, or is contrary to other applicable law, or (2) such black bass or other fish has been either caught, killed, taken, sold, purchased, possessed, or transported, at any time, contrary to the law of the State, territory, or the District of

Columbia, or foreign country, in which it was caught, killed, taken, sold, purchased, or possessed, or from which it was transported, or contrary to other applicable law; and no person shall knowingly purchase or receive any such black bass or other fish which has been transported in violation of the provisions of this Act; nor shall any person receiving any shipment of black bass or other fish transported in interstate or foreign commerce make any false record or render a false account of the contents of such shipment. For the purpose of this section, the provisions of section 10 of title 18, United States Code, shall apply to the term 'interstate or foreign commerce'."

(b) Section 3 of the Black Bass Act (46 Stat. 846), as amended (16 U.S.C. 852a), is amended by deleting the comma after "commerce" and inserting therein "or foreign commerce,".

(c) Section 6(a) of the Black Bass Act (46 Stat. 846), as amended (16 U.S.C. 852d (a)), is amended by adding a new sentence at the end thereof to read as follows: "The provisions of this section and any regulations issued thereunder shall be enforced by personnel of the Secretary of the Interior, and he may utilize by agreement, with or without reimbursement, personnel, services, and facilities of other Federal agencies."

SEC. 12. The second paragraph of section 4 of the Migratory Bird Treaty Act, as amended (16 U.S.C. 705), is hereby repealed.

SEC. 13. The provisions of sections 1 through 12 of this Act shall be effective one hundred and eighty days after the date of enactment of this Act.

SEC. 14. (a) Section 1 of the Act of October 15, 1966 (80 Stat. 926; 16 U.S.C. 668aa), is amended by adding new subsection at the end thereof to read as follows:

"(d) For the purpose of sections 1 through 3 of this Act, the term 'fish and wildlife' means any wild mammal, fish, wild bird, amphibian, reptile, mollusk, or crustacean."

(b) The last sentence of section 2(c) of the Act of October 15, 1966 (80 Stat. 926; 16 U.S.C. 668bb (c)), is amended by changing the "$750,000" to "$2,500,000".

(c) Section 2(d) of the Act of October 15, 1966 (80 Stat. 926; 16 U.S.C. 668bb(d)), is amended by adding a new sentence at the end thereof to read as follows: "The Secretary is authorized to acquire by purchase, donation, exchange, or otherwise any privately owned land, water, or interests therein within the boundaries of any area administered by him, for the purpose of conserving, protecting, restoring, or propagating any selected species of native fish and wildlife that are threatened with extinction and each such acquisition shall be administered in accordance with the provisions of law applicable to such area, and there is authorized to be appropriated annually for fiscal year 1970, 1971, and 1972 not to exceed $1,000,000 to carry out the provisions of this sentence."

(d) The provisions of sections 1 through 5 of this Act and sections 1 through 3 of the Act of October 15, 1966 (80 Stat. 926; 16 U.S.C.

668aa–668cc), as amended by this section, shall hereinafter be cited as the "Endangered Species Conservation Act of 1969."

(e) The second sentence of section 1(a) of the Act of October 15, 1966 (80 Stat. 926; 16 U.S.C. 668aa(a)), is amended by changing the comma after the word "extinction" to a period and deleting the remainder of the sentence.

## Appendix D

### REGULATIONS ON PUBLIC OUTDOOR RECREATION USE OF BUREAU OF LAND MANAGEMENT LANDS INCLUDING AREAS DETERMINED TO BE PRIMITIVE IN CHARACTER*

---

### PART 6000—OUTDOOR RECREATION; GENERAL

Sec.
6000.0-1   Purpose.
6000.0-2   Objective.
6000.0-4   Responsibility.
6000.0-6   Management policy.

Authority: The provisions of this Part 6000 issued under secs. 1, 3, 5, 50 Stat. 874, 875; 43 U.S.C. 1181a, 1181c, 1181e; R.S. 2478; 43 U.S.C. 1201.

§ 6000.0-1   *Purpose.* The lands administered by the Bureau of Land Management are used and managed for a variety of purposes which are described in Subpart 1725 of this chapter. The regulations in this sub-chapter relate to the use and development of these lands for outdoor recreation purposes. The regulations also identify circumstances under which use of such lands may be restricted in order to protect the public health and safety, and natural resources and values.

§ 6000.0-2   *Objective.* The Bureau shall manage lands to promote public use and enjoyment of the lands for outdoor recreation use in a manner which will protect the health, safety, and comfort of the public and preserve and protect natural resources and values.

§ 6000.0-4   *Responsibility.*

(a) Except where specified to the contrary, the authority of the Secretary of the Interior to develop, manage, authorize the use, and stipulate the terms and conditions of such use of lands, and make other determinations in accordance with the regulations of this part has been delegated to authorized officers of the Bureau of Land Management.

(b) The using public has the responsibility to use the lands in a manner which will permit maximum use and enjoyment by all, and will protect and preserve the lands, their resources, and any public recreation facility or value which is added thereon.

§ 6000.0-6   *Management policy.*

(a) Subpart 1725 of this chapter describes the program and multiple-use management policy for public lands, including the development of recreational resources, consistent with the economic and effective development and management of public lands, for use by the public.

(b) Encouragement will be given to State and local governments and

* Published in 34 F.R. 857, January 18, 1969. The BLM is preparing a manual which will expand the primitive area criteria set forth in these regulations. Subchapter F— *Outdoor Recreation and Wildlife Management (6000)*

private agencies to develop additional public recreation facilities when such development is consistent with long-range management plans and programs of the Bureau.

(c) Priority will be given to:

(1) Recreation development and enhancement as follows:

(i) Undeveloped sites currently under heavy, uncontrolled use that threatens public health and safety or damage to the recreation resource.

(ii) Areas in localities where public recreational demand exceeds available opportunities and facilities.

(iii) Areas adjacent to heavily traveled routes or highways near urban areas, bodies of water, and unique scenic attractions.

(2) Preservation and protection of natural and cultural resources, including but not limited to scientific, scenic, historic, and archeological values, and primitive environments.

(d) Reasonable fees in accordance with Part 18 of this title may be established and collected by the authorized officer.

## PART 6010—GENERAL PROGRAM

Sec.
6010.1   Identification of lands.
6010.2   Rules of conduct.
6010.3   Supplemental rules.
6010.4   Closure of lands.
6010.5   State and local laws.

Authority: Same as for Part 6000.

§ 6010.1   *Identification of lands.* To assist the public in the identification of lands, the Bureau shall, where feasible, post signs, publish ownership maps, and otherwise identify public recreation opportunities.

§ 6010.2   *Rules of conduct.*

(a) Permitted activities.—(1) Collecting—hobby specimens. Flowers, berries, nuts, seeds, cones, leaves, and similar renewable resources and non-renewable resources such as rocks, mineral specimens, common invertebrate fossils, and gem stones may be collected in reasonable quantities for personal use, consumption, or hobby collecting. Limitations on this privilege are contained in paragraph (b) of this section.

(2) Collecting—for sale or barter. Gathering or collecting of renewable or nonrenewable resources for the purpose of sale or barter may be done only where specifically authorized by law.

(3) Petrified wood. For regulations pertaining to collection of petrified wood see Subpart 3612 of this chapter.

(4) Vegetative and mineral materials. For regulations pertaining to removal of vegetative and mineral materials under the Mineral Material Sales Act, see Subparts 3610, 3611, and 5400 of these regulations.

(b) Prohibited activities. In the use of lands for public outdoor recreation purposes, no one shall:

(1) Intentionally or wantonly destroy, deface, injure, remove or disturb any public building, sign, equipment, marker, or other public property.

(2) Harvest or remove any vegetative or mineral resources or object of antiquity, historic, or scientific interest unless such removal is in accordance with Part 3 of this title regulations or paragraph (a) of this section, or is otherwise authorized by law.

(3) Appropriate, mutilate, deface, or destroy any natural feature, object of natural beauty, antiquity, or other public or private property.

(4) Dig, remove, or destroy any tree or shrub.

(5) Gather or collect renewable or nonrenewable resources for the purpose of sale or barter unless specifically permitted or authorized by law.

(6) Drive or operate motorized vehicles or otherwise conduct himself in a manner that may result in unnecessary frightening or chasing of people or domestic livestock and wildlife.

(7) Use motorized mechanical devices for digging, scraping, or trenching for purposes of collecting.

§ 6010.3 *Supplemental rules.* Additional rules to protect the public health and safety and protect resources may be established by the authorized officer, as necessary. They shall be posted in appropriate locations to notify the public of requirements for the occupancy and use of lands, outdoor recreation facilities, and roads and trails. The posted rules may provide for, but need not be limited to, protection of public health and safety, protection of the lands from fires, prevention of soil erosion, and utilization and protection of outdoor recreation and other resource values of the Federal lands.

§ 6010.4 *Closure of lands.* In the management of lands to protect the public and assure proper resource utilization, conservation, and protection, public use and travel may be temporarily restricted. For instance, areas may be closed during periods of high fire danger or unsafe conditions, or where use will interfere with or delay mineral development, timber, and livestock operations, or other authorized use of the lands. Areas may also be closed temporarily to:

(a) Protect the public health and safety.
(b) Prevent excessive erosion.
(c) Prevent unnecessary destruction of plant life and wildlife habitat.
(d) Protect the natural environment.
(e) Preserve areas having cultural or historical value.
(f) Protect scientific studies or preserve scientific values.

§ 6010.5 *State and local laws.* Except as otherwise provided by law, State and local laws and ordinances shall apply. This refers, but is not limited, to laws and ordinances governing:

(a) Operation and use of motor vehicles, aircraft, and boats.
(b) Hunting and fishing.
(c) Use of firearms.
(d) Injury to persons or destruction of property.
(e) Air and water pollution.
(f) Littering.
(g) Sanitation.
(h) Use of fire.

———

*Group 6200—Recreation Management*

## PART 6200—GENERAL

Sec.
6200.0-1    Purpose.
6200.0-6    Policy.

Authority: Same as for Part 6000.

§ 6200.0-1    *Purpose.* This group defines outdoor recreation regulations dealing with the administration of lands for specific types of public use, resource conditions, outdoor recreation occupancy and use, and resource development.

§ 6200.0-6    *Policy.* Where appropriate for management and public identification purposes, lands having significant natural values may be (a) designated pursuant to the provisions of Subpart 1727 of Part 1720 of this chapter, and (b) segregated pursuant to the provisions of § 2410.1-4 of this chapter.

---

## PART 6220—PROTECTION AND PRESERVATION OF NATURAL VALUES

6221.0-1    Purpose.
6221.0-2    Objective.
6221.1      Characteristics.
6221.2      Criteria for use.

Subpart 6222—Scenic Corridor-Buffer Zones

6222.0-6    Policy.

Subpart 6223—Wild and Scenic Rivers

6223.0-1    Purpose.
6223.0-2    Objectives.
6223.0-3    Authority.
6223.0-6    Policy.

Subpart 6225—Natural Areas

6225.0-1    Purpose.
6225.0-2    Objectives.
6225.0-5    Definition.
6225.0-6    Policy.
6225.1      Use of natural areas.

Authority: Same as for Part 6000.

§ 6220.0-1    *Purpose.* This part provides guidelines for the management; and criteria for the use, of lands to preserve, protect, and enhance areas of scenic splendor, natural wonder, scientific interest, primitive environment, and other natural values for the enjoyment and use of present and future generations.

Sec.
6220.0-1    Purpose.

## Subpart 6221—*Primitive Areas*

§ 6221.0-1 *Purpose.* This subpart provides procedures and guidelines for the protection and recreation use of lands that have been determined to be primitive in character.

§ 6221.0-2 *Objective.* Lands designated as primitive areas shall be administered for public recreational use in a manner to protect primitive values, and to:

(a) Allow the free operation of natural ecological succession to the extent feasible for scientific and other study.

(b) Preserve solitude, physical and mental challenge, inspiration and primitive recreation values.

(c) Preserve public values that would be lost if the lands were developed for commercial purposes or passed from Federal ownership.

(d) Allow the natural restoration of the primitive character of the lands.

§ 6221.1 *Characteristics.* Natural, wild, and undeveloped lands in settings essentially removed from the effects of civilization are appropriate for designation as primitive areas. Essential characteristics are a natural environment that can be conserved and on which there is no undue disturbance by roads and commercial uses. Primitive areas may be representative of natural environments ranging from the southwest desert to the arctic tundra.

§ 6221.2 *Criteria for use.*

(a) Public use of primitive areas for recreation purposes is encouraged to the optimum extent consistent with the maintenance of the primitive environment.

(b) Travel in primitive areas is restricted to nonmechanized forms of locomotion.

(c) Construction will not be allowed in or on the land except in connection with authorized nonrecreation uses of the lands, and as necessary to meet requirements for the protection and administration of the area (including measures required in emergencies involving the health and safety of persons within the area).

(d) Roads, mechanized equipment, commercial timber harvesting, non-transient occupancy, and the landing of aircraft is prohibited except in connection with activities necessary in the use of the lands for authorized nonrecreation purposes, and then only under conditions specified by the authorized officer.

(e) Grazing of domestic livestock, water storage projects, and rights-of-way for utility lines and other purposes may be permitted by the authorized officer under such conditions and restrictions as he deems necessary to preserve primitive values.

## Subpart 6222—*Scenic Corridor—Buffer Zones*

§ 6222.0-6 *Policy.* Scenic corridors may be established along roads and highways, rivers and streams, trails and other lands for the preservation, protection and enhancement of scenic and natural values. Size and use of scenic corridors shall be consistent with the purposes for which they are established.

Subpart 6223—*Wild and Scenic Rivers*

§ 6223.0-1   *Purpose.* To provide guidelines for management of lands affected by the Wild and Scenic Rivers Act.

§ 6223.0-2   *Objectives.* To assure that all lands affected by the Wild and Scenic Rivers Act are managed in a manner consistent with the purposes of the act.

§ 6223.0-3   *Authority.* (a) The Wild and Scenic Rivers Act (82 Stat. 906) provides that certain selected rivers which, with their immediate environment, possess outstandingly remarkable scenic, recreational, geologic, fish and wildlife, historic, cultural, or other similar values, shall be preserved in free-floating condition, and that their immediate environments shall be protected for the benefit and enjoyment of present and future generations.

§ 6223.0-6   *Policy.* Lands affected by the Wild and Scenic Rivers Act will be identified as soon as possible and will be managed in such a manner as to preserve that characteristic of the area that led to its designation under the act.

Subpart 6225—*Natural Areas.*

§ 6225.0-1   *Purpose.* To describe procedures for management, protection and recreation use of lands having unusual natural characteristics.

§ 6225.0-2   *Objectives.* To provide guidelines for the outdoor recreation use of natural areas.

§ 6225.0-5   *Definition.* The following types of areas may be established under the regulations of this subpart:

(a) Research natural areas. These are established and maintained for the primary purpose of research and education. Scientists and educators are encouraged to use research natural areas in a manner that is nondestructive and consistent with the purpose for which the area is established. The general public may be excluded or restricted where necessary to protect studies or preserve research natural areas. Lands having the following characteristics may qualify:

(1) Typical or unusual faunistic or floristic types, associations, or other biotic phenomena, or

(2) Characteristic or outstanding geologic, pedologic, or aquatic features or processes.

(b) Outstanding natural areas. These are established to preserve scenic values and areas of natural wonder. The preservation of these resources in their natural condition is the primary management objective. Access roads, parking areas and public use facilities are normally located on the periphery of the area. The public is encouraged to walk into the area for recreation purposes wherever feasible.

§ 6225.0-6   *Policy.* Where appropriate the Bureau shall establish and record areas of sufficient number and size to provide adequately for scientific study, research, recreational use and demonstration purposes. These will include:

(a) The preservation of scenic values, natural wonders and examples of significant natural ecosystems.

(b) Research and educational areas for scientists to study the ecology, successional trends, and other aspects of the natural environment.

(c) Preserves for rare and endangered species of plants and animals.

§ 6225.1   *Use of natural areas.* No person shall use, occupy, construct or maintain improvements in natural areas in a manner inconsistent with the purpose for which the area is established; nor shall he use, occupy, construct or maintain improvements unless permitted by law or authorized by the regulations of this subpart.

------

## PART 6250—RECREATION ACCESS

Sec.
6250.0-1    Purpose.
6250.0-2    Objective.
6250.0-6    Policy.
6250.1      Use of trails.
6250.1-1    Hiking and horse riding trails.
6250.1-2    Motor trails.

Subpart 6251—Operation of Motorized Vehicles

6251.0-6    Policy.
6251.1      Motorized vehicles.
6251.2      Motorized vehicle events.
6251.4      Off-road travel restrictions.

Authority: Same as for Part 6000.

§ 6250.0-1   *Purpose.* To provide guidelines for provisions of access to and limitations on travel across lands.

§ 6250.0-2   *Objective.* To assure that persons wishing to use lands have access to them and that outdoor recreation use does not damage the resources.

§ 6250.0-6   *Policy.*

(a) In cooperation with State and local governments and private individuals and associations, the Bureau will endeavor to provide access for public use and enjoyment of lands with outdoor recreation values.

(b) Roads and trails constructed by the Bureau shall normally be available for public access to the lands. However, lands and roads and trails may be restricted to specified authorized use or no use in the interest of public health and safety or preservation and protection of the lands.

(c) The Bureau shall, where feasible, locate, identify, construct, and maintain hiking, horse riding and motor trails, and shall post appropriate signs or markers and use other means to make the existence of such routes known to the general public.

§ 6250.1   *Use of trails.*

§ 6250.1-1   *Hiking and horse riding trails.* Motorcycles and other motor vehicles are prohibited on trails limited to hiking and horse riding.

§ 6250.1-2   *Motor trails.*

(a) Motor vehicles shall remain on established routes or trails.

(b) Drivers of motor vehicles shall yield the right-of-way to pedestrians, saddle horses, pack trains and horse-drawn vehicles.

(c) Motor vehicles shall be operated in accordance with the regulations in § 6251.1.

Subpart 6251—*Operation of Motorized Vehicles*

§ 6251.0-6  *Policy.* Where appropriate, the Bureau will designate vehicle use sites and areas for the operation of motorized vehicles. Such sites and areas shall be selected from lands having terrain suitable to vehicle capability, with low resource production, erosion and siltation potentials. Selection shall be governed by the ability of the land and resources to withstand and sustain cross-country driving and vehicle use impacts. Lands where scenic qualities or other values would be impaired will not be selected for vehicle use sites and areas. Sites and areas will be designed to:

(a) Provide recreation opportunities for owners of vehicles with off-road vehicle use capability.

(b) Provide public use areas where dune buggies, motorcycles, "jeeps", totegotes and other vehicles may be tested and driven under varied conditions.

(c) Concentrate off-road vehicle use into specific areas and sites.

(d) Reduce impacts on other lands and resources by providing suitable locations for cross-country driving.

§ 6251.1  *Motorized vehicles.* The operation of motorized vehicles for outdoor recreation and other purposes is permitted within the following limits unless more restrictive regulations of this subpart apply:

(a) Operators shall maintain safe speeds and drive in a prudent and safe manner with full consideration and regard to public safety and property.

(b) Drivers may be restricted to established roads and motor trails or existing vehicle tracks.

(c) Operators of vehicles shall at all times drive in a manner as to prevent destruction of the land or vegetative resources.

(d) Operators may not drive their vehicles where prohibited by posting or other public notice.

(e) All vehicles shall be maintained in a safe operating condition for public safety and the prevention of fire.

§ 6251.2  *Motorized vehicle events.*

(a) The authorized officer may issue permits in accordance with the regulations in Subpart 2236 of Part 2230 of this chapter for the operation of motor vehicles for organized races, rallies, meets, endurance contests, and other motorized vehicular events.

(b) Permits may be issued to provide a suitable location for motorized vehicular events. Any permit issued will contain provisions to:

(1) Protect the public and participants.

(2) Minimize damage to the land and its resources.

§ 6251.4  *Off-road travel—restrictions.*

(a) The authorized officer may specify areas where the casual operation of motorized vehicles for recreational or other purposes will be restricted if the lands are subject to (1) resource damage and soil erosion, or (2) loss of primitive, scenic or other environmental qualities.

(b) Areas where such use is restricted will be posted by means of boundary signs and identified on maps and diagrams of sufficient detail to make the existence and locations known to the general public.

---

## PART 6260—VISITOR MANAGEMENT

Subpart 6261—*Rules for Visitor Use of Developed Recreation Sites*
Sec.
6261.0-1    Purpose.
6261.0-2    Objective.
6261.0-6    Compliance.
6261.1      Sanitation.
6261.2      Audio devices.
6261.3      Occupancy and use.
6261.4      Vehicles.
6261.5      Public health, safety and comfort.
6261.6      Public property and resources.

Authority: Same as for Part 6000.

Subpart 6261—*Rules for Visitor Use of Developed Recreation Sites*

§ 6261-1   *Purpose.* The rules of this subpart are designed for the comfort and well-being of the public in its use of developed outdoor recreation sites and outdoor recreation facilities provided by the Bureau.

§ 6261.0-2   *Objective.* To promote orderly occupancy and use of developed recreation sites, and other locations where the Bureau has installed outdoor recreation facilities for public use.

§ 6261.0-6   *Compliance.* Rules for public use and occupancy of developed recreation sites, and other locations where the Bureau has installed outdoor recreation facilities, will be posted in conspicuous locations. Failure to comply with rules so posted may result in denial of the use of developed recreation sites and facilities and such other further action as may be required.

§ 6261.1   *Sanitation.* All persons shall:

(a) Dispose of all garbage, paper, cans, bottles, waste materials, and rubbish by burning in authorized fires, removal from the site, or by disposal at places which may be provided for such purpose.

(b) Drain or dump refuse or waste from any trailer or other vehicle only in places or receptacles provided for such use.

(c) Refrain from cleaning fish or food or washing clothing or articles of household use at hydrants or at water faucets located in restrooms.

(d) Avoid polluting or contaminating water supplies or water used for human consumption.

(e) Deposit any body waste only into toilet receptacles provided for that purpose. Deposit of any bottles, cans, cloths, rags, metal, wood, stone or other damaging substance in any of the receptacles in toilet structures is prohibited.

(f) Use refuse containers or other refuse facilities only for the purposes for which they are supplied. The dumping of household or commercial garbage or trash brought from private property is prohibited.

§ 6261.2 *Audio devices.* The following acts are prohibited in developed recreation sites:

(a) Operating or using any audio devices, including radio, television, and musical instruments, and other noise-producing devices, such as electrical generator plants and equipment driven by motors for engines, in a manner to annoy other persons.

(b) Operating or using public address systems, whether fixed, portable, or vehicle mounted unless approved by the authorized officer.

(c) Installing aerial or other special radiotelephone or television equipment unless approved by the authorized officer.

§ 6261.3 *Occupancy and use.* The following rules apply to the occupancy and use of developed camping and picnicking facilities on the public lands. As a condition to such occupancy and use, the user shall:

(a) Pitch tents or park trailers or place other camping equipment only in places provided for such purposes.

(b) Camp within a campground no longer than the period of time established by the authorized officer.

(c) Attend camping equipment within prescribed time limits. Camping equipment which is unattended for more than posted limits, without permission of the authorized officer, is subject to disposition under State and local laws.

(d) Before departure remove equipment and clean any rubbish from the place occupied for recreation purposes.

(e) Build fires only in stoves, grills, fireplaces, or fire rings provided for such purposes.

(f) Camp overnight only in places provided or posted for such purposes.

(g) Maintain reasonable quiet in campgrounds between evening and morning hours as posted.

(h) Enter or remain in campgrounds closed during established night periods only as an occupant, or to visit persons occupying the campground for camping purposes.

(i) Not enter or use a site or a portion of a site closed to public use.

§ 6261.4 *Vehicles.* The following rules apply to driving and operation of motor vehicles in developed recreation sites in the interest of public safety and comfort. Motor vehicles and trailers shall not be:

(a) Driven or operated in excess of posted speeds.

(b) Driven or parked except on roads and places provided for this purpose.

(c) Driven or operated in willful disregard to the rights or safety of others or without due caution and at a speed, or in a manner, so as to endanger, or be likely to endanger, any person or property.

(d) Driven or operated on trails within developed recreation sites, except for purposes of maintaining such sites and facilities.

(e) Driven or operated in developed recreation sites, for any purpose other than access to or from the site.

(f) Driven or operated in developed recreation sites closed to such entrance by the authorized officer.

(g) Driven or operated at any time without a muffler in working order, or in such a manner as to create excessive or unusual noise or annoying smoke or dust, or using a muffler cutoff, bypass, or similar device.

(h) Unnecessarily accelerated when not moving or approaching or leaving a stopping place.

§ 6261.5 *Public health, safety and comfort.* The following rules are adopted to further the public health, safety and comfort in the use and occupancy of developed recreation sites and facilities. The user shall not:

(a) Discharge firearms, firecrackers, rockets, or other fireworks in developed recreation sites.

(b) Be accompanied by a dog, cat, or other animal unless it is crated, caged, leashed, or otherwise under physical restrictive control at all times.

(c) Bring animals, other than Seeing Eye dogs, to swimming areas.

(d) Bring saddle, pack, or draft animals into any developed recreation site except where specifically permitted or authorized.

§ 6261.6 *Public property and resources.* The following rules are adopted to protect public property and to preserve the resources in developed recreation sites for public use and enjoyment. The user shall not:

(a) Intentionally or wantonly destroy, deface, or remove any natural feature or plant.

(b) Intentionally or wantonly destroy, injure, deface, remove, or disturb in any manner any public building, sign, equipment, marker, or other structure or property.

---

## PART 6270—RECREATION DEVELOPMENT

### Subpart 6273—*Transfer of Responsibility*

§ 6273.0-6 *Policy.* State and local governments and private individuals and agencies are encouraged to develop and manage recreation facilities on the public lands for public recreation use and services. Such developments and operations shall be consistent with long-range management plans and authorities of the Bureau, and consistent with leases, licenses, and permits issued under the authority of the regulations in this part.

Stewart L. Udall,
Secretary of the Interior.

January 16, 1969.

## Appendix E

### NATIONAL CONSERVATION BILL OF RIGHTS

Now pending as: H. J. Res. 54; 91st Congress, 1st Session.
In the House of Representatives

January 8, 1969

Mr. Ottinger (for himself, Mr. Dent, Mr. Scheuer, Mr. Edwards of California, Mr. Eilberg, Mr. Podell, Mr. Grover, Mr. Button, Mr. Cleveland, Mr. Saylor, and Mr. Farbstein) introduced the following joint resolution; which was referred to the Committee on the Judiciary.

#### Joint Resolution

Proposing an amendment to the Constitution of the United States relating to the conservation of the natural resources and natural beauty of the United States.

Resolved by the Senate and House of Representatives of the United States of America in Congress assembled (two-thirds of each House concurring therein), That the following article is proposed as an amendment to the Constitution of the United States, to be valid only if ratified by the legislatures of three-fourths of the several States within seven years after the date of final passage of this joint resolution:

"Article—

"Section 1. The right of the people to clean air, pure water, freedom from excessive and unnecessary noise, and the natural, scenic, historic, and esthetic qualities of their environment shall not be abridged.

"Sec. 2. The Congress shall, within three years after the enactment of this article, and within every subsequent term of ten years or lesser term as the Congress may determine, and in such manner as they shall by law direct, cause to be made an inventory of the natural, scenic, esthetic, and historic resources of the United States with their state of preservation, and to provide for their protection as a matter of national purpose.

"Sec. 3. No Federal or State agency, body, or authority shall be authorized to exercise the power of condemnation, nor undertake any public work, issue any permit, license, or concession, make any rule, execute any management policy, or other official act which adversely affects the people's heritage of natural resources and natural beauty, on lands and waters now or hereafter placed in public ownership without first giving reasonable notice to the public and holding a public hearing thereon.

"Sec. 4. This article shall take effect on the first day of the first month following its ratification."

## *Appendix F*

### THE ELEVENTH BIENNIAL WILDERNESS CONFERENCE

#### *March 14 and 15, 1969*

PROGRAM PLANNING COMMITTEE

Dr. Daniel B. Luten, *Chairman*

Maxine E. McCloskey, *General Secretary*

Hasse Bunnelle, *Financial Secretary*

Phillip S. Berry
Mr. and Mrs. David R. Brower
Wes Bunnelle
Dr. James P. Gilligan

George Hall
J. Michael McCloskey
Judge and Mrs. Raymond J. Sherwin
Professor Georg Treichel

Dr. and Mrs. Edgar Wayburn

ARRANGEMENTS CHAIRMEN

Exhibits, Robin Way
Field Trip, Hasse Bunnelle
Hospitality, Fay Golden
Hotel Arrangements, Kent Watson
Poster Distribution, Sonya Thompson
Printing, Wes Bunnelle
Program Design, H. I. Finger
Program Editor, Marcia Tucker
Publicity, George Hall
Registration, Mr. and Mrs. Ken Goodden
Special Assignments, Luella Sawyer
Youth Activities, Bill Devall

As is usual with all Sierra Club functions and campaigns, large numbers of volunteers came forward again to make the wilderness conference possible.

## Appendix G

### BIOGRAPHICAL SKETCHES

RICHARD W. BEHAN is now associate professor of resource policy and administration in the School of Forestry, University of Montana, Missoula, where he earned the B.S. and M.S. degrees in forestry. He is now completing his dissertation for the Ph.D. degree from the University of California at Berkeley. Previously he served for six years with the Forest Service in the Tongass and Chugach National Forests in Alaska. While serving at the Chugach National Forest he helped originate, in cooperation with the Alaska Department of Fish and Game, a Copper River Delta Wildlife Management Area.

DAVID BROWER has been active in the conservation cause since 1933 when he joined the Sierra Club. He was elected director of the club and from 1952 to 1969 served as its first executive director. He edited the *Sierra Club Bulletin*, and initiated and edited the Exhibit Format Series, winner of the Carey-Thomas award in 1964. He led the club's successful defense of the Grand Canyon against proposed dams. He has received an Honorary Doctor of Science degree from Hobart College and has been given a number of awards for his books and films. He is president of the Friends of the Earth, which he founded in 1969, and is director of the John Muir Institute for Environmental Studies.

CONGRESSMAN JEFFERY COHELAN has been representing California's Seventh District (Berkeley, North Oakland) since first elected in 1958, and serves on the House Appropriations Committee. A San Francisco native, he did undergraduate and graduate work in economics at the University of California. He was a Fulbright research scholar to the universities of Leeds and Oxford, 1953-54. Active in labor union affairs in the 1940's, he served as consultant to the University of California Institute of Industrial Relations. His record in Congress demonstrates his concern for the environment. Since 1960 he has been working for measures to control water pollution; he was coauthor with the late Clem Miller of the Point Reyes National Seashore Bill; he introduced legislation to establish a Redwood National Park; he sponsored the 1964 Civil Rights Act; and he is a leader in the fight against the antiballistic missile system.

RICHARD A. COOLEY, associate professor of geography, University of Washington, Seattle, is an authority on international resource problems. His contributions to economic and geographical studies for state agencies and scientific journals are many. He has served as consultant for the Outdoor Recreation Resources Review Commission, the governor of Alaska's State Division of Planning, and the Department of the Interior on the proposed Rampart Dam. For his book *Politics and Conservation* he was given the Western Political Science Association Award. In 1967 he published *Alaska, a Challenge in Conservation*. He received the Ph.D. degree from The University of Michigan's School of Natural Resources.

HARRY B. CRANDELL is the planning officer of the Division of Wildlife Refuges, Bureau of Sport Fisheries and Wildlife, Washington, D.C., where he directs planning and wilderness programs in the National

Wildlife Refuge System. Prior to being stationed in Washington in 1964, he served for 12 years as refuge manager and wildlife biologist in Arizona, Colorado, New Mexico, Oklahoma, and Wyoming. His home state is Colorado where he graduated from Colorado State University in Fort Collins.

ROBERT R. CURRY is now assistant professor of geology, University of Montana, Missoula, following his position as assistant professor of environmental sciences at the University of California at Santa Barbara. Additionally, he is a hydrologist and geologist for the United States Geological Survey's research on riverbed load transportation. The most recent of his numerous published scientific articles is a report to the Senate Subcommittee on Air and Water Pollution on the geological hazards associated with offshore oil exploration and production. He works with several conservation organizations on state and national environmental legislation and is an advisor to the United States Senate Public Works Committee on matters of environmental geology, ecology, and policy. He earned his Ph.D. degree in geology and geophysics at the University of California at Berkeley.

PAUL R. EHRLICH, author of the book The Population Bomb, is one of the world's experts on the subject of population. A member of the Stanford University faculty since 1959, he is professor of biology. He was National Science Foundation senior postdoctoral fellow at the University of Sydney, Australia. His present research includes investigations into density effects in human populations, experimental studies of natural and laboratory populations, and plant-herbivore coevolution. He has authored or coauthored more than 80 scientific papers and articles in the popular press, and several books on biology and evolution. Dr. Ehrlich and Anne H. Ehrlich have recently published Population, Resources, Environment: Issues in Human Ecology. He earned the Ph.D. degree in 1957 from the University of Kansas.

BROCK EVANS is the northwest representative in Seattle, Washington, for the Sierra Club and the Federation of Western Outdoor Clubs. Active in the conservation movement, he holds other positions including director, North Cascades Conservation Council; founder and director, Washington Environmental Council; and vice-chairman and trustee, Western Washington branch of The Nature Conservancy. He was born in Columbus, Ohio. After graduation from Princeton University and The University of Michigan Law School, he practiced law in Seattle.

R. BUCKMINSTER FULLER is an inventor, mathematician, philosopher, poet, cartographer, architect, engineer, and professor of comprehensive design at Southern Illinois University in Carbondale. He has received degrees in science, the arts, humane letters, and architectural engineering from 18 universities and institutions. The recipient of awards from the American Institute of Architects, the Royal Institute of British Architects, and many other institutions, he makes frequent contributions to journals and is in demand as a speaker at conferences. He serves as consultant to a number of foundations, and is a fellow of the World Academy of Art and Science, the American Academy of Arts and Sciences, and the National

Academy of Design. Among the most famous of his structural designs are the Dymaxion House and the geodesic dome.

*JOHN L. HALL* joined The Wilderness Society staff as assistant executive director in December, 1967. He directed the study of proposals for the addition of federal lands to the National Wilderness Preservation System. In September, 1969, he became special assistant to the regional forester, Alaska region, United States Forest Service and lives now at Juneau. As a professional forester he has had 16 years of experience with the Forest Service, previously serving in Montana, and as a deputy division chief of the Information and Education Division of the Eastern region. He earned the B.S. degree in forestry from The Pennsylvania State University and the M.S. degree from Yale University.

*GARRETT HARDIN*, professor of biology at the University of California at Santa Barbara, has been a member of that faculty since 1946. He was elected faculty research lecturer for the Santa Barbara campus because of his concern with questions related to the logical basis of the sciences and to the cultural, ethical and emotional values involved in scientific thought. He earned the Ph.D. degree in biology at Stanford University. He has published more than 70 articles and reviews that stress the humanistic bearings of biology. His book *Nature and Man's Fate* has been called one of the best general introductions to the problems of evolution. *Population, Evolution and Birth Control*, his most recent book, was published in 1964.

*H. ALBERT HOCHBAUM* is director of the Delta Waterfowl Research Station at Delta, Manitoba, and thus is a Canadian resident. In 1933 he graduated from Cornell University and later completed his M.S. degree at the University of Wisconsin. After serving in the National Park Service for three years he began his career at the Delta Research Station. He has published numerous scientific articles on waterfowl habitat and biology, and is the author of *The Canvasback on a Prairie Marsh* and *Travels and Tradition of Waterfowl*. The University of Manitoba honored him with an LL.D. He has been awarded the Brewster Medal of the American Ornithologists' Union, the Literary Award of The Wildlife Society (twice), and the John Guggenheim Fellowship. He serves as director of the Wildfowl Foundation and The Nature Conservancy of Canada, and is fellow of the American Ornithologists' Union and American Association for the Advancement of Science.

*CELIA HUNTER* is the chairman of the Alaska Wilderness Council, which she helped organize at the first All-Alaska Wilderness Workshop in February, 1969, in Juneau, and also serves on the Citizen's Multiple Use Advisory Board of the Bureau of Land Management for Alaska. One of the charter members of the Alaska Conservation Society, she has since served as its executive secretary. She is also a member of the Council of The Wilderness Society. A native of Washington's Puget Sound, she earned her pilot's wings with the Women's Air Force Service Pilots, serving in the Ferry Command of the A.T.C. during World War II. After the war she ferried a plane from Seattle to Fairbanks on an arduous 27-day midwinter flight, and has been an Alaskan ever since. She operates in partnership with Ginny Hill Wood a wilderness tourist camp, Camp Denali, on the northern boundary of Mt. McKinley National Park.

*SENATOR HENRY M. JACKSON* of Washington was first elected to the Senate in 1952 and is now chairman of the Senate Interior and Insular Affairs Committee. He has been instrumental in the passage of important conservation legislation—the Redwood National Park, the North Cascades National Park, the Land and Water Conservation Fund, and the National Water Commission. He was a major influence in defeating two proposed dams in the Grand Canyon. He serves on the Government Operations and Armed Services committees, and has published four books based on his investigations into the role of the National Security Council and the Department of Defense. A graduate of the University of Washington, he was chairman of the Democratic National Committee in 1960.

*W. HOWARD JOHNSON* is regional forester, Alaska region, United States Forest Service. A native of Colorado, he studied forestry at the University of Washington, served with the Forest Service in Washington and Montana, and moved in 1964 to to his present position in Juneau. He provides administrative and technical leadership in the activities of the Alaska National Forest Region and also serves as the appointed representative of the secretary of agriculture on the Federal Field Committee for Development Planning for Alaska.

*NORMAN B. LIVERMORE, JR.,* is secretary of The Resources Agency of California. In a key position for conservation, he coordinates the work of the Departments of Conservation, Fish and Game, Harbors and Watercraft, Parks and Recreation, and Water Resources, as well as that of seven state boards. His long association with the Sierra Club began when he was a summer guide in the High Sierra. He has written numerous articles on wilderness and conservation subjects. He formerly served as treasurer of the Pacific Lumber Company. A native of California, he graduated from Stanford University and did graduate work at the Harvard Business School.

*WILLIAM B. LORD* is director of the Center for Resource Policy Studies and Programs, School of Natural Resources, University of Wisconsin, Madison, where he also teaches natural resource economics. The center recently completed a study of federal public land law and policy in Alaska. Previously he served as a research forester in the United States Forest Service and as economic advisor to the secretary of the army on the Corps of Engineers water resources program. His publications are about forest and water economics, planning and policy. Active in many conservation organizations, he serves as an outings leader and a member of the executive committee of the John Muir Chapter of the Sierra Club. He received a Ph.D. degree from The University of Michigan's School of Natural Resources.

*DANIEL B. LUTEN,* conference chairman, is lecturer in geography at the University of California at Berkeley where he earned his Ph.D. in chemistry. Dr. Luten had a distinguished career in chemistry, and from 1935 to 1961 produced many patents and publications with Shell Oil and

Development Companies. He also served as technical adviser to the chief of the Natural Resources Section, Civil Administration of Occupied Japan. Later, his compelling interest in conservation and ecology turned his career to environmental concerns. He provides leadership in several conservation organizations and has published many papers on population dynamics and conservation.

GEORGE MACINKO is professor of geography at Central Washington State College, Ellensburg. His interest in the environment began during boyhood in Pennsylvania where he saw the devastation caused by strip mining. He received both the M.A. and Ph.D. degrees from The University of Michigan where he did postdoctoral work in 1965 and 1966 at the School of Natural Resources. He has been awarded the Horace W. Rackham Dissertation Travel Grant, a National Science Foundation Faculty Fellowship, and study grants from Planned Parenthood-World Population, The Conservation Foundation, and Office of Water Resources Research.

FERREN MacINTYRE is assistant professor of oceanography, Scripps Institution of Oceanography, University of California at San Diego. He studied under a fellowship at Massachusetts Institute of Technology, where he earned the Ph.D. degree in physical chemistry. He held positions as teaching assistant at M.I.T. and at the Musée d'Histoire Naturelle in Paris. His publications include such technical articles as "Ion Fractionation," "Vibrating Capillary for Production of Uniform Small Bubbles," and "Elimination of Eccentric Error in High Precision Counting." He conducts conservation studies at John Muir College in San Diego, and is active in organizing an adequate college curriculum on caring for the natural environment.

J. MICHAEL McCLOSKEY was appointed executive director of the Sierra Club in 1969. Before transferring to the national office of the club in 1965, he represented the Sierra Club and the Federation of Western Outdoor Clubs in the Pacific Northwest. As conservation director he coordinated the club's successful campaigns to establish a Redwood National Park, a North Cascades National Park, and various wilderness areas. He received an award from the California Conservation Council in 1969 for his staff work in the redwood campaign. Listed in *Leaders in American Conservation*, he is also a director of the Citizens Committee on Natural Resources and the North Cascades Conservation Council. He has published numerous articles in conservation and law journals. He earned an A.B. degree in American government from Harvard University, served in the U.S. Army from 1956-58, and received his LL.B. degree from the University of Oregon.

JOHN P. MILTON is director, Office of International Affairs, The Conservation Foundation, Washington, D.C. He has worked for the foundation since receiving the bachelor's and master's degrees in conservation and ecology at The University of Michigan. Additionally, he has served as consultant in national park planning to the governments of Peru, Ecuador, and Costa Rica, and as technical specialist and secretary for the Organization of American States in their Inter-American Conference on Renewable Resource Conservation. His publications appear in a variety of professional journals, and he coedited *Future Environments of North America*, the proceedings of the conference he organized in 1965. He also organized "Ecological Aspects of International Development," a recent conference sponsored by The Conservation Foundation. He worked on the development of the Sierra Club's Exhibit Format book *Galapagos: The Flow of Wildness*.

MARGARET E. MURIE has had an intimate association with wilderness throughout her life. She grew up in Alaska, was the first woman graduate of the University of Alaska, and married government biologist Olaus J. Murie who later became director of The Wilderness Society. From 1927 on, the Muries made their home in Jackson Hole, Wyoming. She worked closely with him in his wildlife studies and conservation work, and on field expeditions to Alaska, New Zealand, and Europe. Mrs. Murie is the author of the book *Two in the Far North* and, with her husband, of *Wapiti Wilderness*. She continues her conservation work as consultant to The Wilderness Society.

RODERICK NASH, associate professor of American intellectual history, University of California at Santa Barbara, is recognized as an authority on wilderness history. He has published many articles on wilderness and conservation and numerous books (including *The American Environment: Readings in the History of Conservation* and *Wilderness and the American Mind*), and edited the Sierra Club's *Grand Canyon of the Living Colorado*. He earned the Ph.D. degree at the University of Wisconsin. In 1968 he served as consultant on the conservation of natural resources, Democratic Party Platform. He is editorial consultant for *American Quarterly*, and advisory editor on ecology and conservation of the University of Kentucky Press. A member of the executive committee of the Los Padres Chapter of the Sierra Club, he was recently elected to the Explorers Club of New York.

URBAN C. NELSON is conservation consultant of The Nature Conservancy and the Alaska Sportsmen's Council. He led in establishing modern game management in Alaska; was instrumental in studies and negotiations leading to the dedication of the Arctic, Izembek, and Clarence Rhode national wildlife ranges; and organized the first large-scale effort to band migratory waterfowl on northern Alaska breeding grounds. For these accomplishments he was presented with the Department of the Interior's highest honor, the Distinguished Service Award. He began his career in 1935 with the United States Soil Conservation Service. Formerly, he was commissioner of the Alaska Department of Fish and Game, and Alaska regional director for the Bureau of Sport Fisheries and Wildlife.

CONGRESSMAN RICHARD L. OTTINGER has been representing New York's Twenty-fifth District (Westchester and Putnam counties) since 1965 and currently serves on the House Interstate and Foreign Commerce Committee, Communications and Power Subcommittee. He has led efforts to promote conservation and air safety, upgrade congressional ethics, and reform tax and welfare laws. During his first term in office he authored the Hudson River Compact Act of 1966 to help preserve and develop the Hudson River Valley, and opposed the Hudson River

Expressway project. Resulting from his legislation were electric car research and a study of the effects of jet air pollution. He received the LL.B. degree from Harvard University and did graduate work in international law at Georgetown University.

DOUGLAS R. POWELL is now associate in geography, University of California at Berkeley, where he is a candidate for the Ph.D. degree in geography. A native of California, he has wide knowledge and experience of the state's history, land, and people. Every winter since 1957 he has worked as a snow surveyor and hydrographer in the Sierra Nevada for the California Department of Water Resources. An experienced mountaineer, he has guided a wide variety of geographical reconnaissance trips to Alaska, as well as a number of Sierra Club outings and private mountaineering groups.

GEORGE W. ROGERS, professor of economics at the University of Alaska, has since 1956 been engaged in long-range research on the economic development of Alaska, his home for 25 years. This work has been supported by Resources for the Future, Inc., the Arctic Institute of North America, and the University of Alaska. Books published as the result of his investigations include *Alaska in Transition* and *The Future of Alaska*. Formerly an economist for the Department of the Interior and chairman of the Alaska Field Committee, he served for one year as visiting fellow at Clare College, University of Cambridge, England. He received the Ph.D. degree from Harvard University.

RAYMOND J. SHERWIN is judge, Superior Court, Solano County, California. Long active in Sierra Club affairs, he is chairman of the Minaret Summit Road Task Force which has thus far kept the route out of the California and federal highway systems. He is a member of the National Audubon Society, The Conservation Law Society of America, the Planning and Conservation League, and the California Roadside Council. He was elected to the board of directors of the Sierra Club in 1969, and appointed secretary and member of the executive committee. He earned the LL.B. degree at Boalt Hall, University of California, Berkeley.

BURTON W. SILCOCK is state director for Alaska, Bureau of Land Management. His career in government work spans 25 years, first in Texas with the Soil Conservation Service, later with the Bureau of Land Management in Wyoming, Idaho, and Montana, and since 1965 in Alaska. He holds a B.S. degree in forestry from Utah State University. He is a member of The American Forestry Association, the American Society of Range Management, and the Society of American Foresters.

ELVIS J. STAHR is now president of the National Audubon Society after a distinguished career in education and in government service. After graduating from the University of Kentucky, he was a Rhodes Scholar at University of Oxford where he received four degrees including one in law. He earned a diploma in Chinese language from Yale University and is the recipient of 20 honorary degrees. He has been dean of the University of Kentucky College of Law and later provost of that university, vice-chancellor of the University of Pittsburgh, and president of West Virginia and

Indiana universities. During the Korean War he served as special assistant to the secretary of the army, and was secretary of the army from 1961 to 1962.

*LEE M. TALBOT* is resident ecologist and field representative for international affairs in ecology and conservation at the Smithsonian Institution in Washington, D.C. He is the author of more than 100 scientific or technical publications emphasizing land use and wildlife. A world traveler because of his research, he is a consultant to many professional conservation societies. He has served on the staff of several international scientific and conservation conferences including the 1961 Pan-African Conservation Conference, the 1965 Bangkok Conference, and others sponsored by the International Union for Conservation, and the United Nations' Food and Agricultural Organization and Educational, Scientific and Cultural Organization. He is a graduate of the University of California at Berkeley where he received the Ph.D. degree in ecology and range ecology.

*MARTHA HAYNE TALBOT* is a Smithsonian research associate in the Office of Environmental Sciences at the Smithsonian Institution. A graduate of Vassar College, she was cofounder and codirector of the Student Conservation Program. Marty and Lee Talbot first met at a Sierra Club wilderness conference some ten years ago, were married, and traveled to Africa. She works with her husband organizing and participating in international scientific conservation projects, and also serves on the staff of the International Biological Program. She has written many scientific and technical publications and coauthored with Dr. Talbot the 1963 Wildlife Society Award-winning *Conservation in Southeast Asia*. She has led a National Parks Association tour to East Africa.

*WILLARD A. TROYER* is superintendent of the Kenai Moose Range. A wilderness biologist, he is the author or coauthor of technical papers on the brown bear, bald eagle, and moose; and has done extensive research on the Kodiak bear in preparation for a forthcoming book. With the Bureau of Sport Fisheries and Wildlife since 1952, he formerly was the manager of the Kodiak National Wildlife Refuge, and continues to conduct field wilderness studies for the 18 national wildlife refuges in Alaska. He received the B.S. degree in wildlife management from Oregon State University and the master's degree in wildlife technology from Montana State University. He is active in the Alaska Chapter of the Sierra Club, the Alaska Conservation Society, and The Wilderness Society.

*EDGAR WAYBURN* has been a member of the Sierra Club since 1939, a director since 1957, and twice president. In May, 1969, he was elected vice-president of the club. He also serves as director and treasurer of the Sierra Club Foundation. He led the club's successful effort to establish a Redwood National Park, and was instrumental in expanding California's Mt. Tamalpais State Park. Additionally, he has served as president of the Trustees for Conservation and the Federation of Western Outdoor Clubs. For his leadership in conservation campaigns, he has received many honors including the California Conservation, the American Motors Conservation, and the KTIM Marin County Conservation awards. A physician by profession, he is chief of the endocrine clinic at Pacific Medical Center, and associate clinical professor of medicine on the faculties of Stanford University Medical School and the University of California Medical Center in San Francisco.

ROBERT B. WEEDEN became Alaska representative for the Sierra Club and The Wilderness Society in October, 1969. He has been studying Alaskan wilderness and wildlife since 1959 when he joined the Alaska Department of Fish and Game as a game biologist. Known for his extensive research on ptarmigan and grouse, he has led research planning for waterfowl and fur animal programs. He earned the Ph.D. degree in zoology at the University of British Columbia, was instructor in zoology at Washington State University and later was associate in wildlife at the University of Alaska. He also serves as a fellow in the Arctic Institute of North America, and as president of the Alaska Conservation Society.